Orcus

Jeremy Allan Neal

.

Table of Contents

For Teddy,

my fine, beloved boy.

Acknowledgements

There are a great many people who have helped me, both wittingly and incidentally with this work. As my constant, wise and measured advisor I most of all want to express heartfelt and loving gratitude to my Alice.

Also to the esteemed Steven Forrest whose wisdom, encouragement and generosity have been more valuable than words can easily express.

To my dear friends Marek, Nina, Angus and Julie who have been constant and true through dark days and whose companionship, trust, belief and encouragement has been invaluable, thank you.

To all the many friends, colleagues and teachers, near and far, who have so bravely shared their stories, their fears, and their wisdom and have contributed so many threads to the tapestry of this work, thank you:

Erin Sullivan, Neeti Ray, Deirdre Tanton, Shannon Brianne, Shyama Persaud, Sarah Molea, Verena Heinrich, Jessica Shepherd, Honey Romero, Rick Levine, Kelly Karalis, Jeff Kishner, Mia Davis, Adiaha Ruane, Elsa Panizzon, Donna Cunningham, Noel Tyl, Anthony Louis, Robert Hand, Angie MacDonald, Lucinda & Paul Hallam, Deborah Houlding, Sharon Marshall, April Elliott Kent, Alan Oken, Annie Nijhuis, Tash Forrest, Dom and Char Downes, Carole Venthem, Ben Postnikoff, Lukasz Bicki, Tony Brookes, Vicky Steward, Lin Cook and Jan & George Oldham.

Part I

Doria

Be in me as the eternal moods
of the bleak wind, and not
As transient things are –
gaiety of flowers.
Have me in the strong loneliness
of sunless cliffs
And of grey waters.
Let the Gods speak softly of us
In days hereafter.
The shadowy flowers of Orcus,
Remember thee.

Ezra Pound

Mythology

On they went, hidden in solitary night, through gloom,
through Dis's empty halls, and insubstantial kingdom,
like a path through a wood, in the faint light
under a wavering moon, when Jupiter has buried the sky
in shadow, and black night has stolen the colour from things.
Right before the entrance, in the very jaws of Orcus,
Grief and vengeful Care have made their beds,
and pallid Sickness lives there, and sad Old Age,
and Fear, and persuasive Hunger, and vile Need,
forms terrible to look on, and Death and Pain:
then Death's brother Sleep, and Evil Pleasure of the mind,
and, on the threshold opposite, death-dealing War,
and the steel chambers of the Furies, and mad Discord,
her snaky hair entwined with blood-wet ribbons.

Virgil: The Aeneid – Book 6

The Swearing of Oaths

The Roman deity Orcus makes few appearances in the mythological sources. A shadowy and terrible figure, he is first identified in early Etruscan records, promoted as an agent of divine vengeance to the Greeks, a kind of bogey-man to the Romans and makes a brief appearance, mostly as a proscribed focus of pagan practice, in early medieval sources. He is a divine terror, inexhaustible pursuer of the wicked, angel of death and our own Grim Reaper. His is the Roman name for hell, and the relentless demon whose task it is to mark those souls which are to be sent down into the earth for eternity. He is the later personification of the Wild Man, the Green Man and the King of May.

He exists though only in fragments, and even in those places where modern scholars have investigated his import, the insights are fleeting or contradictory.

Any exhaustive study of the ancient texts reveals that Orcus was used most frequently as an epithet or derivation of the lord of the dead and the underworld, often interchangeably with 'Pluto', who was also referred to by the Romans as Dis, in the street vernacular of Rome, but most especially by her soldiers, for whom he held an especial familiarity in this nomenclature:

"Dis Pater, Dispater or simply Dis is a name Caesar and other Romans preferred for the God we call Pluto or Hades, deity of the nether world, ruler of the dead. The preference for 'Dis Pater' was not simply a euphemism for dreaded Pluto, whose name actually translates as 'giver of wealth'. Dis from the Latin Dives, also implies wealth."[1]

So Dis was probably preferred over Pluto's other epithets for no reason other than the fact that it retained Pluto's association with wealth, and men throughout time have dreamt of riches. But Dis *Pater* was preferred for other reasons too: the name signified a patriarch and protector; and Caesar used the term in his diaries and presumably in his speeches and letters and Caesar was adored by the fighting men of Rome. Orcus, as an epithet for Pluto was less commonly employed.

Etymologically, the name Orcus itself is most likely derived from *Horkus* who, in the Greek, was a son of Eris[2] making him a nephew of Ares or Mars. Orcus therefore straddles both Greek and Roman sources; Horkus is Greek for "oath", while Orcus most closely corresponds to the Greek ἕρκος which translates as a "lock-up" or prison.

This correlation between 'oath' and lock-up' is profoundly important, but not in a manner which is immediately apparent due to a vastly

---

[1] *Myths and Legends of the Celts* (2006), James MacKillop, Penguin p 40.
[2] Roman: Discordia

differing world-view from that of ancient times. To the ancient Greek or Roman an oath was a sacred and solemn undertaking, not viewed in remotely the same vein as a promise made in this day and age. The key is to understand that for the Roman an oath was a contract that would in effect *bind*. An oath taken in the name of a God was especially fearsome:

> "*...our word fantasy derives from Latin and Greek roots meaning to make visible, visionary, unreal. The fantastic seems both opaque and transparent, like a poetic image. We feel incomplete and yet are filled with wonder in one and the same instant. This is akin to the effect of promising, which functions as an ordinary speech convention and yet magically creates a future where there was none, formalises commitment and obligation where none existed before. The ancient Greeks and Romans simultaneously represented and repressed this doubleness by according Hades, the Unseen, the supplementary names Pluto and Dis, which both mean wealth, abundance, excess. As a location, Hades is often imagistically represented as forbiddingly empty and terrifyingly full (e.g. Virgil and Dante). The Latin designation Orcus, yet another conventional name for Hades, both the God and the place is most likely derived from the Greek Horkos, oath. In his guise as Orcus, Hades emerges as a spirit who avenges perjury and who enforces the keeping of promises. The ancients did not view promises and vows as merely legalistic, but as essentially mysterious and magical relations with unmistakable links to the world of mythic shadow, the underworld, which was construed as a place of threatening loss and of promising reward[3]*"

This cuts to the core of the concept of Pluto for the Roman. If Pluto is the totality of the dread Lord Hades, then we can deduce that Dis Pater

---

[3] *Mindscapes: the geographics of imagined worlds* (1986), George Edgar Slusser, Eric S. Rabkin, Southern Illinois University Press.

represented his honourable, wealth-promising face, and Orcus, his punishing and imprisoning face. Swearing an oath on Pluto contained the positive potential of reward, via Dis, as a natural consequence of being a person of virtue that honoured the covenant, and at the same time the negative potential of purgatory, via Orcus, as a natural consequence of being a scoundrel and an oath-breaker.

Looked at in this way then, we can appreciate that for the Roman, an oath was more than a casual proposition: once taken it was in effect a lock-up, or a prison. Once uttered in earnest the covenant could not be escaped and any attempt to do so would bring down the wrath of Orcus, the avenger of broken promises. Even this though is only half the story, because the only true requirement of a good Roman oath was for it to be sworn in good faith. The fates might always take a hand, rendering the promise unfulfilled and mortals were, in Roman life, ever at the mercy of the whims of the Gods. Orcus was most likely to be invoked as punisher of wilfully taken false oaths, as related by Herodotus:

> *"There was at Sparta a man named Glaucus, famed over all Greece for his justice and integrity: into his hands a certain Milesian fearing some danger at home and being encouraged by the character of the man, deposited a large sum of money. After some time the sons of this Milesian came to Sparta and showing Glaucus the bill demanded the money. Glaucus pretended he was wholly ignorant of the matter yet promised to recollect with himself and if he found any thing due to them to pay it. To do this he took four months time and having gained this delay immediately took a journey to Delphi on purpose to ask Apollo's opinion whether it was lawful to perjure himself thereby to secure the money. The god moved with indignation at the impudence of the man returned him this answer*
>
> *No, Glaucus, no, I think you need not fear,*
> *To bilk your easy creditor, and swear*

He lent you no such sum you'll gain thereby
And this consider'd you may death defy
Death of the just alike an enemy.
But know that Orcus has a monster son,
Ghastly of shape who ever hastens on
To o'ertake perjuries; he'll ne'er forget
Your heinous crime, but with revengeful hate
Send losses, racking pangs, destructive woe,
Till he yourself, with your whole race undo."[4]

The distinction is subtle, but crucial nonetheless: Orcus did not punish the breakers of oaths, but rather those who wilfully took them in vain in order to deceive and thereby to profit. This is why *perjury* was to the Greek or Roman the gravest of crimes and was only practised by the worst of characters[5].

Culturally, the gravity of oath-taking in a world without recourse to contractual or legal penalties was essential to the proper functioning of society and indeed, the oath stood in stead of the signed agreement, duly witnessed and notarised, of today. Quite as a matter of necessity, in order that society function, a man's word had to be his bond.

The Greek, and later, Roman belief then, that a promise was no trifle, but in fact a spell, binding the party taking the oath and calling the Gods as witness is a proscription that we are familiar with, at least with an echo of the ancient reverence, but it might be argued that even in

---

[4] For a full account of the story of Glaucus, see *The History of Herodotus: a new English version, Volume 3* (2010), Herodotus, George Rawlinson, Sir Henry Creswicke Rawlinson, Sir John Gardner Wilkinson, Nabu Press.

[5] "*As Chaos had spontaneously produced offspring, now her daughter Nyx does likewise. Among the fifteen children she bears - mostly fell creatures of dark and trouble - are numbered Cer 'Destiny', Geras 'Old Age', Moerae 'Fates', Nemesis 'Retribution', and Eris 'Strife', who herself parthogenetically produces fifteen similar beings - such as Ponus 'Toil', Machae 'Wars', Pseudea 'Lies', and Horkus 'Oath' "who brings the greatest ruin to men on earth, when willingly they swear falsely.*" From *The Cambridge Companion to Greek Mythology*, (2007), Roger D. Woodward, Cambridge University Press p. 87.

matters of the greatest solemnity, oaths are taken legalistically in this day and age without the awareness of old for the magical component of this ritualised act of *promising*. Roman legionaries, by contrast would habitually swear oaths by Dis, their preferred facet of the Hadean triumvirate of Pluto, Orcus and Dis Pater, with a reverent awareness of the forces thus invoked. These dread epithets or 'faces' of the principle of death and the Underworld gave true gravity to a man's word and backed their resolve with the threat of Hades' myriad terrors, tortures and punishments, meted out over eternity.

Orcus the Implacable

Orcus, Hades, Pluto, all of these were used interchangeably to describe the location of the Greek Underworld Tartarus. It may be that Orcus, as an entity, rather than a geographic catch-all, was used to describe Pluto when adopting a specifically punishing persona or face in the same way that Jupiter Victor was a face of Jupiter that, adorned with armour and armament, was called upon to lead the legions to glory. Herodotus and Hesiod both state that Orcus was the demon sent to punish the swearers of false oaths, and not necessarily by direct intervention, but through the gradual destruction of life, ambition, reputation and contentment. Orcus wears down the target of his rage, implacably.

This implacability is yet another important tenet of Orcus, an Orcan quality espoused by the Roman poet Horace, who tells us that Orcus is "pitiless":

*It makes no difference whether you're wealthy, born
a descendant of ancient Inachus, or whether you live out
in the open, a poor man and of a humble family --
[you're still] the prey of pitiless Orcus.*[6]

---

[6] *Diuesne prisco natus ab Inacho
nil interest an pauper et infima
de gente sub diuo moreris,
victima nil miserantis Orci.* (Horace Ode 2.3 lines 21-24)

There is no suggestion here that Horace is referring to any deity distinct from Pluto. However, where Orcus is used as an appellative, both by Horace and Virgil (as well as a few other less celebrated Roman poets) the tone of the passage is deliberate and implies implacability. This is because the duality of the Latin terminology which, when not obscured in translation, implies much more literally a prison or lock-up, something which therefore cannot be escaped. Orcus was, to the Roman poet, a name of Pluto which described his implacable nature very directly, whereas Pluto has a more generalised intimation of benefit, being the Latin form of Ploutōn, meaning 'the wealth-giver' (Greek. ploutos, 'wealth'), because in the ancient world all wealth came from the earth. The *resonance* of "Orcus" therefore is of an implacable punisher even though *technically* it is a reference to Pluto, brother of Jupiter and Neptune, Persephone's husband.

So we see, Pluto and Orcus are facets of the same deity, but in practice, the cultural translation from the earlier Greek to the more pragmatic Roman worldview contained a fair few efficiencies and expediencies and entire deities were lost. Rome was a borrower of culture, cherry-picking the best of their vassal states' mores and customs, rejecting the superfluous and streamlining the unwieldy. Eris became Discordia and her son Horkus was amalgamated into a persona of the Lord of Hades. Archetypically, we honour all sources and Orcus the punisher has – for the most part – been demoted to a *function* of Pluto. It is germane though to understand that the selected epithet for the lord of the underworld was far from casual to the Roman poet; the name described the mood of Pluto if you like, and, rather like a case of multiple personality disorder, there are distinct organic personalities contained within a single entity. They all perform distinct functions which, when drawn together, formulate the totality of the Plutonic purpose, which is a type of *emergence*, the whole being greater than the sum of its parts. In many ways, to the Roman at least, the concept of Pluto is indeed vastly more dimensioned than the narrow remit of the Greek Horkus, who has this initial intimation of being little more than an *aspect* of the dread Lord of Hades.

The Etruscan Orcus and the Grim Reaper

That is not to imply that Orcus, the autonomous entity, has vanished entirely. The Etruscans, Gauls and provincial Italians of the Roman era all recognised Orcus, or facsimiles of him, and his works and his nature were well-known:

"It would hardly be worth while to mention Orco, the Italian form of Orcus, who has passed into innumerable fairy tales as the Ogre, and who is known to every Italian child, were it not for the peculiar description of him given by my chief authority. "Orco," she said, "is a terrible spirit who was once a great wizard." For this is all the world over the earliest conception of spirits, and especially of those who are feared. Among savage tribes in the early stages of Shamanism, like the Red Indians of America, every remarkable spirit was once a man, always a magician. We may say that the Latin Orcus was a personification of hell, or of the horrible, just as Jupiter was of lightning, but, etymology to the contrary, it is a fact that rude races apply such names as hell and lightning to men. According to Euhemerus of Messina, who derived all gods from men, in which he appears to have been, to a certain degree, right, so far at least as rude races are concerned."[7]

Etruscan scholars ascribe to Orcus the role of psychopomp thus laying the foundation for a more contemporary version of Orcus as the Grim Reaper thus:

"In what shape Death was personified by Euripides, in his Alcestis[8], cannot be made out from the insufficiency of data afforded by the lines relating to

---

[7] *Etruscan Roman Remains in Popular Tradition* (1901), Charles Godfrey Leland, T. Fisher Unwin

[8] Alcestis, Euripides' earliest surviving play – a tragedy – tells the tale of the wife of Admetus who is taken by Orcus only to be resurrected after 3 days (a Christian prototype therefore) after Heracles fights Orcus and forces her release; an outcome that Apollo attempted to engineer through argument in the play's opening scene.

his appearance on the stage. It is, however, plain that the poet brought forward Θάνατος in a bodily form, perhaps considering him the same with Aïdoneus, for he styles him "King of the Dead;" and Macrobius, speaking of the same event, uses for his name the Roman equivalent, 'Orcus.' All that can be gathered from the incidental allusions of the other dramatis personæ to this apparition, is that he was robed in black, and carried a sword, wherewith to sever a lock from the head of his destined victim, and so devote it to the subterranean gods." [9]

Psychopomp derives from the Greek ψυχοπομπός, *psychopompos,* "guide of souls" an entity whose task it is to transport the newly expired to their eternal resting place in the afterlife. Psychopomps are ubiquitous throughout human culture, and Orcus was one example of such, although he did not fulfil all the criteria of a *guide* of the dead; rather, he marked souls for death. In the Greek pantheon it was more properly the job of Hermes to act as escort, whereupon the doomed mortal was given over to Charon to be ferried across the Acheron (Styx in the Roman). Mercury fulfilled this same role in Roman myth, as illustrated by Virgil:

...Mercury made ready
to follow his great father's orders. First
he laces on his golden sandals: winged
to bear him, swift as whirlwinds, high across
the land and water. Then he takes up his wand[10]*;*
with this he calls pale spirits up from Orcus
and down to dreary Tartarus sends others;
he uses this to give sleep and recall it,
and to unseal the eyes of those who have died.[11]

Inevitably the God failed: Orcus is pitiless. The altercation between Apollo and Orcus is further discussed in 'Orcus the Punisher', page 26.

[9] The Gnostics and Their Remains, Ancient and Medieval, (1887), Charles William King, Bibliobazaar

[10] The Caduceus

[11] The Aeneid, Book IV 319-326, Virgil

Orcus then was not a judge (a role more properly ascribed to Rhadamanthus, Aeachus or Minos), but rather he was the executioner, the symbolic removal of a lock of hair being the incontrovertible act of condemnation; as we have seen, even mighty Apollo could not change Orcus' mind once his target was determined. As the Biblical story of Samson illustrates, hair is symbolic of life, vigour and power, so to cut the hair is to effectively cut the life-force; it is indeed a metaphor for death or execution.

Orcus is therefore the personification of death, most neatly conflated with the Grim Reaper, a figure of dread who is a derivation of various death-bringers in human culture manifesting as an avenging angel, spirit, god or demon. His corollary can be found in Anglo-Saxon – as Wōden – and in Norse as Odin, Ankou of the Celts and as Yamaraj in Hindu culture. The Archangel Azrael of the Old Testament fulfilled this exact function. The Riffian people of Northern Morocco:

"...are recognisable by their wild appearance and garb, their different language, and the shaven crown, whence grows the scalp-lock by which Azrael, the Angel of Death, is to pull them up to heaven on the Last Day. This appendage is cultivated with the care its importance demands, for on its reliability rests the Riffian's hope of a blessed immortality."[12]

Azrael is shared by both Christian (Hebrew) and Islamic theosophies, the Qu'ran names him *Malak al-Maut* meaning literally "Angel of Death", fulfilling the identical function as a subordinate to the will of God as he does in the Roman, a personification of Pluto's judgement, whereby the living, once condemned, are hunted down by Orcus who performs the symbolic execution that presages their journey to Hades.

Gauging the quality of Orcus' demeanour though is not straightforward; he is described as both coldly implacable (as in Virgil) or terrifyingly furious or vengeful in various other sources (such as

---

[12] *El Maghreg: 1200 Miles' Ride Through Morocco* (2008), Hugh Edward Millington Stutfield, p.30

Herodotus). In any case, the intimation remains that Orcus is retributive and punishing, and *inescapable*.

This refers, as we have seen, to both the *function* of Pluto and the geographical context of Tartarus, both are inescapable (except in very rare and specific circumstances), in the *Codex Nazareus*[13], one of the ancient Kabbalistic texts contemporaneous with the bible, the word Orcus is used to name the "bottomless pit" into which Lucifer was hurled by Jahweh when he was cast down from heaven. Once again this concurs with the idea that Orcus is – as a locale – a prison, a place of torment and of isolation. It is the place of banishment, of the outcast. Then too, the *entity* that is Orcus facilitates the capture of souls to be incarcerated therein, most evidently as a form of divine retribution or punishment for sinners, and most especially those who, with malice aforethought, commit the crime of oath-breaking.

Orcus is not alone in the heavens however, since in 2009, Orcus' lone Moon was named Vanth by the same team that discovered Orcus in 2004. This provides another mythic cryptogram that we can decode, but rather than elucidating the themes of Orcus, the astronomical perspective has rather muddied the waters. Vanth is a direct reference to an Etruscan death deity, also a psychopomp who was described as being of a benevolent nature. Despite her gentle quality, in many depictions she was a companion to an avenging and punishing Etruscan death deity named Charun. It is generally accepted that Vanth has no counterpart in the Greek, although some have claimed – probably without foundation – that she is a prototype for the Erinyes of Greek myth and in appearance her garb appears to correspond to that of a huntress of the period:

"The Erinyes may have furnished the model already for the first type of Vanth in a long garment, but the demoness or goddess Vanth is certainly older, as the inscription on an aryballoss[14] of the second half of the

---

[13] *Liber Adami*, "The Book of Adam", an early Gnostic text written around the time of Jesus , translated into English by Matthew Norburg 1815.

seventh century clearly proves. Weber-Lehmann 1997 stresses too much the Greek influence in the genesis of Vanth. Vanth originally was, as far as a demon of death can be that, a kind guide, like the Greek Hermes Psychopompos, and not an interpretatio etrusca of the Erinyes[15]. She maintained this manner even when the West Greek huntress type of the Erinyes with a short chiton or skirt, and crossed shoulder straps and boots was adopted for her. Only slowly, under the influence of those West Greek furies, her character began to include less benevolent aspects."[16]

The fact that Vanth has been paired with Orcus is an astronomical anomaly which creates an uncomfortable cultural dissonance. Pluto and his moon Charon make a natural pairing but in the case of Orcus we witness a benevolent Etruscan deity alongside a punishing Roman facsimile of Pluto. It may be that the anomalous association is based upon a misapprehension about the subject of an Etruscan tomb painting excavated in 1868 by a French army officer in Tarquinia, Italy. He wrongly determined that the mural of a hairy, tusked demon within the newly excavated chamber was a depiction of Roman Orcus, and so he named the tomb *Tomba dell'Orco*, the Tomb of Orcus. Despite the fact that the entrance to this chamber displayed paintings of Vanth and Charun, the erroneous association was made. It has been surmised that the hairy demon was in fact a representation of Polyphemus[17], Geryon[18] or a more generic image of a Cyclops.

The observant will naturally wonder at the similarity between the names Charon and Charun, but it is generally agreed that there is no

---

[14] A small spherical or globular flask with a narrow neck containing perfume or oil, often depicted in vase paintings attached by a strap to an athlete's wrist, or is hung by this strap from a peg on the wall.

[15] Erinyes meaning "the angry ones", adopted by the Romans as the Furies who are cited in the Iliad as "those who beneath the earth punish whosoever has sworn a false oath." (iii.278ff; xix.26off).

[16] *The Religion of the Etruscans* (2006), Nancy Thomson De Grummond, Erika Simon

[17] The Cyclops of Homer's Odyssey fame, blinded by Odysseus.

[18] A fearsome giant who dwelt on the Mediterranean island of Erytheia, killed by Heracles in the execution of his 10th labour.

correlation between the two deities, except the broad Chthonic and psychopompian themes which they share. Does the cultural disconnect matter? In terms of gleaning astrological perspective, we can test the various hypotheses. Naming anomalies aside, the mythic imprecision which faces us must be tempered with various practical considerations. In this sense the astronomy can help us and it is worth considering the words of Mike Brown, the astronomer who discovered Orcus:

"We discovered Orcus in early 2004. At the time it was the 4th largest known Kuiper belt object, though by now it has dropped to something like 8th. The most interesting thing about Orcus to me was that it appeared to be the anti-Pluto.

Pluto has what was originally thought to be a peculiar orbit. ...It is so elongated that, for a brief time during its revolution about the sun, it actually comes closer to the sun than does Neptune. So does Orcus. When Pluto comes close to the sun, though, it is never actually close to Neptune, partially because at that point in its orbit it is high above the disk of the planets, hitting the most extreme spot of its tilted orbit. Just like Orcus.

In fact, if you look at the orbits of Pluto and Orcus ... you will see that they are nearly identical except for 2 things. Their elongated orbits point in nearly opposite directions, and, right now, Pluto is nearly as close as it ever comes to the sun while Orcus is nearly as far away as it ever comes. In fact, because Pluto and Orcus are forced by Neptune to have precisely the same orbital period, they will always stay in opposite phases of their orbits.

Orcus is the anti-Pluto.

Several years ago, when searching for a name for what was then known only as 2004 DW, we decided to concentrate on the anti-Pluto aspect of the object's personality, and we came up with Orcus. In the version of the Orcus myth that I like to tell, Orcus was, essentially, the early Etruscan grim reaper, collecting the dead and bringing them to the underworld where another god – Pluto – ruled. As the Etruscan mythology was incorporated into Roman mythology and blended with Greek mythology, Orcus lost his separate identity and Pluto became the master of all of the functions of the dead. Orcus became in some ways simply an alternate name for Pluto, but it also remained a slightly more evil and punishing incarnation of Pluto. In that incarnation, the Latin word Orcus was the origin of words such as ogre and orc. "[19]

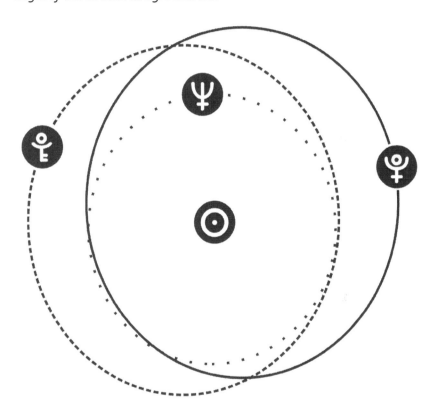

This discussion leaves a few breadcrumbs for us to follow with regard to the original motivation for the naming of Orcus. Clearly, the case for Orcus' mistaken identity is revealed, since in fact, Charun was "the early Etruscan grim reaper" and I find no evidence in any ancient source for the 'version of the myth' that Dr Brown prefers. He is correct nonetheless when he implies that there was a mish-mash made from

---

[19] http://www.mikebrownsplanets.com/2009/03/s1-90482-2005-needs-your-help.html

various Hellenic and early Italian sources which were ultimately drawn together into a Chthonic catch-all in the form of Pluto. Once again we infer from this that Orcus was a function of Pluto, conveying the imprisoning and punishing aspects of Pluto as both a 'reaping' entity and as a location beneath the earth, and these themes are indeed reflected in the earlier Etruscan models which were undoubtedly incorporated into later Roman thought and culture. This leaves little doubt, however, that were the Etruscan pantheon the source for Orcus' naming then Orcus would have been named Charun, the true Etruscan counterpart to Vanth. Clearly this would have created a confusion with Charon, the moon of Pluto. Of further interest is the astounding similarity between the astronomical characteristics of Orcus and Pluto, which intimates that the astronomical Orcus is not so much the anti-Pluto, as his twin.

Orcus the Wild Man

Orcus remained prevalent in European culture long after his Roman counterparts had become dim historical recollections in the form of the Wild Man or Green Man of Medieval European rural society. In this tradition, the dance of Orcus and Maia – most probably a fertility rite – was specifically outlawed by the Catholic Church:

"It would seem that the dance of Orcus and Maia, or... of the wild man and his spouse which is castigated in a Spanish penitential of the 9th or 10th Century in which Orcus is mentioned as the dance partner of Maia, and was, after all simply one of the names of the virgin mother goddess whose cult seems to have spread from the lands bordering the Eastern Mediterranean." [20]

How much meaning we can derive from the characteristics and development of the Wild Man in human culture is uncertain, for as a derivation of Orcus he is likely to evolve in tandem with cultural concepts rather than maintaining archetypal qualities. The Wild Man's

---

[20] *Wild Men of the Middle Ages: a Study in Art, Sentiment and Demonology*, (1970) Richard Bernheimer, Octagon Books

fundamental nature is, however, concomitant with certain key tenets of Orcus, those being his hairiness and outlandish, frightening appearance, a generally untamed and inhuman nature (thus implying a lack of reason), and his propensity for violent acts. The Wild Man, like his Roman prototype, was a character to be avoided at all costs.

It is intriguing however that Orcus, an underworld deity, should be conflated with fertility practices and paired with Maia, who was the Roman goddess of spring, representative to Romans of fruitfulness and fecundity. This creates a very powerful union of opposites, with the god of death and the goddess of new life emphasising, through their fusion, the chthonic cycle embodied in numerous mythological motifs throughout human culture. The same sacred marriage is enacted by Pluto in his union with Proserpina the daughter of Ceres, Goddess of cereals, and thus another example of the same death and birth/fertility polarity blended through marital union. Upon realising that her daughter had been abducted, Ceres mourned and spring did not come. The same symbolism is ubiquitous in the ancient world and reflects the monomyth of life, death and rebirth:

"From the preceding examination of spring and summer festivals, we may infer that our rude forefathers personified the powers of vegetation as male and female, and attempted, on the principle of homoeopathic or imitative magic, to quicken the growth of trees and plants by representing the marriage of the sylvan deities in the persons of a King and Queen of May, a Whitsun Bridegroom and Bride and so forth. Such representations were accordingly no mere symbolic or allegorical dramas, pastoral plays designed to instruct or amuse a pastoral audience. They were charms intended to make the woods to grow green, the fresh grass to sprout, the corn to shoot and the flowers to blow." [21]

---

[21] *The Golden Bough: A Study in Magic and Religion*, (1936) Sir J. G. Frazer, Robert Frazer, Macmillan & Co. Chapter 7, *The Sacred Marriage*

The marriage rite of Orcus and Maia then was a ritual enactment of the *hieros gamos*, one of the most ancient of festivals and, incidentally, one of the most enduring:

"*The idea of a primal marriage is more than myth – it has an important role in cult. In Nauplion there was a spring Kanathos:*

> Here the people of Argos say that Hera, when she is washed yearly, becomes a virgin. This is from the rite they conduct for Hera and is one of the secrets. Pausanias 2.38.2f

Thus, the magic of cult brings us back to the starting point for a theogony, or for a marriage, and the marriage of Zeus and Hera is a way of restarting the clock. It is what we refer to as a hieros gamos, a sacred marriage, which can be ritually enacted."[22]

The ritual enactment of union was a method of attuning the human with the divine, and keeping time with the mystical cycles of creation. Zeus and Hera represented an early example – although much earlier facsimiles can be found in Mesopotamian, Assyrian, Cretan and Egyptian sources to name but a few – and a festival which fell in the month of *Gamelion*, the month of weddings was widely practised in Attica whereby married couples would stay at home in seclusion for two days in January and renew their marriage by assuming the mystical roles of the deities. This tradition survives in countless folklore traditions and are the basis for much later stories, for example the Arthurian legends which show:

"*Kings unable to rule unless they possessed the queen whose name was often given as Guinevere – also rendered Cunneware, Gwenhwyfar, Jennifer, Ginevra or Genevieve. King Arthur married all three. Repeated abductions of her by Meleagant, by Lancelot, by Melwas, by Arthur and by Mordred signified many would-be kings' claim to sovereignty. The*

---

[22] *Zeus* (2005), Ken Dowden, Routledge, p.31

collapse of Arthur's kingdom was intimately related to the loss of the Queen." [23]

And this is because, in order for the kingdom to thrive, the 'equation' must be balanced. Zeus requires Hera, Pluto, Persephone and Arthur, Guinevere. The King's dominion becomes symbolically impotent when he has lost his Queen.

To this day, Mayday rituals in the English countryside continue to celebrate the hieros gamos, which represents as we have seen a union of opposites. This suggests that to the Medieval European mind Orcus corresponded to, in some manner, the antithesis of the fertility Goddess Maia and was equated quite directly with kingship, for the hieros gamos always represents a *regal* marriage, even if it is primarily designed to echo a *divine* one.

This association might seem unlikely were it not for the fact that in ancient societies the power to punish, to take life and to enforce oaths was embodied in the person of the king. The queen and king in this scenario therefore respectively correspond to the divinely echoed power of life and death.

Hubris
The right of taking life with impunity, because one is operating from a position of innate superiority, is an Orcan mandate. In this context, Orcus instantiates the punishing oath, the promise to destroy, which finds its highest expression in the Royal death warrant, which when expressed by the unconscious as a base identification with the archetype becomes the belief that:

"concentrated, intense venomous hatred, or will can kill. And there are many who, believing themselves to be thus hated, do die. And when the hate has really been awakened by a deep wrong, be it from conscience or

---

[23] *The Woman's Encyclopaedia of Myths and Secrets* (1987), Barbara Walker, HarperSanFrancisco

the mysterious working of destiny, and causes beyond our ken, it is wonderful to see how often the arrow strikes--sooner or later! Believe in nothing if thou wilt, neither in the heaven above or in the earth below, but "cast up the account of Orcus--the account thereof cast up," and if there is one on earth whom thou hast deeply, deliberately wronged, thou shalt find thy Nemesis. Dread him whom thou hast struck." [24]

This rather wonderfully encapsulates one of the key precepts of Orcus, which invokes, out of intense feelings of anger and a sense of injustice, a metaphysical death warrant. Thus, just as the entity Orcus condemned mortal souls to death and acted therefore as a literal executioner, those same archetypal energies, debased and adulterated are in human life oft repurposed in the pursuit of revenge. While such extreme reactions to conflict are inappropriate, it is nonetheless an old and tired human story. The privileges of the Gods are enacted *in principle* as the blind servant of human craving and resentment, often with the most petty of motives and justifications. Mortals however, do not have divine privileges. They are not permitted to wield the powers of the Gods with impunity. This tells us that even if the impulse to wish others dead is, in some individuals, a sad inevitability, such unrestrained malice cannot ever have a positive outcome because mortals do not possess the divine right to issue a death warrant. Unleashing the power of Orcus is Pluto's privilege alone, and it can only have unexpected and unfortunate consequences for anyone so powerfully – and negatively – motivated. Assuming the impunity of the Gods is classically termed hubris and punishments[25] for those who were found guilty of this most heinous of crimes were typically beyond the pale.

---

[24] Etruscan Roman Remains in Popular Tradition (1901), Charles Godfrey Leland, T. Fisher Unwin

[25] For examples of the general tone of punishments for hubris it is worthwhile to research the stories of Tantalus, Sisyphus, Arachne, Niobe and Ixion, all of whom angered the Gods with their singular entitlement and lack of humility and suffered dreadful consequences.

In this respect, another mythic touchstone of Orcus is centred upon the double-edged sword of the oath of vengeance. This becomes in a very real sense an invocation of Orcus, a summoning of the most dread demon of Hades, and if the conjuror's motives are at all tainted or impure, if the oath is not uttered with absolute integrity, then there is no circle of protection, and the oath-swearer may well become the victim of his own intended vessel of revenge.

As we shall see in the course of this journey, Orcan power carries heavy responsibility and, misused, creates grave karmic consequences.

The mythology of Orcus, from ancient to Medieval times encompasses themes and tenets of integrity, revenge, judgement, isolation, desolation, implacability and imprisonment and these form the foundation of the astrological lexicon for this dark, distant and enigmatic entity.

Imprisonment

So who is free? The wise man: in command of himself,
Unafraid of poverty, chains, or death, bravely
Defying his passions, despising honours, complete
In himself, smoothed and rounded, so that nothing
External can cling to his polished surface, whom
Fortune by attacking ever wounds herself. Can you
Claim any of this for your own?

Horace: The Satires, Book II – VII – 68-94

Stacy Keach

"I just played a warden in a movie for television, now I'm probably fairly well-known as the warden in Prison Break [Warden Henry Pope] *because that's a very popular show, but I did a warden prior to that, so when I think of that period of my life I think of the trilogy of wardens."[26]*

This 'trilogy of wardens' was played by Stacy Keach who, with Sun in Gemini and conjunct Orcus by a mere 32 minutes of arc, is a man that experiences several (Gemini) Orcan identities (Sun) and has used them extensively in his work. Mercury rules his Midheaven and disposits the Sun, so that identity and his distinctive voice are the key qualities which make him, in the eyes of casting directors and audiences, the perfect personification of a prison warden.

What is even more intriguing is the fact that Keach spent nine months in a British prison, after being convicted of attempting to smuggle cocaine.

---

[26] Stacy Keach on InnerVIEWS, http://www.youtube.com/watch?v=4eStFmZMSkg

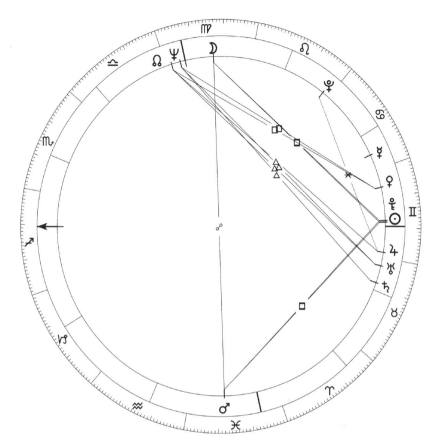

Stacy Keach: 2nd June 1941, 19:15, Savannah, Georgia, USA

Here is a direct exposition of Orcus' mythic energy which creates an association with prisons and places of incarceration. Upon his release after a nine month stay at Reading Jail he said: "*I feel like I've just woken up from a bad dream. I also learned something about freedom. I never realised how precious it is until I lost it... And the saying is true; anything in prison that doesn't kill you can only make you stronger.*"[27]

In 1983, a few months before his imprisonment, Keach experienced Pluto square Orcus by Solar Arc, and thus still well within orb at the time of his arrest. Indeed, considering that there are 90 years between

[27] http://www.youtube.com/watch?v=r3Tq6Xvu-Fk

4th harmonic Solar Arc aspects, this is astonishingly precise. Pluto's arc applied from the 9th house of long distance travel too, and Pluto, the ruler of his 12th house of imprisonment was conjunct Moon in the 9th by Solar Arc at the time of his incarceration: a foreign (9th) prison (12th) quite literally became his home (Moon).

Stacy Keach came to prominence through playing the character Mike Hammer, a detective with an uncompromising attitude toward criminals and their nefarious deeds. Hammer would fight crime with the most brutal and merciless methods, reasoning that the perpetrators of the most heinous crimes deserved no consideration and, as a result of their selfish choices, had forfeited their legal and human rights. He was intolerant and dismissive of the legal system, believing it an obstacle to natural justice, which was his ordained mission to deliver to the guilty. Most episodes ended with his delivering his verdict and executing the perpetrator without remorse or compassion. Mike Hammer, in his unwavering pursuit of vengeance and wrongdoing was a literal archetypal caricature of Orcus. Who better to play him than the man with Sun-Orcus?

Orcan themes run like a freight train through Keach's life and career which gives us, as astrologers, the first clue that the astrological Orcus is much more potent in effect than previously suspected. Indeed, it could be argued that a thorough and relevant astrological insight into Keach's motives, drives and personality would not have been possible without understanding the key themes of Orcus.

His imprisonment was a major surprise too, because it tied into major Orcus transits with almost perfect precision. What I subsequently found in my research is that instances of imprisonment are almost always presaged by major transits or directions from or to Orcus, and the matrix of Orcan contacts describes with uncanny accuracy the conditions and nature of the incarceration.

In Keach's case this bears out very precisely. He was arrested at Heathrow Airport on April 3rd 1984; Uranus was transiting radix Orcus at this time making exact hits on 30th January, 7th May and 15th November. He was arrested in between the first two contacts, and began his sentence at Reading Jail on December 4th, a mere 19 days after the final pass of Uranus-Orcus. He then spent six months in prison and was released just as Chiron applied to Orcus weaving together myriad and complex themes; wounding, healing, incarceration and loss of liberty and ultimately evolution. Keach developed a measure of wisdom (a common Chirotic theme) under the transit to Orcus, as he learnt a profound and painful lesson about the true value of freedom.

Mike Tyson

The theme therefore of being "sent down" appears to be a most natural expression of these various transits to radix Orcus. Consider the case of Mike Tyson, one of the most notorious and dominant heavyweight boxers of modern times, who has a partile conjunction of Orcus with the asteroid Toro in Cancer. Toro is:

"...Spain and corridas and the streets crowded with men who prove their courage in the running of the bulls. Tests of testosterone! Real men don't eat quiche! Toro is... embodied in Rambo and Rocky stereotypes; in football and prizefights... body-builders, machismo and bullies. Toro is cave-man mentality and the worst of blue-collar attitudes; it is unnecessary roughness. Toro is seeing red and charging blindly; it can be somewhat coarse, unpolished and unrefined! It is attempting to use force to get your way. It's being "pushy" and overly assertive and aggressive. Toro uses anger to intimidate."[28]

On July 27th 1991, Tyson was arrested and charged with the rape, 8 days earlier, of beauty contestant Desiree Washington in a hotel room in Indianapolis. Tyson experienced an opposition of Neptune to Orcus on the 22nd, a mere three days after the alleged crime. He was convicted of

---

[28] *Mechanics of the Future: Asteroids* (1991), Martha Lang-Wescott, Treehouse Mountain

the rape by a jury on February 10th 1992, only 18 days after the first pass of Uranus opposition Orcus. Tyson has always claimed innocence of the charges. Desiree Washington did appear, upon subsequent examination, to have sustained injuries consistent with rape and was, according to Tyson's driver who took her back to her own hotel later that night "frantic and disorientated."[29] The conjunction of Toro with Orcus suggests that excessive force, brutality and roughness is conjoined with the theme of imprisonment, while the opposition to Neptune hints that there is some deception at work. The most obvious astrological deduction that can be made about the incident certainly suggests that Tyson may have been telling the truth, the tryst was consensual, but Washington was shocked by Tyson's habitual brutality and (perhaps understandably) changed her mind sometime during the proceedings and afterwards may have seen some retrospective opportunity to avenge her abused right to change her mind. Whether or not that is the case, and we shall never know what happened in that hotel room (Neptune transited in opposition to Tyson's Orcus through the 4th house), the fact remains that Neptune's signature was writ large into the Orcan theme for the heavyweight. Tyson converted to Islam while incarcerated, and was actively engaged in "exploring religion, exploring his roots"[30] which very neatly encapsulates the Neptune in the 4th dynamic, expressed under the influence of Jupiter trine Orcus, a single pass contact which was exact at the time of his soul-searching and really does describe very succinctly how one might use incarceration as a deepening and positive experience.

And it underlines too, the manner in which, in both these examples, imprisonment has instilled within the individual a greater reverence for freedom, spirituality and life purpose and meaning.

---

[29] New York Times: *Tyson's Driver Says Woman Was Dazed* By Phil Berger, Published: February 2, 1992
[30] New York Times: *The Tyson, Olajuwon Connection* By Dave Anderson, published: November 13, 1994

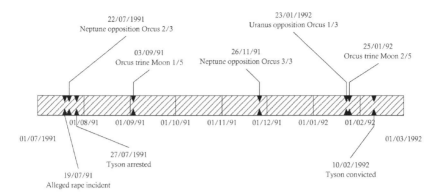

It is the first hint that Orcus, not unlike his counterpart Pluto, has a transformative potential and with it, a possibility of realising a great benefit. It is, if you like, in keeping with the underlying principle of the penal system, which when understood as an enforced *penitence* – prisons are termed penitentiaries or correctional facilities – further underlines the *modus operandi* of Orcus: *isolation that transforms*.

We can see in both examples a man who has experienced both positive and negative potentials of Orcus. Enforced incarceration is a facet of the punishing face of Orcus, here there is retribution for wrongdoing and in each instance, the subject has eventually realised some measure of the exaltation of Orcus through a profound and irrevocable shift of perspective, either through a deeper appreciation for liberty or through finding a more spiritual basis for living. Orcus, like Pluto therefore, is a transformative power operating through the adversity of isolation, incarceration and loss of freedom.

Terry Waite
Possibly an even better example of this principle is that of Terry Waite, the Church of England's Special Envoy who was himself taken hostage while on a mission to Lebanon to try and secure the release of John McCarthy and Brian Keenan. In total, Waite endured 1,763 days in captivity, four years of which were spent in solitary confinement. Upon his release he wrote a book about his experiences "Taken on Trust", wherein much of the early focus was on the principle of trust. His

captors had solemnly sworn to afford him safe passage to visit
McCarthy and Keenan. He went on to say that:

*"The five years I spent in captivity, four of which were in total solitary
confinement, gave me a unique opportunity to learn how to appreciate
being alone but more importantly how to value silence."* [31]

Once again there is a powerful Orcan theme at work in the life of a man
who is *identified* with his captivity and too we see a nativity
characterised by an exact conjunction of an otherwise unaspected Sun
with Orcus, in the sign of Gemini. As an intriguing aside, Waite was kept
hostage, chained to a radiator in an ordinary house in Beirut. He was
taken hostage just as transiting Orcus applied to the asteroid House
4950 at 8° Leo in his chart. Upon his release, he began to write, and he
said of that process:

*"In Beirut, I relived my past, and in Cambridge, where this book has been
written, I have relived it yet again. There have been days where I have
been gripped by fear and days of pure joy when I have experienced the
beauty of solitude and the harmony of family and friendships. Living for
years deprived of natural light, freedom of movement and
companionship, I found that time took on a new meaning... This is the
story I wrote when I was totally alone. It concludes when after four years,
I was moved to be with other hostages. If you read this book as a captive,
take heart. Your spirit can never be chained."* [32]

Waite's account of his years in solitary confinement is a singularly
Orcan dialogue.

Nelson Mandela
Perhaps the most celebrated example of an Orcan transformation
exists in the example of the former President of South Africa and Anti-
Apartheid Campaigner, Nelson Mandela. There is a great irony in his life

---

[31] *The joy of inner quietness*: Terry Waite, http://www.maturetimes.co.uk/node/7572
[32] *Taken on Trust* (1994), Terry Waite, Coronet

arc, for Mandela was a vocal proponent of armed struggle[33], but after his release from prison he was awarded the Nobel Prize for Peace. That is certainly a transformation, albeit one that operates on a polarity.

Mandela's Orcus is not involved in any aspectual arrangement of *obvious* note. However, with Orcus at 3°20" of Taurus, we are drawn to the observation that the asteroid Toro falls at 3°20" of Leo, closely conjunct Sappho at 3°02" Leo. The exactitude of these contacts is noteworthy in the extreme. Orcus in the 5th squares Toro/Sappho in the 8th and Leo: here themes of leadership identity are creating enormous tension with the traditional order of the day (5th house, Taurus, the square). Mandela was South Africa's first black lawyer working in partnership with Oliver Tambo in 1952, and was sentenced along with a number of other men whom he counted as friends, although Tambo was, at the time of Nelson Mandela's arrest, already living in exile in London.

Once again, the transits of Orcus are writ large on the story of Nelson Mandela's time in prison. He was sentenced to life imprisonment as Orcus made the 3rd of 5 passes to Mandela's natal Mars. Incredibly at the exact moment he was making his closing speech during his Pretoria trial and the judge was handing down the sentence, Orcus was at the exact midpoint in time of these Mars squares.[34]

If Mars – Orcus was the characterising astrological event presaging his incarceration, it ought to be no surprise that Orcus square Mars, this time by Solar Arc was partile within 3 days of his release on 11th

---

[33] In his trial statements, Mandela asserted that the ANC had attempted to bring about reform of apartheid through peaceful means for many years and that to continue with a policy of peaceful protest was tantamount to surrender, because of its ineffectiveness. He argued therefore that a campaign targeting the symbolic places of apartheid was the only workable means of realising their objectives. He later expressed regret for those civilians who were killed or injured during these attacks.

[34] The precise midpoint in time of the 5 Orcus squares to Mars beginning 08:23 a.m. on August 11th 1963 and ending 04:11 a.m. on April 30th 1965 is 04:47 a.m. 20th June 1964, a few hours before Mandela was sentenced later that day.

February 1990.[35] The Orcus effect was complete and Mandela was transformed:

Mandela invited to his inauguration his arch enemy P W Botha and also Percy Yutar, the lawyer who had tried to get him executed in the Rivonia trial. He then went out of his way to support the all-white national rugby team, the Springboks, wearing a team shirt during the 1995 World Cup. And he threw his weight behind Desmond Tutu's idea for a Truth and Reconciliation Commission, which offered amnesty to all those who came forward to fully confess their crimes during the apartheid regime. This policy of reconciliation averted a bloodbath and eased the transition to multi-racial democracy.

This was his most extraordinary achievement. Ironically its roots lay in the long years of imprisonment.

In jail, he said, "You come face to face with time: there is nothing more terrifying." There he learned the power of forgiveness. Though as a boy he was educated at Methodist colleges, Mandela had no personal religious faith as motivation. But his long years in prison inculcated in him an extraordinary tolerance and compassion, and brought him a sense of perspective that enabled him to see beyond day-to-day politics to more ultimate ends.

It enabled him to exert authority over the warders, and eventually over the South African government itself until they were virtually his prisoners and he was the warder. Afterwards he never reminded anyone of their past support for apartheid or its horrors. And when angry young ANC activists called for vengeance he replied that if he could work with enemies who sent him to jail for a third of his life, so could they.

---

[35] Orcus squared Mandela's natal Mars on February 8th 1990 by Solar Arc, an astrological event of astonishing precision in the context of the degree for a year system of prediction.

Reconciliation was the price of future peace. "Men of peace must not think about retribution or recriminations," he said. "Courageous people do not fear forgiving, for the sake of peace".[36]

These unbending principles, painstakingly accrued in the darkness of incarceration and the silence of isolation are, together with personal dignity and depth of character, the rare and incomparable gifts of the astrological Orcus.

---

[36] From "*A monument to Mandela: the Robben Island years*", by Paul Vellely: Independent on Sunday, 2 September 2007.

Punishment

What god opposes my prayers with his divine will?
Might I be suffering from some crime of yours that harms me?
Whatever one deserves to suffer should be borne lightly:
what comes undeservedly, comes as bitter punishment.
Ovid: Heroides V

It would be possible to fill an entire tome with examples of how, with uncanny precision, transits to and from Orcus correspond with periods of jail-time[37]. What this intimates is that there is an unerring connection between the underlying and foundation principles of Orcus in the mythological context, as both an entity and a place of incarceration; somewhere in the no man's land between these mythic principles there is a meeting point where the principle of imprisonment meets the inner human condition and the soul resonates with the imperative of Orcus. One might naturally suspect that this thematic quality ought therefore to be extant in the nativities of arch-imprisoners of the most heinous type, in the recent and horrific cases, for example, of Philip Garrido and Joseph Fritzl, however, the astrology does not support this perspective. There is first and foremost – it would appear – a rational element to

---

[37] As an example, the actor Robert Downey Jr. was on numerous occasions between 1996 and 2001 arrested for drugs and firearms offences. He was ordered into rehab several times but repeated violations of his parole agreements eventually left the judge no choice but to 'send him down'. He was sentenced to rehab on June 23rd 1999, and was transferred to prison on August 5th. Orcus moved to within a degree of squaring Downey's Neptune in August 1997 (when he was ordered to attend rehab), and moved out of orb in July 2000, one month before he was released from prison. His transfer to prison occurred 15 days before the last pass of his Orcus – Neptune squares on 20th August 1999. It would have been deeply problematic to have predicted Downey's prison-time without an understanding of Orcus.

Orcus, which requires some measure of analytic judgement and at least a tip of the hat to some underpinning principle of justice. Orcus does not appear to operate clearly in cases of complete derangement and dysfunction, usually a rationalisation is required, no matter how skewed or off-kilter and in these kinds of cases, though there is profound compulsion, both Fritzl and Garrido are at some level aware that their actions are not promulgated through any sense of rational justice.

These last two words are key operators in the invocation of Orcus. Those examples we have contemplated thus far demonstrate how Orcus operates through a dispassionate system that, although often flawed, as its name implies, is fundamentally allied to the principle of justice. The justice system is replete with the myriad checks and balances that are required by a civilised society, so that, even if the solution to the problem of wrong-doing is an ineffectual and blunt instrument, it does at least arrive at its judgements with as much impartiality as is possible.

The *principle* of Orcus though, operates regardless of the rigour, or lack thereof, of the framework within which it is constrained.

No better example of this can be presented than that of Die Endlösung – the Final Solution – of Nazi Germany's Jewish "problem" and its architect, Heinrich Himmler.

Unconscious Programming
A detailed analysis of the psychology of German anti-Semitism of the period would be too wide in scope to reasonably explore here, but it is nevertheless important to understand the rationalising component of Orcus, which is apparent in all human life, just as it was in the ideals of German National Socialism. A judgement is *required* before the target can be condemned. There is no guarantee of any objective standard of fairness in any Orcan judgement that is handed down. One has but to be convinced that 'the accused' is guilty - regardless of the legitimacy of the accusation - and Orcus is unleashed.

"*The house in which my twin brothers and I were born stood in a street off the Kurfurstendamm. As far as I can recall, the majority of the occupants were always Jews. My parents were only on friendly terms with our Gentile neighbours. From old remarks of theirs, I gathered that Jews were "foreigners": our neighbours pronounced the word with scorn. Contact with the other Jewish inhabitants of the house was limited to an exchange of greetings if one met them on the stairs.*

Whether I had any Jewish classmates at my primary school, I no longer remember, but at the secondary school Jewish girls, at times, made up one third of my class. My parents often complained about this situation. Why it was lamentable I did not understand, but then our parents also complained about the unemployment although we did not suffer from it ourselves.

I ask myself now how my Jewish schoolfellows struck me. First, almost without exception, by their physical and mental precociousness. They were "ladies" already, while I felt I was still a child and the ostentatious clothes many of them wore annoyed me. Not one of them came from a poor home. Most of them, indeed, were rich and there were some who sought to impress with their fathers' cars in which the chauffeurs sometimes came to fetch them. The fact that these airs particularly upset me may have been connected with my mother's frequent complaints about "nouveau riche". If this expression refers to the time a family's prosperity dates from and not to a style of life, then my mother came from a nouveau riche family herself anyway. Her father was a tradesman who had worked his way to the top.

The first political conversations I can remember having with other girls at school were provoked by a girl in my form whose father had been an officer in the First World War and belonged to the Stahlhelm [a nationalist paramilitary group]. These consisted of boasting about the exploits of one's brothers and cousins which were directed against the new German Republic and even before 1933 against the Jews...

One day Gerde brought me a railway ticket which looked like an ordinary one. It was only on closer examination that I realised this was a political joke. It carried the imprint "to Jerusalem". Underneath was written in smaller print "and no return". We gave this ticket to Rachel K for her father. We chose Rachel because she was a particularly good-natured girl, somewhat simple in her friendliness. I was then 12 years old."[38]

These subtle but invidious shifts of perspective are the first requirement for the Orcan invocation. As the account later unfolds it is clear that the manipulation of young (and more impressionable) minds by those in positions of authority began with an appeal at the level of archetype[39].

The use of archetypes by the Nazi leadership was raised to a level hitherto unseen in all history, although it is probably fair to say that the designers of this propaganda did not fully understand the psychological mechanics of their approach. By today's standards their unconscious programming was crude, cynical and naive, but it was nonetheless completely effective. Contemporary western culture is more sophisticated in its understanding of symbols and therefore more resilient to manipulation of archetypal imagery, but the sheer psychological naïveté of the German people offset the relative lack of sophistication of the propagandists. This archetypal reverberation echoed throughout the whole of the German collective unconscious, which manipulated symbolism consistent with the entire improbable edifice of Nazism. The enemies of Germany were depicted as bestial, evil and sly, while German figures were rendered as chivalrous Teutonic

---

[38] *Account Rendered* (1964), Melita Maschmann, Abelard-Schuman, p.37-39
[39] Jung's work with psychotic patients at the Burgholzli mental clinic in Zurich, led him to postulate a 'collective unconscious'. He found that many of the delusions experienced by patients could not be explained as products of the patient's personal history and his extensive knowledge of human symbols, myths and comparative religion led him to detect parallels with psychotic material which argued a common source, a myth-making level of mind common to all humanity. This collective unconscious consists of mythological motifs or primordial images which Jung termed 'archetypes'.

knights, or protective and fatherly figures. Jung saw the difficult potentials of this misuse of archetypal manipulation from its inception:

"Nobody called Charlemagne's kingdom the First Reich, nor Wilhelm's the Second Reich. Only the Nazi's call theirs the Third Reich. Because it has a profound mystical meaning: to every German the expression 'Third Reich' echoes in his unconscious of the biblical hierarchy." [40]

This biblical connotation was exploited by the Nazi propaganda machine at every opportunity, particularly in addresses to the Hitler Youth who, their minds unformed, were more vulnerable to even the most blatant of appeals to archetype. On one occasion, Hitler proclaimed to the massed ranks of German youth: *"You are flesh of our flesh and blood of our blood"* [41] while at an earlier rally he told the assembled youth to either be: *"hot or cold, but lukewarm should be damned and spewed from your mouth."* The Book of Revelation contends that *"Thou art neither cold nor hot... So then because thou art lukewarm... I will spew thee out of my mouth."* [42]

In this way the Nazi propagandists manipulated biblical archetypes to mould and manipulate the minds of the young and vulnerable. Biblical archetypes echoed across the length and breadth of Germany at this time, with Hitler cast as the nation's messiah. This suited the party line

---

[40] Jung believed that individual self-knowledge and the capacity for human relationships that this brings is the only power to resist the collective dominance of the state (or of malicious authoritarian figures). On this theme he commented in 1957: *"anyone who has once learned to submit absolutely to a collective belief and to renounce his eternal right to freedom and the equally eternal duty to individual responsibility... will be able to march with the same credulity and with the same lack of criticism in the reverse direction, if another and manifestly better belief is foisted upon his idealism. What happened not so long ago to a civilised European nation? We accuse the Germans of having forgotten it all already, but the truth is that we don't know for certain whether something similar might not happen elsewhere. It would not be surprising if it did and if another civilised nation succumbed to the infection of a uniform and a one-sided idea."* The Undiscovered Self (1957), C.G. Jung, Routledge, Chapter 1, The Plight of the Individual in Modern Society.

[41] Compare Genesis Chapter 2 Verse 23, *"This is now bone of my bones, and flesh of my flesh"* attributed to Hitler by Albert Speer, September 5th 1934.

[42] The Book of Revelation, chapter 3, verse 15-16.

since before 1933 he was able to pose as a kind of saviour and he was conflated with the rescuer archetype in an overt and blatant manner. The people loved him, believing that he had been sent to deliver them from their discontent. This elevation of Hitler enabled him to create a party system that depended on his autocratic style of management. The glorious Fuhrer was above reproach. His subordinates rarely dared to exercise initiative, resulting in the gradual disintegration of the whole structure of government through a lack of balance. None dared gainsay the now deified leader. The most potent example of this deliberate association of Hitler with the Messiah archetype and its cynical insertion into German consciousness is evidenced by the following dictation approved by the Ministry of Enlightenment and Propaganda (a rather dissonant title in itself), first used in German primary schools on the 16th of March 1934: "*Jesus and Hitler. As Jesus freed men from sin and hell, so Hitler freed the German people from destruction. Jesus and Hitler were persecuted, but while Jesus was crucified, Hitler was raised to the Chancellorship... Jesus strove for heaven, Hitler for the German earth.*"[43]

In art, literature and propaganda of the period within Germany, archetypes, repurposed in this deliberate manner, abound, mostly thematically focused on the image of the German as a form of mythical warrior, usually in the chivalric tradition, battling heroically against the various evils of Bolshevism, 'International Jewry', contamination of the racial character by *Untermenschen* (sub-humans) and the inequalities of Versailles.[44]

---

[43] During an interview in 1938, which appeared in Hearst's International-Cosmopolitan magazine, widely circulated in the US, the interviewer, H.R. Knickerbocker asked Jung: "*As he [Hitler] said just after his Czech victory, Germany stands today on the threshold of her future. That means he has just begun and if his voice tells him that the German people are destined to become the lords of Europe and perhaps of the world and if his [unconscious] voice continues to always be right then we are in for an extremely interesting period aren't we?*" To which Jung replied: "*Yes, it seems the German people are now convinced they have found their Messiah.*"

[44] For Hitler, the Marxist tenets held dear by the German labourer came as a great shock during his time in Vienna. "Are such men worthy of belonging to a great people?" He asked, from Mein Kampf. The denunciation of Marxism was assured for Hitler with

The subject of Hitler's racism, and indeed, that of the party as a whole, intimates an increasingly skilled and cynical use of archetypes, even if they were not understood in those terms at that time. It is difficult to say if this manipulation was however, entirely deliberate; in many ways it is naively shameless, but certainly, there is no questioning its effectiveness. Whether or not the methods were understood as an archetypal manipulation is moot, they worked. The same methods which so effectively exalted Hitler and decent Germans, cast down a host of 'inferior' types; most especially the Jews.

"There is no mystery. They killed them [the Jews] *because violent anti-Semitism which preached extermination as the 'solution to the Jewish problem' permeated German society... Hitler was merely adapting mass popular belief to his own political purposes. As early as the beginning of the Nineteenth Century this obsessive certainty that the Jews were the main source of all that was wrong in Germany had become German 'common sense'"*.[45]

---

the knowledge that Karl Marx was a Jew. The Untermenschen were a unique category consisting mainly of non-Jewish Poles and Russians whom he considered to be inferior races. Bullock ascribes to Hitler the belief that "in international affairs Jewish capitalists sought to divert nations from their true interests and plunge them into wars, gradually establishing their mastery over them with the help of the power of money and propaganda. At the same time the Jewish leaders of the international Communist revolution had provided themselves with a world headquarters in Moscow from which to spread subversion internally through the propagation by the Marxist parties of internationalism, egalitarianism and pacifism, all of which Hitler identified with the Jews and saw as a threat to Aryan values." *Hitler and Stalin, Parallel Lives,* (1991), Alan Bullock, Harper Collins

[45] *Hitler's Willing Executioners: Ordinary Germans and the Holocaust,* (1997), Daniel Goldhagen, Abacus. Goldhagen believes that the Holocaust was participated in by all Germans; not just a few hard-line fanatics. The German weekly "Die Zeit" announced a *"Historikerstreit"* – battle among historians – in response to the publication of this book. The first was in the early 1960s when Fritz Fischer wrote a book to prove that the First World War had been deliberately started by Imperial Germany. The second began in the late 1980s, when several historians suggested that the Nazi genocide of the Jews was not entirely a German initiative but had some relationship to the massacres already perpetrated by Stalin and his henchmen against sections of the Soviet Union's population.

Certainly, anti-Semitism was not new to Hitler, or even his generation but the Nazis contaminated the archetypal imagery of 'the Jew' with a new level of symbolic negativity, playing on the unconscious insecurities of the German people most typically with scenarios of the degradation and corruption of Aryan women, conjuring *"the nightmare vision of the seduction of hundreds of thousands of girls by repulsive, crooked-legged Jew bastards."*[46] This style of propagandist hysteria was typical and yet it was even so remarkably effective because any type of rational appeal inciting anti-Semitism would have been dismissed perfunctorily. In psychoanalytic terms, it is only through the manipulation of primitive archetypes that such appeals can possibly bear fruit. Hitler understood this principle, that successful manipulation of people could be achieved, not by argument, but by appealing to their emotions, when he said *"The psyche of the broad masses is accessible only to what is strong and uncompromising. They have very little idea of how to make a choice... They see only the ruthless force and brutality of [their leaders'] utterances to which they always submit in the end."*[47]He reinforced this view somewhat more succinctly when he wrote *"for the great majority of a nation.. thought and conduct are ruled by sentiment rather than sober reasoning."*[48] Jung too allowed for this principle, that there is no evidence of a collective rationality, indeed *"if you choose one hundred of the most intelligent people in the world and get them all together, they are a stupid mob... ten thousand of them together would have the collective intelligence of an alligator."*[49] This principle is

---

[46] From *Mein Kampf* (2007), Adolf Hitler, Jaico Publishing House. Another form of archetypal persuasion used by Hitler to denigrate the Jews was through pejorative nomenclature: 'worm' was most popular, although any insect of a parasitic nature was utilised in this way. For Hitler's purposes this enabled Aryans to feel justified in his assurances of superiority; *"as soon as I began to investigate the matter... Vienna appeared to me in a new light... Was there any shady undertaking, any form of foulness, especially in cultural life, in which at least one Jew did not participate? On putting the probing knife to that kind of abscess one immediately discovered like a maggot in a putrescent body, a little Jew who was often blinded by the sudden light."* This literary dehumanisation of the Jews allowed the subsequent progression to their actual dehumanisation at a later point. This process is fundamentally Orcan.

[47] From *Mein Kampf.*

[48] From *Mein Kampf.*

characterised by Jung as the tendency toward mediocrity by the average individual, although in Jung's system, unlike Hitler's social Darwinism[50] this does not imply inferiority, merely a preference for convention which the "great" do not possess. The impetus to resist the collective is correctly termed, in Jungian parlance, to have a "vocation", the etymology of which is "to be addressed by a voice" so, while Hitler had vocation, the vast majority of Germans did not and therefore had no power to resist the pull of the collective. This also to a large extent explains the success of archetypal sublimation on the nation. From the Jungian perspective, any established archetype exists *a priori* and thus has truth to the individual regardless of any experience to the contrary. In this way, by presenting the Jewish archetype as parasitic, the unconscious imagery remains unaffected by conscious evidence. This dissonance is demonstrated perfectly in the testimony of ordinary Germans at the time:

"We never thought of identifying our Jewish school friends with "The Jew". This confused attitude later made it possible for me to feel and think as an anti-Semite without realising how inhuman this was. My hate was directed against a bogey [or archetype], *not against actual people."*[51]

---

[49] From *C.G. Jung Speaking: Interviews and Encounters* (1980), William McGuire (ed.); R.F.C. Hull (ed.) C. G Jung; Macmillan.

[50] Specifically the belief that success in the human sphere is the natural reward of the superior type. Hitler's views were encapsulated within 'rassenpolitik' or race-policy. Jung stated that *"nature is aristocratic and one person of value outweighs ten lesser ones"* which, though it might resemble social Darwinism, is a statement lacking a racial component. From *The Relations Between the Ego and the Unconscious* a subtext of *Two Essays on Analytical Psychology* (1967), C.G. Jung, Princeton University Press.

[51] Melita Maschmann's testimony is an excellent source for exploring the psychological confusion of an entire people. "My twin brother and I were enraptured at that time by the heroes of the ancient German myth, the Nibelungelied. We loved the heroic Siegfried and hated the evil Hagen. These symbols gave us an inkling of what the grown-ups meant when they spoke of the 'dagger-thrust'. The enemy [the perpetrators of the Versailles injustice] had fallen upon Germany as she lay prostrate on the ground, like robbers upon a wounded hero. Almost all her neighbours had torn away parts of her territory as one might tear flesh from a living body. The phrase 'The Bleeding Frontier' made such a deep impression that I could not hear it in later years without feeling physical pain... At 15 I learned the endless calls to arms of Theodor Korner: 'Wash the soil of your German land with your pure blood', and so on. I read the works of Ernst

From Jung's teachings it can be seen that she would have struggled to control the effect of this kind of archetypal manipulation:

"irrational yet undisputed and indisputable moods and opinions... are so difficult to influence because of the powerfully suggestive effect emanating from the archetype. Consciousness is fascinated by it, held captive, as if hypnotised."[52]

This process gives rise to an important understanding. The reason that I have used the example of the Jews in Nazi Germany is to leave no doubt as to the power of archetypal subversion, the deliberate contamination of archetypes, whereby a human being is associated with an inhuman or unconsciously revolting archetype for the purpose of undermining their relative human rights. When that *process* has reached its conclusion all sorts of horrors are unleashed because the target individual is no longer accorded basic human rights or respect. They become a legitimate scapegoat and thus *deserve* punishment and ultimately death. The reason that this is fundamental to the Orcan drive is that the meting out of punishment can only operate under a Hadean imperative: the 'death-warrant' must be signed off by a higher power. Where Orcus is concerned, the punishment impulse has to be justified; because that is a fundamental of the Orcan principle.

And it is crucial to place this in its proper context, because Orcus *is* the punishment impetus in the human soul; it is retribution, vengeance, rightful and divine in its justice, because it has to be in order to operate. When there are two opposed views, an argument results, and while one person cannot 'win' the dispute, Orcus cannot be invoked. *Judgement* must precede *sentence*. If the argument does not suffice then – precisely because the desire to punish and seek retribution against

---

Moritz Arndt aloud, and wrote school essays about Schiller's 'Wilhelm Tell' in which I drew bold parallels with the contemporary situation in Germany. The Fatherland, in reality unhappy and miserable, was in our dreams a kind of Holy Grail of perfect purity and beauty, for which no sacrifice could be too great." From *Hitler Youth: Growing Up in Hitler's Shadow* (2005) Susan Campbell Bartoletti, Scholastic Nonfiction
[52] C.G. Jung: *The Relations Between the Ego and the Unconscious* 1967.

those who have resisted your intent is compulsive and therefore (to the self-unaware) irresistible – the next best thing to winning the argument and thus being justified in meting out punishment is to render your opponent's argument superfluous. A God does not have to argue with a man any more than a king has to prove his superiority over a commoner, any more than *a man is required to demonstrate his ascendancy over a worm...*

Dehumanisation

Dehumanisation is a prime tool of the misdirected Orcan imperative. Death is not interested in the doomed mortal's pleas for understanding because his mission is divinely ordered: in Euripides' *Alcestis*, Apollo attempts to argue with Orcus for the life of Alcestis to be spared:

From the right comes ORCUS, with a drawn sword in his hand. He moves stealthily towards the Palace; then sees APOLLO and halts abruptly. The two Deities confront each other.

ORCUS: *Ha! Phoebus! You! Before this Palace! Lawlessly would you grasp, abolish the rights of the Lower Gods! Did you not beguile the Fates and snatch Admetus from the grave? Does not that suffice? Now, once again, you have armed your hand with the bow, to guard the daughter of Pelias who must die in her husband's stead!*
APOLLO: *Fear not! I hold for right, and proffer you just words.*
ORCUS: *If you hold for right, why then your bow?*
APOLLO: *My custom is ever to carry it.*
ORCUS: *Yes! And you use it unjustly to aid this house!*
APOLLO: *I grieve for a friend's woe.*
ORCUS: *So you would rob me of a second body?*
APOLLO: *Not by force I won the other.*
ORCUS: *Why, then, is he in the world and not below the ground?*
APOLLO: *In his stead he gives his wife-whom you have come to take.*
ORCUS: *And shall take-to the Underworld below the earth!*
APOLLO: *Take her, and go! I know not if I can persuade you...*
ORCUS: *Not to kill her I must kill? I am appointed to that task.*

APOLLO: *No, no! But to delay death for those about to die.*
ORCUS: *I hear your words and guess your wish!*
APOLLO: *May not Alcestis live to old age?*
ORCUS: *No! I also prize my rights!*
APOLLO: *Yet at most you win one life.*
ORCUS: *They who die young yield me a greater prize.*
APOLLO: *If she dies old, the burial will be richer.*
ORCUS: *Phoebus, that argument favours the rich.*
APOLLO: *What! Are you witty unawares?*
ORCUS: *The rich would gladly pay to die old.*
APOLLO: *So you will not grant me this favour?*
ORCUS: *Not I! You know my nature.*
APOLLO: *Yes! Hateful to men and a horror to the gods!*
ORCUS: *You cannot always have more than your due.*
APOLLO: *Yet you shall change, most cruel though you are! For a man comes to the dwelling of Pheres, sent by Eurystheus to fetch a horse-drawn chariot from the harsh-wintered lands of Thrace; and he shall be a guest in the house of Admetus, and by force shall he tear this woman from you. Thus shall you gain no thanks from us, and yet you shall do this thing-and my hatred be upon you*

APOLLO *goes out.* ORCUS *gazes after him derisively.*

ORCUS: *Talk all you will, you get no more of me! The woman shall go down to the dwelling of Hades. Now must I go to consecrate her for the sacrifice with this sword; for when once this blade has shorn the victim's hair, then he is sacred to the Lower Gods!*

This interchange demonstrates that Orcus is not amenable to persuasion; once Orcus is invoked therefore, argument becomes superfluous: the target is condemned and no words will change the sentence.

No amount of rational argument about such principles as humanity, compassion or decency would have deterred the Nazis from condemning the Jewish people to annihilation. Even if an argument had been presented that was on its own merit convincing, it could be discounted, because the Jew was less than human. They were parasitic worms who 'deserved' to be destroyed. Human rights are only applicable to humans after all.

Dehumanisation takes many forms. It is only required to demonstrate that the target has motives or characteristics which are out of step with *normal* or *healthy* motives and characteristics for the target to be dehumanised. They can be labelled stupid, illiterate, evil, dangerous, violent, abusive or cruel. They might be power-mad, lustful or out of control. This style of dehumanisation is more subtle, because of course, on occasion, any person might be lustful or dangerous – indeed, most people are capable of being self-interested and unpleasant under certain circumstances. The manipulation lies in creating the impression that the target individual or group has these negative motives or characteristics at all times.

Less subtly, the target might be labelled verminous or parasitic. This is an outright dehumanisation and is a favourite of megalomaniac rhetoric. Mein Kampf is liberally littered with references to Jewish rats, worms and parasites. Once dehumanised, the target becomes a justified target and must be dealt with.

Punishment is therefore the lower function of Orcus, whilst *reform* is the higher order. Nowhere in the many philosophic depictions of National Socialism is there any intimation to reforming the parasitic Jewish tendency, they are a problem with only one solution, and a *final* solution at that.

Heinrich Himmler

Nobody better espoused the base impetus of Orcus than the architect of the Holocaust, Heinrich Himmler. Himmler was a devout Roman Catholic and claimed that his religious views were what allowed him to do his work, because the understanding that he was engaged in God's work relieved him of guilt about having to destroy the Jewish people. He saw himself as a mythical warrior, devoted to the purification of his people, rescuing them from the indignity of moral and racial pollution by lesser peoples. Delinquents of all types were identified: the Jews, gypsies, homosexuals, the disabled and those racial types considered to be subhuman: Slavs, Poles and Russians:

"I am now referring to the evacuation of the Jews, the extermination of the Jewish people. It's one of those things that is easily said: 'The Jewish people are being exterminated', says every party member, 'this is very obvious, it's in our program, elimination of the Jews, extermination, we're doing it, hah, a small matter.' [...] But of all those who talk this way, none had observed it, none had endured it. Most of you here know what it means when 100 corpses lie next to each other, when 500 lie there or when 1,000 are lined up. To have endured this and at the same time to have remained a decent person - with exceptions due to human weaknesses - had made us tough. This is a page of glory never mentioned and never to be mentioned. [...] We have the moral right, we had the duty to our people to do it, to kill this people who wanted to kill us."[53]

Himmler has associated the onerous duty of destroying the Jews with a moral imperative, necessary to the survival of upstanding Germans. Himmler manages to turn the moral question upon its head, refashioning black as white and vice-versa:

"Another question which was decisive for [us] was the Jewish question. It was uncompromisingly solved after orders and rational recognition. I believe, gentleman, that you know me well enough to know that I am not a bloodthirsty person; I am not a man who takes pleasure or joy when something rough must be done. However on the other hand, I have such good nerves and such a developed sense of duty - I can say that much for myself - that when I recognise something as necessary I can implement it

---

[53] Heinrich Himmler, in a speech to Nazi officials in October 1943. Full text of the Poznan Speech at http://www.holocaust-history.org/himmler-poznan/speech-text.shtml

without compromise. I have not considered myself entitled - this concerns especially the Jewish women and children - to allow the children to grow into the avengers who will then murder our fathers and our grandchildren. That would have been cowardly."[54]

It was Himmler's divine duty to exterminate the Jews, and it would have been *cowardly* to have shirked this great responsibility to murder women and children. See how the language of Orcus is employed here to expedite the Final Solution to the Jewish 'Problem' with the employment of a lexicon of Orcan words and phrases, most succinctly summarised in 'without compromise'. See how Orcus takes no heed of methods because objectives are exalted to a level beyond reproach or equivocation. This type of expedience is typical of the base energy of Orcus. Objectives and outcomes are raised to a level of outright imperatives – "at any cost" – and the actions and choices made in pursuit of the outcome are automatically sanitised. Even the murder of children is justified because other, "worthier" children are being saved from the spectre of future revenge. On the dark side of Orcus the end always justifies the means.

The nativity of Heinrich Himmler evinces a fascinating structure wherein Orcus is at the apex of a Thor's Hammer aspect pattern from a square between Mercury and Mars.

---

[54] Himmler, in a speech of May 24 1944, Sonthofen, from *Holocaust Denial on Trial, Trial Judgement: Electronic Edition* (2004), Charles Gray, Lewis H. Beck Center for Electronic Collections and Services, Emory University, Atlanta

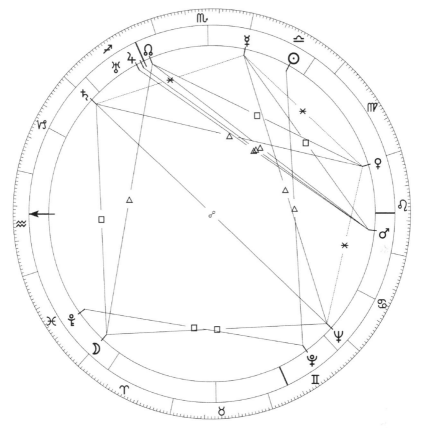

Heinrich Himmler: 7th October 1900, 15:30, Munich, Germany

What is more intriguing perhaps is the placement of Orcus at the precise midpoint (a 4 minute contact) of the Mercury Mars square in the fixed signs. With Orcus ruled by a Neptune that squares the Moon and opposes Saturn, we can surmise that this 'punishment instinct' was learned from mother, who was undoubtedly stern and authoritarian and had little time for the young Heinrich's sensitivities.

Even a cursory study of his chart clarifies Himmler's propensity toward speaking in such peculiarly implacable language; it also explains, in potential, his commitment to the annihilation of an entire culture. Expedience and rationalisation litter his every utterance. Note that astrologically, he is the perfect instrument for this grim task: Sun makes a single Ptolemaic contact with Pluto, and Sun – Pluto connections (whatever their ambience) always give a capability for annihilation and a certain disconnection from one's core humanity. Orcus *squares* Pluto and is thus brought into the matrix, the angel of death is made manifest in the person of Himmler, through the medium of a double-Thor's Hammer, with Orcus and Mercury fizzing tense energy between them, connecting tautly with Mars and Pluto and adding their brutal undercurrent to the merciless sentiments.

The Thor's Hammer (also known as a 'Fist of God') is an interesting pattern; it generally connotes a difficult energy (represented by the square) which has to find an outlet through the apex planet. This is why – like Thor's Hammer – it is a weapon of great destructive potential. Generally – as with the underlying evolution of the human soul – the nature of the pattern requires a gradual education, the wielder of the Hammer must learn to manage the power of the weapon. In earlier years they may find themselves doing great damage with it, but ideally, as life progresses, discernment and restraint temper the damaging power of the Hammer and it can be used as a force for good. Thor the Thunderer was a good example of this principle: his power was used to destroy evil, rather than for self-aggrandisement and the furtherance of selfish aims. The Thor's Hammer pattern represents a difficult energetic conundrum that one must learn to 'handle' and express to positive effect through the medium of the apex planet.

In Himmler's case, there are distinctly complicating factors at play. Consider that on its own the square of Orcus with Pluto must be expressed through Mercury in Scorpio and the 8th house. That's an awfully intense, dreadful and infernal imperative with an almost charnel and biblical quality. In word (Mercury) at least, he was pressured by his nativity to express these black concepts; with Plutonic and Orcan disregard for the gentle human qualities of life. Clearly, if you were to take an objective view of this nativity, you can understand how he attained his dread power, whilst finding scant sympathy for a soul that was not the master of his astrology, but rather, was its servant. Had this Thor's Hammer existed in isolation then perhaps he might simply have talked a good genocide, but the interconnection with a second Thor's Hammer, of Mercury-Mars to Orcus, means there is no escape. Here, Mercury squares Mars, so there is anger (and low self-esteem because of a controlling and powerful mother-figure) which is catharsised through the daily business of genocide (from the 6th to the 8th house)[55].

The interconnecting Thor's Hammer has Orcus as its apex and this requires therefore that Himmler should express Mercury square Mars through the medium of Orcus itself. Mercury is an exceedingly neutral planet and he takes on the ambience of connecting placements and signs more so than any other point in the nativity, Gemini the mimic ensures therefore that in Himmler's chart the Martian propensity toward 'plain-speaking' is extant. There are likely to be episodes of brutal candour – both Mars and Pluto make energising contacts with Mercury here and too Mercury falls in Scorpio, ruled therefore by Mars and Pluto, so the pallor of Mercury is decidedly intense, incisive and on its shadow side, destructive. This then is the style of communication: unadorned, plain-speaking, aggressive and unsentimental. Sun in Libra is a detached and unsentimental position too, and in the 8th with an easy trine to Pluto, there is a potential to further rarefy the emotional atmosphere which in turn, provides the breath for personal identity. To express those rather emotionally disconnected concepts through Orcus then is no great leap for Himmler: indeed he could state plainly what others could only allude to. Here was a man who could talk of solutions rather than problems, because through the medium of Orcus he could remove all human dimension from the conundrum. That is the gift and the curse of Orcus.[56]

---

[55] The nativity inclines, it does not dictate. This is why it is near-enough a nonsense to 'predict fate' with astrology, the map does not delineate the soul which animates the being.

[56] The gift of Orcus in this context could only be beneficially applied to oneself. In this way the unsentimental drive could push one to great efforts and cut away self-serving delusions. Orcus applied to others, of course, cannot have a spiritual dimension.

There are many other factors and it is always important to consider that we are analysing a matrix that is greater than the sum of its parts: hard aspects to Orcus alone do not an architect of Holocausts make. In Himmler's case Mars is parallel Toro[57] and Ceres is semisquare Orcus (once again underlining mother's casual brutality – since Mars rules the 2nd house of self-worth and squares Mercury, ruler of the 4th, mother, early childhood and home conditions) and the entire configuration of the nativity, coupled with the enormous strength of peculiar conviction denoted by the chart-ruler culminating and nigh-crushed by a strong Jupiter, gives a very difficult potential, but crucially, *one that could not be understood without reference to Orcus.*

---

[57] See the previous discussion of Mike Tyson for more on Toro, page 28.

Pursuit

*He stretched his arms towards his child, but the boy cried and
nestled in his nurse's bosom, scared at the sight of his father's
armor, and at the horse-hair plume that nodded fiercely from his
helmet. His father and mother laughed to see him, but Hektor took
the helmet from his head and laid it all gleaming upon the ground.
Then he took his darling child, kissed him, and dandled him in his
arms, praying over him the while to Zeus and to all the gods.
"Zeus," he cried, "grant that this my child may be even as myself,
chief among the Trojans; let him be not less excellent in strength,
and let him rule Ilion with his might. Then may one say of him as he
comes from battle, 'The son is far better than the father.' May he
bring back the blood-stained spoils of him whom he has laid low,
and let his mother's heart be glad.'"*

*With this he laid the child again in the arms of his wife, who took
him to her own soft bosom, smiling through her tears. As her
husband watched her his heart yearned towards her and he
caressed her fondly, saying, "My own wife, do not take these things
too bitterly to heart. No one can hurry me down to Hades before
my time, but if a man's hour is come, be he brave or be he coward,
there is no escape for him when he has once been born."*

Homer: The Iliad, Scroll VI

Orcus' mythic remit was not limited to taking people down: the logical
precursor to imprisonment required hunting them down first. This was
one of the key insights that came to light in extensive studies of Orcus:
athletes are invariably influenced to a high degree by the planet. We
understand of course that Olympic competition would invariably
constitute one of the positive manifestations of Orcan energy although

the same pursuing drive debased, could be exploited for considerably more nefarious purposes.

Carl Lewis

Carl Lewis, of whom it has been said that it is "hard to argue that he is not the greatest athlete ever to set foot on track or field", [58] has a nativity that evinces yet another conjunction of Sun with Orcus, although in this instance, the conjunction is *Cazimi*, an Arabic term meaning "in the heart of the Sun". Technically this placement is defined as being within the arc of the solar disc in the sky, a measurement of precisely 34 minutes of arc. Thus any planet or body within 17 minutes of the Sun's position has this status. The ancients contended that any planet or body thus placed would be exalted and purified by the Sun's rays[59]. Examples of the power of Cazimi placements abound, and in Lewis we find no exception. Note how the conjunctions of Orcus in the charts of Stacy Keach and Terry Waite are within a degree but – crucially – more than 17 minutes from partile. They do not therefore experience the exalting and purifying effect of Cazimi, allowing the shadow-side of Orcus to manifest in equal, if not greater measure to the positive[60].

At one time or another, Carl Lewis has broken eleven world records and has accrued 8 Olympic gold medals, and part of his secret is

---

[58] *Track and Field News*, November 1991, vol. .44, #11, p. 8

[59] The positive view of Cazimi placements is not universally accepted. Many contemporary astrologers (such as James Wilson) consider the distinction to be misleading and that a body in Cazimi must be as combust as is possible and therefore such placements are without any redeeming quality. I disagree with this view. Examples of the beneficent influence of Cazimi planets are myriad, not least in the case of Carl Lewis, the supreme Olympian, with Cazimi Orcus. Annie Lennox, Carole King, Jimmy Page, Alan Watts all share Cazimi Mercury. Oprah Winfrey with Cazimi Venus, Tim Burton with Cazimi Pluto and Denzel Washington with Cazimi Node all attest to the sheer power of such placements. To contend that Annie Lennox's Mercury in Capricorn is as benighted as can be is such a nonsense that it is impossible to make any sensible defence of such a position.

[60] With Terry Waite his experience of combust Orcus (identified with difficult incarceration) was tempered by an (in all likelihood) Cazimi Rhadamanthus 38083. This point undoubtedly confers great integrity.

undoubtedly the close alliance of male identity with Orcus' relentless power of pursuit. The conjunction is in truth a Cazimi stellium with the inclusion of the asteroid Terpsichore which is Cazimi by parallel. Terpsichore addresses...

"...*grace, balance and coordination. In practice, the Muse of Dance governs not only dance but any physical training, discipline or specialised activity. It is mobility, grace and coordination (and the sports that require it.) Runners, joggers and folks into aerobics have Terpsichore prominently placed in their charts.*"[61]

If you couple, then, Terpsichore's physical precision with Orcus' relentless power to pursue (the leading pack, the world record, the gold medal) and a close conjunction of Mars with Pluto in Virgo rising, then you can understand why Lewis believed that "Life is about timing."[62] It is also about never giving up, which is an Orcan mantra. Lewis is the only man to have successfully defended a track and field Olympic title in four consecutive games (in the long jump) and his epic battle to take the world long jump record over fellow competitor Mike Powell during the 1991 competition is one of the iconic sporting moments of the 20th Century.

Examples of this abound in the world of sporting excellence. Florence Griffith-Joyner, "Flo-Jo", still the fastest woman ever to have lived, had Orcus conjunct the Midheaven, precisely sextile Moon, trine Neptune and opposition Saturn. Mary Decker, who set seventeen world records in women's middle distance running had Orcus on the Ascendant and at the precise midpoint of a Mercury – Mars trine, thus in sextile to both. In a great number of athlete's charts, of all disciplines, Orcus is heavily featured. Muhammad Ali's nativity is no exception, with Orcus conjunct Jupiter, in the 10th house, and precisely sextile a Leo Chiron in the 12th, it appears Orcus ameliorated a particular sense of not being given enough respect (Chiron/Leo) and with Chiron precisely conjunct

---

[61] *Mechanics of the Future* (1988), Martha Lang-Wescott, p223
[62] Sports Illustrated article *"Ode to Joy"* by Kenny Moore, August 17 1992.

Nemesis in the 12th, themes of victimisation and scapegoating are the basis for this sense of woundedness. Ali found the perfect tool for self-improvement through using the power of Orcus to promote his status and public persona. We have already seen how Orcus configures into the nativity of that other renowned boxer of the 20th Century – "Iron" Mike Tyson – so the dynamic appears quite pronounced, especially in one-on-one competitive scenarios.

This is a positive expression of the Orcan energy, but the same 'pursuer' dynamic can be expressed with extreme negativity.

Ian Brady and Myra Hindley became notorious for a string of child murders in the North of England during the 1960's. Both their nativities show pronounced configurations involving Orcus. In Brady's case, Orcus is precisely conjunct Eros and square Mars, which suggests that hunting boys was a distinct turn-on for him. Hindley has Orcus in partile conjunction with Ascendant and (like Ali) precisely sextile Chiron in Leo, although in her case from the 4th house. This clearly suggests that Hindley was not adored by her father, or rather that she perceived a distinct lack of warmth from him which was deeply wounding to her, and with Orcus opposing Panacea precisely, she determined that being the pursuer and the punisher would solve her relationship problems. She followed the path of evil because it was what Brady wanted and her Orcus – Panacea opposition tee-squared a stellium in Virgo and the 5th house (of children) of Psyche, Siva and Odysseus. It might be argued that by destroying those children she could alleviate her own psychological sense of isolation and damage.

It is of course risky to attempt to draw too many conclusions – astrological or otherwise – from the biographies of the deranged. As stated previously, serial imprisoners (like Josef Fritzl and Philip Garrido) do not appear to have any especial configurations involving Orcus (although we cannot know without an accurate birth time for sure that there is not some intriguing connection to the scope of the nativity), however, Elizabeth Fritzl (Josef Frtizl's imprisoned daughter) does have a precise semisquare between Orcus and Minerva, a prisoner to keep father happy therefore, and clearly she was not in any manner deranged.

At the end of 1946 a unique event occurred as Orcus made a series of precise conjunctions with Uranus around 20 degrees of Gemini[63].At the same time, Saturn joined with Pluto in Leo[64]; a combination which Ebertin referred to as the 'mass-murderer' conjunction[65]. Whilst this should not for one minute imply that people born at this time will be mass-murderers, it does describe a general issue with this very specific subset of the Pluto in Leo generation , since the sheer force of this collection of influences requires very careful handling. It can make for a great measure of worldly success: Saturn – Pluto in any guise supercharges 10th house values, thus status is a major motivational factor for these people: and when you add in Uranus – Orcus, there is a surfeit of rational ruthlessness brought to bear on an already single-minded combination.

Uranus has this ability, to look at facts remotely and dispassionately, and if the agenda is Saturn-Pluto's – getting ahead, being respected and obeyed – then there is a real danger of power and control issues running amok. A list of those who share these conjoined planetary energies reads like a veritable Who's Who of movers and shakers in all fields of human endeavour. Bill Clinton, Al Gore and George Bush, Arnold Schwarzenegger, Edwina Currie, Steven Spielberg, Elton John, Glenn Close, OJ Simpson, Camilla Parker-Bowles, Stephen King and -

---

[63] Partile conjunctions occurred on 16th September and 18th October 1946, and on 24th May 1947.

[64] A series of approaches in orb between October 1946 and June 1948, falling partile on 11th August 1947.

[65] Ebertin contends that the conjunction confers a propensity to violence, that at best it gives the ability to *"perform the most difficult work with extreme self-dsicipline, self-denial and renunciation"*, but at worst denotes *"a hard and unfeeling disposition, also cold-heartedness, tendency to violence, a fanatical adherence to one's principles once they have been adopted. A martyr."* From *The Combination of Stellar Influences* (1972), Reinhold Ebertin, Ebertin-Verlag.

if, as Ebertin would have it, serial-killing can be considered a field of human endeavour – Ted Bundy, to name but a few.

In every case, we have a group of individuals who might be considered 'super-achievers' in this select group, and it is worth analysing a case study to understand the manner in which Orcus has lent his unique energy into this narrow spectrum of influences to such remarkable effect. One of the key lessons of applied astrology has to be the reality that a single placement does not describe behaviour any more than a lone tree describes an ecosystem, but it does provide clues, which when considered alongside other flora and fauna can give a very accurate impression of the environment.

Arnold Schwarzenegger

There is no better example of this than the son of an Austrian policeman, from a remote town in Europe, who is at this time a self-made millionaire, a box-office superstar, the most acclaimed bodybuilder in history and the former governor of California. Arnold Schwarzenegger has created a remarkable legacy of achievement from a life marked out by humble origins and, against incredible odds of location, language, wealth and opportunity, has become a household name the world over. It seems an almost impossible rise to prominence, and yet it was (allegedly) in Schwarzenegger's mind from the earliest age that he would strike all of these lofty targets with unerring ease and accuracy.

This last suggests that perhaps it has been easy, where, of course, it cannot have been. Here the fanatic impulse of Saturn – Pluto in Leo is in the earthy 2nd, there is therefore a financial connotation, and Schwarzenegger is truly wealthy, but the house (and the sign of Leo too) is now dominated by the Sun, partile to the cusp in its domicile; creating an enormous ego and huge personal and physical power.

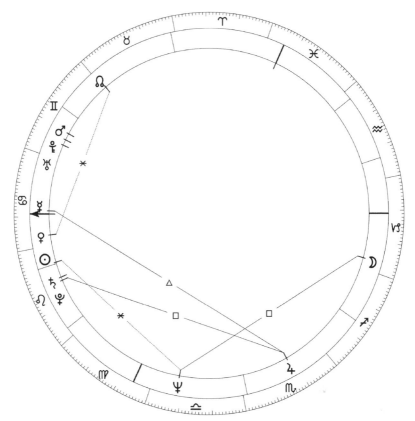

Arnold Schwarzenegger: 30th July 1947, 04:10, Graz, Austria

The square to Jupiter in Scorpio creates a leadership issue as well, but the Ascendant is trine Jupiter giving an easy outlet for the tension into the body itself. Arnold's physique becomes a channel for all that power, leadership and dominance; he can quite literally manifest the driving angst into his muscles. In the 5th as well, Jupiter introduces an element of joy into proceedings, from which we surmise that Schwarzenegger enjoys flexing his biceps and showing off his great power. But let us not forget that he has a peregrine (unaspected) Venus, he really wants to be beautiful and admired for his physical perfection (Venus rising) and in the sign of Cancer and with Moon quindecile to Mars in the 12th, he probably feels compelled to do that because his mother didn't nurture him very well.

When we consider Orcus, we see that he is placed at the precise midpoint of the Mars – Uranus conjunction in Gemini and the 12th house, ruled by Mercury rising and therefore expressed through the *appearance*. This is quite remarkable, because Orcus is of course the pursuer, the punisher, the implacable, not to be deterred avatar, hell-bent on tracking down and executing its target. Mars – Uranus alone creates an image of technological (Uranus) warfare (Mars), machines designed for the purpose of attack, and Orcus pursues. That is, without doubt a Terminator, and ruled by Mercury (appearance is key, also a voice marked by the imprint of the homeland – Mercury in Cancer), in the 12th house (of movies), then we can see the unique imprinting. As Michael Biehn's character said in the first film of the Terminator franchise: "*you still don't get it, do you? He'll find her, that's what he does. It's ALL he does! You can't stop him!*"

He could have been describing Orcus.

If you consider too that in Schwarzenegger's case, Saturn rules the 7th and Pluto the 5th, we are drawn to the observation that these are both relationship houses. Status is sought, at least in part, through relating, and his marriage to Maria Shriver, the niece of John F. Kennedy certainly fulfilled this criteria. The 2nd house influence manifests in the fact that Schwarzenegger was a millionaire before the age of 30; status derived from wealth therefore, which provided the platform for his subsequent acting career and allowed him to court a member of one of America's most prestigious families.

Wendy Leigh, Schwarzenegger's unauthorised biographer, went to Austria to research his roots, and came away convinced he plotted his political rise from an early age, using body-building and films as stepping stones to escape from a depressing home. There was certainly a lot to escape from. His father, Gustav, a frequently drunk local police chief who had signed up for the Nazi party after the 1938 Anschluss, apparently made no secret of his preference for the elder, more strapping of his two sons, Meinhardt.

Leigh portrays Schwarzenegger as obsessed with the pursuit of power and at one point quotes him as saying: "I wanted to be part of the small percentage of people who were leaders, not the large mass of followers. I think it is because I saw leaders use 100% of their potential... I was always fascinated by people in control of other people." [66]

The Terminator Effect
We understand the classic principle of conjunction; in this case Pluto supercharges Saturn's desire for status and to be respected and considered respectable, but it also works in the other direction. Saturn makes Pluto's control desires inflexible and rigid and there is enormous anxiety about unconventional forms of human expression and behaviour. This aspect, unchallenged, narrows the focus such that the only accepted forms of success are in keeping with prevailing societal values and norms. What this means is that *conventional* success, wealth and prestige is the engine which drives the reach for power and status. This desire exists wherever Saturn connects with Pluto; however, the years 1946 to 1948 were noteworthy because Orcus combined with Uranus to create a highly compatible new dimension to the overarching need to be considered special and to be admired that is the trademark, more generically, of the Pluto in Leo generation as a whole. To that royal, Leonine compulsion was added the ability to rationalise and employ ruthless strategies in the drive to realise superior status.

With Uranus, a cauterisation of emotional normalcy is achieved and there is an ability to view oneself as if from a great distance. That distance provides perspective, but it can also cut a person away from their human, compassionate core. Uranian rationalisation, which is the

---

[66] The Governator by Julian Borger and Duncan Campbell, The Guardian, Friday 8 August 2003

11th house expression of the polarity to Leo's 5th, provides in this instance, a tendency to step away from human warmth and 'for the greater good' (whatever that is rather calculatedly determined to be) take action. When you couple this with Saturn in Leo: an *early difficulty* with spontaneous and natural warmth and affection combined with a rigid expectation that one should be obeyed, and then finally, you add Orcus; you actually have a potentially inhumane and dominating combination of influences. It really can create Terminators.

At best it creates superhuman self-discipline and determination; but the other side of that coin is a great deal of suffering in those relationships that are sacrificed to the reach for power and control.

Looking at other examples from the same narrow milieu supports this same conclusion. The control impulse is extremely strong for these people which, when thwarted, can have devastating results, and is not helped by the fact that Saturn/Pluto was semisquare Orcus from October 1946 until June 1947, which I consider to be the 9 month long period of critical intensity. In my own consultation experience I have noted the disproportionate number of now adult children of this narrow generation, who endured emotionally abusive childhoods at the hands of their Terminator parents, and who have yet to reconcile their history with any relevant perspective of who they are. For the most part they suffer from chronically annihilated self-esteem because of growing up within a narcissistic family dynamic that is off the charts in terms of scale and intensity. Some may never recover a balanced sense of self, while others have had to develop astonishing powers of discrimination to free themselves from this crippling legacy[67].

And once again, in astrological counselling terms, this simply could not have been understood if it were not for the inclusion of Orcus, who is

---

[67] It should be noted that this same generation suffers from a third Hadean imperative with a conjunction of Ixion and Neptune in Libra. Pluto, Orcus and Ixion form a triumvirate of Hadean energies as they are all in 2:3 resonance with Neptune (along with Huya, 2003VS2 and 2003AZ84).

every bit as meaningful in understanding the context of these individuals as Saturn, Uranus or Pluto! It is hardly a coincidence that a significant proportion of the children of this narrow generation has Orcus in the sign of Cancer, and thus experiences isolation and alienation as a result of a punitive family dynamic which blighted their formative years and continues to affect them long into adulthood.

It makes sense to expand upon the underlying theory here, because we are examining a difficult legacy: difficult for those who are required to relate with this narrow generation and, in truth, difficult for those who live with the natal energies too. In my view there is no greater obstacle to spiritual progress than the Saturn-Pluto conjunction, most especially in the signs Leo and Libra. This is because the transformation of a rigid, inflexible and calcified Pluto is much less likely than a Pluto less encumbered.

Volguine[68] extrapolated the brilliant theory of planetary strength but it puzzled me greatly to read his estimations of Pluto. He determined that Pluto in Scorpio had little or no power, while Plutonic energy manifested most strongly in the signs Leo, Libra and Sagittarius. It seems clear, upon reflection that these are the most dominating Pluto placements, and with time I came to understand that this is because these signs are in their fundamentals the *least* compatible with the principle of Pluto. Pluto is *hidden* and therefore most accustomed to subtlety, privacy and darkness and prefers obscurity to the spotlight. Leo has almost diametrically opposed needs to this. To be ignored, overlooked and obscured is death to the Leo principle, but where Pluto falls in Leo, that Hadean energy has to take centre stage and put on a show. There is nothing more debilitating to the spiritualising mechanism of Pluto than to be put on show, but nonetheless, Pluto's naked *but subtle* power cannot fail but to create a 'strong' and formidable character, especially in conflict. Plutonic conflict is never

---

[68] For more on this fascinating topic please refer to *The Ruler of the Nativity* (1973), Alexandre Volguine, ASI Publishers Inc

overt remember, and therefore you have an energy signature where the compulsive need to be dominant is measured in terms of Leo energy. This signature dictates that dominance is aristocratic and therefore Pluto in Leo has to be better than everyone else. All is well if others accept their inferior status, but should anyone have the temerity to claim equality then the power struggle is begun.

The same methodology applies to Libra which needs to be admired, not as superior, but as desirable. So it is not the same as Leo energy, which makes compulsive kings or queens (but, most likely, queens, as I shall explain) because this energy is much more likely to manifest in close relationships and financial affairs: very little unmasks Pluto in Libra so much as the spectre of divorce.

Similarly with impulsive Sagittarius, which is probably the sign least inclined to self-control in the entire zodiac. It is not coincidence that the phenomenon of ADHD in children has corresponded precisely with the transit of Pluto through Sagittarius (compulsive impulsivity). This phenomenon will almost certainly go into complete abeyance as children born with Pluto in Capricorn move into the school system.

In each case we can see that the modus operandi of Pluto is dissonant with each of these signs, whose natures are to some extent showy, outgoing, and desirous of attention. This is why Scorpio is Pluto's most natural and most powerful position. The domination energy is kept under wraps, it is hidden, subtle and out of sight.

Pluto in Leo has another hidden dimension. Because Leo is the solar principle it is most naturally expressed through the male archetype. As with Sun-Pluto contacts in a female chart, therefore, the Pluto in Leo woman is most likely to delegate her Plutonic anxiety onto important male figures. What this means (in effect) is that for a man with Pluto in Leo, he has not had any place to put that anxiety, so he had to deal with it. Pluto in Leo males were undoubtedly quite dominating before midlife, but either catharsised that energy through midlife (rare but not unheard of), or became the focus of that energetic medium through their Pluto in Leo wives. This is why Pluto in Leo is most problematic in a female chart. (As a philosophic aside we can say that the same will be true for Pluto in Sagittarius, but the converse for Pluto in Libra: the men of this generation will be mild in early life and dominating after midlife, most especially toward their partners and beyond all reason should they get divorced from that partner).

This explains why there is such a number of married Pluto in Leo men who are sick, alcoholic or workaholic that are married to very strong, uncompromising and dominating Pluto in Leo women.

By the same token, the subtle and modest signs, Cancer, Virgo, Scorpio and Capricorn should all prove to be excellent repositories of Plutonic energy, greatly maximising the potential for a successful Plutonic conversion after midlife.

So when Volguine spoke about power, he was not referring to any sort of sympathetic concurrency. He simply meant it as a measure of raw energy, a little like a Geiger counter reading. Where Pluto is concerned though, as with radioactivity: less truly is more[69].

---

[69] The spiritual ramifications of Pluto energies are immense, deep and subtle, as with Pluto himself. It will be seen that the misuse of Plutonic power (employed to control others) is a guarantee of spiritual collapse, while its converse, practising only self-control, will result in spiritual advancement.

Expiation

Not far from thence, the Mournful Fields appear
So call'd from lovers that inhabit there.
The souls whom that unhappy flame invades,
In secret solitude and myrtle shades
Make endless moans, and, pining with desire,
Lament too late their unextinguish'd fire.

Virgil: The Aeneid, 447-452

Expiation, like absolution and penance are concepts closely allied to the pursuit of spiritual progress and it is in this aspect of religious life that Orcus begins to render his latent rewards of self-improvement and purification. In many of the cases we have examined we see an enforced Orcan transformation which, when meted out by some external agent as a punishment for perceived wrongdoing has had the effect, regardless of the veracity of the original judgement, of inculcating within the subject an inner transformation of perspective. The Orcan fuel consumed by this process takes the form of reflection and a gradual quietening of subjective drives in the face of time and solitude's overwhelming implacability.

What has been known by saints, sages and ascetics over the ages is that this principle of "spiritual fermentation", which is an extant principle of Orcus, can be leveraged purposefully, to propel one more intently along the path of spiritual improvement. If, as we see, a transformation of perspective occurs when people are incarcerated and isolated from society for long periods – whether against their will or otherwise – then it should be no surprise to learn that voluntary isolation – by dint of the refinement of one's inner silence which is its product – has long been understood to be one of the keys to enlightenment.

Solitude vs. Loneliness

John Lubbock[70] said: *"The whole value of solitude depends upon one's self; it may be a sanctuary or a prison, a haven of repose or a place of punishment, a heaven or a hell, as we ourselves make it."* He is describing Orcus most succinctly, but his perspective suggests that the value of solitude is dependent upon one's attitude to it. If we can accept that solitude does have the potential to change people in ways which make them more compassionate, patient and peaceful, then this hints at new dimensions of astrological insight. Every major spiritual practice underlines the transforming potential of solitude and isolation and this is reflected in each faith's adherence to various principles of meditative practice. The sitting Zen monk and the kneeling Christian monk are engaged in the same work, despite their theological differences. They are actualising Orcan energies, transmuting the discipline of facing inner quiet into inner peacefulness and communion with an impersonal reality. It is tempting for the sceptical to discount the courage of such an act too, for facing one's inner chaos is difficult and not for the faint-hearted. Certainly, whilst most people would cope with the necessity of enduring the potential boredom of sitting quietly for a time with nothing to 'do', very few would welcome it as a regular daily practice, and even fewer would follow the way of isolation as a lifestyle choice.

This strength of character that is an essential for the business of solitude speaks to the heart of the matter. Aldous Huxley said that *"the more powerful and original a mind, the more it will incline towards the religion of solitude."* In our modern society, the constant blaring of the radio or television, the never-ending cascade of information with which to distract the mind unused to the rigour of silence, masks the

---

[70] John Lubbock, the 1st Baron of Avebury was a politician and biologist and a close friend of Charles Darwin.

discomfort of quietude which is so suddenly thrust onto those who are unwillingly incarcerated.

This does not mean that all prisoners will become deepened and made spiritual by their time in prison, but for those who are able to approach their plight with a willingness to contemplate eternity and who have, innate, a strength of spirit, it is invariably the case that this tempering of the soul takes place, and it is that precise alchemical mechanism which is actively sought by spiritual seekers.

Spiritual Transformation

In "A Path with Heart", the spiritual teacher Jack Kornfield explains *"spiritual transformation is a profound process that doesn't happen by accident. We need a repeated discipline, a genuine training in order to let go of our old habits of mind and to find and sustain a new way of seeing. To mature on the spiritual path we need to commit ourselves in a systematic way."*[71]

Later he relates the story of a writer of his acquaintance who *"didn't know much about meditation, but after some preliminary instruction he decided that enlightenment was for him. He went off to a hut in the mountains of Vermont and brought his few books on meditation and enough food for six months. He figured six months would perhaps give him a taste of enlightenment. As he began his retreat he enjoyed the forest and the solitude, but in just a few days he began to feel crazy because as he sat all day in meditation his mind would not stop. Not only did it think, plan and remember constantly, but worse, it kept singing songs. This man had chosen a beautiful spot for his 'enlightenment.' The hut was right on the edge of a bubbling stream. The sound of the stream seemed nice on the first day, but after a while it changed. Every time he sat down and closed his eyes, he would hear the noise of the stream, and immediately in tune with it, his mind would begin to play marching band songs like 'Stars and Stripes Forever' and 'The Star Spangled Banner.' At*

---

[71] *A Path with Heart* (1995), Jack Kornfield, Rider & Co. p31.

one point the sounds in the stream got so bad he actually stopped
meditating, walked down to the stream, and started moving the rocks
around to see if he could get it to play a different tune."

These first, small anguishes which are experienced when isolation and lack of distraction first begin to affect the human spirit are absolutely typical. For the meditation student the initial forays into a regular daily practice can be broken up into small episodes and masked within the hurly-burly of life's vicissitudes. For those prisoners, like Nelson Mandela in particular, who were kept in solitary confinement, there is no such escape. The inner tumult has to be faced down. What this facilitates, most especially in the man or woman of strong character, is undoubtedly a deepening and further strengthening of the spirit.

The key insight therefore is that this Orcan imperative, when consciously employed, positively manifested, can be a powerful catalyst for spiritual evolution. In fact it can be argued that without Orcus, enlightenment is simply not viable. The struggle against Orcus (as denoted by hard aspects, poor placements) can manifest as a great discomfort with solitude, a fear of facing the inner self and a craving for distraction. It is not comfortable to gaze at eternity after all, but some, a rare few, learn to welcome that exchange, because within it they see their own immortality and their oneness with creation. With that being so, it suggests that in keeping with his shadowy twin Pluto, Orcus has a breaking down effect on the false self, which has been variously called the ego, the personality or, perhaps most pertinently of all, the individual nature. Faced with the implacable and impersonal power of Orcus, the sense of one's insignificance assumes proportions that are impossible to any longer ignore.

All the great prophets of the world's major religions endured the trial of wandering alone in the wilderness. Christ, at around the age of 30, met the devil there who offered him dominion and glory, Muhammad retreated to a cave at the age of 40 and here he received his first revelation from God. Krishna died while meditating in a lonely forest (killed by an arrow wound to the left foot, like Chiron, Pholus and Achilles) while Buddha, after 49 days of meditation under the Bodhi tree achieved enlightenment at the age of 35. In Egyptian lore, Horus wandered in the desert where he was tempted by Set, the God of evil and chaos, who, identically to the story of Jesus and indeed Buddha, made offers of glory and dominion in return for his allegiance. These stories from all the world's major religions are identical in their key elements.

What all of these stories imply is that the act of 'going into the wilderness' is a prerequisite to spiritual evolution. Jesus, Buddha and Muhammad all began their ministries between the ages of 30 and 40 as a direct result of facing the devil (a facsimile for the Plutonic transformation) in the wilderness (through Orcan solitude or meditation). It hints at an inner transformation that can only be attained through a commitment to facing something within the self and it also suggests a state of inner maturation that is required, which is reflected in the ages of these great prophets. It is not a path which is easily accessible to the young; or as Moliere said it: *"solitude terrifies the soul at 20."*[72]

Emily Dickinson

So what of the astrology of those who voluntarily choose solitude? These are not nearly the celebrated types which make headlines, except perhaps for reasons of strangeness. Emily Dickinson, the reclusive American poet who almost never left her home, penned these lines:

The soul selects her own society,
Then shuts the door;
On her divine majority
Obtrude no more.

---

[72] Célimène, in *The Misanthrope*, act 5, sc. 4 (1666). Célimène refuses to move from Paris to the country.

Unmoved, she notes the chariot's pausing
At her low gate;
Unmoved, an emperor is kneeling
Upon her mat.

I've known her from an ample nation
Choose one;
Then close the valves of her attention
Like stone.[73]

Suzanne Juhasz interprets this early work of Dickinson's through an Orcan lens:

"[The poem] is a strong statement about the power of the self alone. The soul is shown living within a space defined by door, gate, and mat. The external world, with its nations and their rulers, is kept outside. . . .

Traditional ideas about power are reversed here. Not control over vast populations but the ability to construct a world for oneself comprises the greatest power, a god-like achievement, announces the opening stanza. Not only is the soul alone "divine," but it is also identified as "Society" and "Majority": the poem also challenges our ideas about what constitutes a social group. Consequently, the enclosed space of the soul's house is more than adequate for a queenly life, and ambassadors of the external world's glories, even emperors, can easily be scorned. Yet while the speaker claims her equality with those most powerful in the outer world--they may be emperors, but she is "divine Majority," at the same time she asserts her difference from them; for her domestic vocabulary of door, low gate, and mat establishes her dwelling as not a grand palace but rather a simple house.

While associating power with the enclosed space of the mind, the poem also implies how isolation is confinement, too. When the soul turns in

---

[73] Emily Dickinson Everyman Poetry, (1997), Emily Dickinson, Helen Mcneil (Ed) Phoenix.

upon her own concerns, she closes "the Valves of her attention-- /Like Stone--."

Valves permit the flow of whatever they regulate in one direction only: here, from outside to inside. Either of the halves of a double door or any of the leaves of a folding door are valves. Valves seen as doors reinforce the poem's house imagery, while their association with stone makes the walls separating soul from world so solid as to be, perhaps, prison-like.

Prison-like because they allow no escape from the kinds of conflict, the kinds of terror, even, that must occur within.[74]

Dickinson had Orcus rising on her Scorpio Ascendant precisely conjunct the asteroid named House[75], which is as perfect an image as you could conjure for somebody who chose to make such a solitude of their home.

In more general terms, we might expect to see the astrological motifs for home associated with Orcus in the nativities of those who choose to live in isolated locations, conditions or communities. Myriad examples of Orcan narratives can be gleaned from the lives of those who have, through necessity or design, opted to live in remote places, or experienced periods of incarceration.

Henri Charrière, the infamous French prisoner Papillon, who made several daring escapes from some of the most remote prisons in the world (including the notorious French penal colony on Devil's Island) had a precise trine of Orcus with Icarus! The trine covers an arc of only 38 minutes and of course Icarus was immortalised as a result of his attempt to escape an island prison too.

---

[74] *The Undiscovered Continent: Emily Dickinson and the Space of the Mind.* (1983), Suzanne Juhasz , Indiana University Press
[75] 4950 House (1988 XO1) is a main-belt asteroid discovered on December 7, 1988 by E. F. Helin at Palomar.

John Inman

One of the research cases for this book was that of British comedy actor John Inman, whose Moon was conjunct Orcus by a mere 11 minutes. Inman, who was famously 'undecided' in his sexual orientation, was described as being the most witty and inventive of actors by Wendy Richard, his co-star of many years. *"Of course he never said he was gay, he just said he was a young man who was very good to his mother."* When I was researching John Inman's life story, I was struck by how little information was available about his life outside of show business. Indeed, there is a great deal of insight about John Inman's various roles – particularly that of Mr Humphries in the 1970's British sitcom *Are You Being Served*, but it is impossible to find out anything more about John Inman's private life. Unusually for a high-profile celebrity, he never wrote or authorised a biography, despite his enduring success on stage and screen and the high regard in which he was held by the British public. It seems therefore that John Inman's private life, which we can understand to be represented by the lunar principle, was itself isolated, remote and, if you like, locked away from public view. Insofar as his home was concerned, Inman grew up in a boarding house, spent the first half of his life living in hotel rooms before eventually settling down at his home with his civil partner of 30 years, Ron Lynch, in Maida Vale, West London. No information about his home exists, nor about his private life, which appears to be an uncannily well-guarded secret. It seems that Inman's privacy was simply inaccessible to anyone on the outside, which is completely at odds with the stereotypical celebrity life story.

Anne Frank

For Anne Frank, whose home became a literal prison, Orcus squared her 2nd house Moon. There are clear safety issues in any lunar square and with a Moon-ruled Pluto in the 12th, which is also peregrine (unaspected), clearly the life and death nature of needing to stay hidden is stressed. Intriguingly, Orcus transited to a semisquare with her Ascendant on the exact week[76] that she and her family went into hiding from the Nazi occupiers in the loft rooms of an Amsterdam apartment building. It is perhaps no coincidence that after receiving a humanitarian award from the Anne Frank Foundation in 1994, Nelson Mandela addressed a crowd in Johannesburg, saying he had read Anne Frank's diary while in prison and *"derived much encouragement from it."* He likened her struggle against Nazism to his struggle against apartheid, drawing a parallel between the two philosophies with the comment *"because these beliefs are patently false, and because they were, and will always be, challenged by the likes of Anne Frank, they are bound to fail"*[77]

Helen Keller

For Helen Keller, deaf and blind from childhood, we ought not be surprised to discover that Orcus was in exact opposition to her Mercury, and Orcus' ruler, Uranus was precisely conjunct her Midheaven. Her struggle to communicate became the subject of her vocation and with Mercury in the 9th and Orcus in the 3rd, she communicated that struggle by writing her biography, *Story of my Life.* [78] In it she states: *"Everything has its wonders, even darkness and silence, and I learn whatever state I am in, therein to be content."*

Orcus creates a sense of isolation that must be transformed, in the Plutonic mould, from loneliness and isolation into solitude and acceptance, and with Keller's 3rd house placement, we apprehend the familiar day to day environment, those things which are immediate, close at hand, taken for granted. The familiar and close at hand then, became for her remote and isolating and it was through the alchemy of Orcus that she realised acceptance and ultimately freedom from her 3rd house prison.

---

[76] Orcus 15GE06 semisquare Ascendant 00LE06, 12th July 1942 00:59am. The Franks moved into the secret annex on July 6th, but were joined by another family, the van Pels, on July 13th.

[77] Address by President Nelson Mandela at the Johannesburg opening of the Anne Frank Exhibition at the Museum Africa: http://www.anc.org.za/3670

[78] *Story of my Life* (1997), Helen Keller, Dover Publications Inc.

Orcus with Sun and Moon

We can appreciate how Orcus might offer insights of contrast when associated particularly with solar and lunar principles. When connected to the Moon we can see how much more Orcus is internalised than when associated with the Sun, the point where, astrologically, identity is forged. The Moon says "this is who I am", while the Sun says "this is who I want to be." Incrementally, life offers the opportunity to forge this solar identity and gradually the lunar self is overshadowed. We begin lunar and learn to become solar. The Moon, private, vulnerable, is not for sharing; it is the Freudian *id* and thus escapes us in moments of distress or shock; it is the self that takes over when we are not trying to be ourselves but are simply *reacting*. The solar self on the other hand is much more deliberate. It is the projection of identity that we aspire to, that we carefully foster and practise being. Our role models are embodiments of our solar nature that we easily identify with. It is no surprise therefore that fathers are especially accessible as role models for the child. A strong Sun is a strong paternal role model. So we see that with Emily Dickinson and John Inman, the lunar blend with Orcus created a sense of deepest and most profound privacy. For Dickinson it created a great isolation within that most lunar of mansions, the home. For Inman too, his home was a 'lock-up' of the Dickinsonian type; it kept the world imprisoned *outside*.

We have already seen that those with a strongly Orcan solar influence have been profoundly affected in terms of identities. But if we are going to perceive the nature of Orcus as a spiritual indicator, then we have to appreciate that wherever Sun and Orcus are combined there is going to be especial intensity. The focus and implacability of Orcus must inevitably become encapsulated by the identity at some level or other. We have seen that with Terry Waite, the hostage negotiator, he incorporated into his identity a need to *communicate* with *imprisoners*. He became so well known for it, that it *became* his identity. Terry Waite's powerful experience was to become a precise motif for Sun conjunct Orcus in Gemini. With Stacy Keach we see the same combination, except here Gemini's quality as the mimic allowed him to impersonate or mimic *a variety* of imprisoners, of prison warden roles. With Carl Lewis, the supreme Olympian, we see a Cazimi Orcus, thus exalted and purified; creating an all-American sports star. His dominance of the Olympic field reflected his identity as an icon of his home country and as a *representative* of the United States at the world's oldest, most *traditional* and *historic* sporting competition. Cancerian themes all.

Emily Dickinson had Orcus rising on her Scorpio Ascendant precisely conjunct the asteroid House. It might also be noteworthy, to those with an interest in the 5th harmonic, that Orcus quintiles Saturn and both planets form biquintiles to Mars conjunct Pluto in Aries and the 5th house. This 'Golden Yod' aspect pattern is invariably powerful once actualised for creative purposes, or even for more nefarious ones[79]. In Dickinson's case the 5th is the natural house of creative work and the Golden Yod from sombre Saturn and isolated Orcus can be felt tangibly in the body of her work.

Alan Watts, who possibly ranked among the finest philosophical minds of modern times, had Orcus precisely conjunct Imum Coeli (by a few minutes of arc only), and thus opposition Midheaven. He taught meditation theory to a vast number of students throughout the 1960s and 70s. Watts began each and every day of his adult life with a period of meditation and spent many months of his later years in contemplation in an isolated cabin on Mount Tamalpais in Marin County, California.

---

[79] I have done a fair amount of research on the quintile; it is a fifth harmonic aspect which John Addey associated with the use and abuse of power; because of the occult significance of the pentagram it is considered by some to be an aspect which requires activation lest it be triggered into its base expression with often uncomfortable results. Bill Tierney, in his *Dynamics of Aspect Analysis* noted that it is often found in the charts of composers and artists, but also mass-murderers and murder victims.

Philip Kapleau who wrote the seminal *Three Pillars of Zen* had a close trine of his strong Sun in Leo with Orcus in Aries. He identified very comfortably with the struggle to achieve inner quiet:

"You must realize that no matter how intently you count your breaths you will still perceive what is in your line of vision, since your eyes are open, and you will hear the normal sounds about you, as your ears are not plugged. And since your brain likewise is not asleep, various thought forms will dart about your mind. Now, they will not hamper or diminish the effectiveness of zazen unless, evaluating them as "good", you cling to them or, deciding they are "bad", you try to check or eliminate them."[80]

---

[80] *The Three Pillars of Zen, Teaching, Practise and Enlightenment* (1989) Philip Kapleau, Anchor Books

Torture

I see, Prometheus;
and over my eyes a mist of tears and fear spread
as I saw your body withering ignominiously
upon this rock in these bonds of adamant.
For there are new rulers in heaven,
and Zeus governs with lawless customs;
that which was mighty before
he now brings to nothing.

Aeschylus, Prometheus Bound, lines 144-151

The shadow side of Orcus is implicit in the understanding of the difference between solitude and loneliness. One empowers while the other debilitates. We already understand the power of Orcus as a principle of transformative suffering, but the energy can easily be abused, where the objective of Orcan expressions is not to exalt the human condition, to improve society or one's own relationship to the eternal, but is instead debased as a means to garner power or advantage for selfish purposes. It is a sad truth that this is the statistically prevalent manifestation of Orcus in human life.

Possibly the basest expression of Orcus is found in the act of torture. Torture has a long and colourful history and has been found in most cultures throughout history in one form or another. In more recent times, the Catholic Church has been the major proponent of torture up until as recently as 1816 when it was finally decreed unlawful by papal bull. The majority of civilised institutions had outlawed torture in any form many years previously – for example in England, the practice was banned in 1640, although the use of torture was exceptional even before this time – torture was seen as a last resort or as fit only for extraordinary situations (such as high treason), unlike the Catholic Church, for whom it was often employed as a first resort.

Dick Cheney

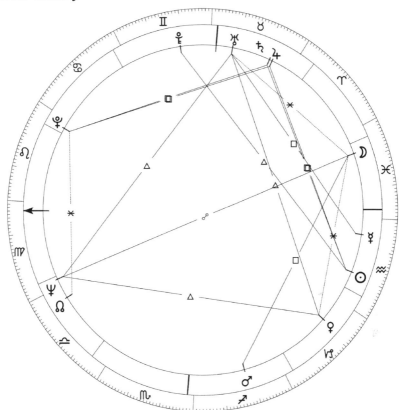

Dick Cheney: 30th January 1941, 1930, Lincoln, NE, USA

In recent times, torture is rightly vilified and outlawed by all progressive, free societies and it would seem correct that it would be roundly condemned by the statesmen and leaders of those societies, without reservation. As is often the case, though, wherever expedience rears its ugly head (itself a shadow-play of mismanaged Orcus), a case for torture might be made.

Such is the case with former US Vice President Dick Cheney who has stated his support for the use of torture, albeit under the guise of the more innocuous nomenclature of 'enhanced interrogation.'[81] These enhanced techniques, which include the use of 'waterboarding'[82] and sleep deprivation, are clearly at odds with the United Nations statement on the definitions of torture.[83] Cheney's support and approval of these enhanced interrogation techniques is, according to many, a violation of the UN Convention against Torture.[84] Regardless of the semantic debate that surrounds the use of these techniques and whether or not they constitute a legal definition of torture (the consensus being that they do and that they are therefore illegal, however the issue is currently mired, not so much in the question of whether or not it was wrong, but who was to blame?) the fact remains that Dick Cheney is a public proponent of the use of torture.

---

[81] This Week on ABC News, 14 February 2010. Transcript available from http://abcnews.go.com/ThisWeek/week-transcript-vice-president-dick-cheney/story?id=9818034

[82] The water board technique dates back to the 1500s during the Italian Inquisition. A prisoner, who is bound and gagged, has water poured over him to make him think he is about to drown. Current and former CIA officers tell ABC News that they were trained to handcuff the prisoner and cover his face with cellophane to enhance the distress. According to Sen. John McCain, R-Ariz., himself a torture victim during the Vietnam War, the water board technique is a "very exquisite torture" that should be outlawed. From History of an Interrogation Technique: Water Boarding: New Debate Sparked on What Constitutes Torture ABC News 29 November 2005.

[83] The United Nations Convention against Torture and Other Cruel, Inhuman or Degrading Treatment or Punishment (UNCAT) came into force in June 1987, it stated that: For the purposes of this Convention, the term "torture" means any act by which severe pain or suffering, whether physical or mental, is intentionally inflicted on a person for such purposes as obtaining from him or a third person information or a confession, punishing him for an act he or a third person has committed or is suspected of having committed, or intimidating or coercing him or a third person, or for any reason based on discrimination of any kind, when such pain or suffering is inflicted by or at the instigation of or with the consent or acquiescence of a public official or other person acting in an official capacity.

[84] Article 2.2 states: "No exceptional circumstances whatsoever, whether a state of war or a threat of war, internal political instability or any other public emergency, may be invoked as a justification of torture."

Cheney's chart contains several remarkable features, the most noticeable of which is a Kite to Neptune in a difficult placing within Virgo, but more compelling than this is a trine between Sun and Orcus in the 10ᵗʰ house within two minutes of arc.

The astrology here is remarkable. Orcus trines Sun; identity is formed around an Orcan core, in the 10th house, and he publicly supports the use of torture. Cheney is immensely wealthy, mostly due to his association with Halliburton, the world's second largest oil services corporation. Halliburton is purported to have made enormous profits as a direct result of the Iraq conflicts. Cheney's Orcus makes hard contacts with the asteroids Atlantis (invasions of privacy, conspiracies) and Eos (unconsciousness). Thus torture (Orcus) involving getting at hidden information (Atlantis) through forcing unconsciousness (Eos) – a common side-effect of waterboarding. Cheney's Sun-Orcus trine becomes a grand-trine with the inclusion of Panacea. In the air element there is enormous rationalising power here and, crucially, if the Grand Trine requires no external validation it suggests a persona that can rationalise torture as a solution. What though, is the problem that is truly being solved? Note how this Grand Trine in the air element falls across the earth houses. Cheney has arguably grown rich as a direct result of the War on Terror. The opposition of Orcus to Eos/Atlantis actually forms the spine to this grand air trine and it suggests therefore that the yielding benefit of Orcus (as the Kite's focus) is realised through the Eos/Atlantis conjunction. Cheney receives some form of Orcan and 10ᵗʰ house payoff therefore as a result of obtaining information through enforced unconsciousness.

We could spend a great deal of effort in speculating about what that payoff might be, and perhaps that is too diverse a question for this text[85]

---

[85] The wide opposition of Sun to Pluto, tee-squaring the Jupiter/Saturn conjunction in Taurus does suggest a drive based around the typically existential anxiety that affects the Sun-Pluto native in difficult ways. There is enormous anxiety about identity, so wealth and power (Plutonic compensations) are often sought to shore up a flailing sense of personal meaning and effectiveness. Jupiter with Saturn in Taurus receives this tension, so conventional (Saturn) means of improvement (Jupiter) through wealth

. It does raise another intriguing issue however: does Orcus represent a path to riches, in the same manner that Pluto appears to? We already understand perhaps the potential for realising an inner richness, a wealth of the spirit within the context of Orcus, but might it also connote some potential for, if not Plutonic, then Orcan wealth in the material sense?

Orcan Wealth

Bill Gates' nativity also evinces a Sun – Orcus trine, with a very close parallel between Orcus and that other lord of the underworld, Pluto. Leona Helmsley, the so-called "Queen of Mean" who swindled the poor out of their cash while retaining her own billion dollar fortune has a stellium of Sun, Venus and Pluto in sextile to Orcus (again in Taurus); the sextile between Orcus and Pluto falls within a few minutes of arc. Lee Iacocca, former President of Chrysler and business guru who has amassed a personal fortune of many millions has a Yod to Orcus (in Taurus!) from Mercury sextile Jupiter, and talking (Mercury) about better ways of doing things (Jupiter) has been his trademark[86] and the basis for his success. Intriguingly, the newspaper magnate Rupert Murdoch, like Dick Cheney, has an exact matrix of hard contacts between Orcus, Panacea and Atlantis, invasions of privacy are seen as the 'solution' to the problem of wealth: his Orcus falls in Taurus also. Lakshmi Mittal, currently rated Britain's wealthiest man has a close

---

(Taurus) are seen as the way to remedy this anxiety. Pluto is ruled by a rather weak Sun in the 6th and Aquarius while Jupiter/Saturn are ruled by Venus in the 5th. Here is somebody who could not express his uniqueness easily in mundane daily activities and experienced a sense of powerlessness as a result. Venus in Capricorn, while clearly an expression of early difficulty with love relationships (he married his high school sweetheart and has had no other intimate relationship) also has a material component, the attitude to wealth is conservative and conventional and in the 5th it becomes an important component of identity. Ultimately it is another solar problem: Cheney appears to have struggled to connect with his father (the common denominator of all difficult Sun-Pluto contacts and the wellspring from whence existential anxiety originates).

[86] Throughout the 1980s, Iacocca appeared in a series of commercials for the Chrysler company's vehicles, using the ad campaign "The pride is back" to denote the turnaround of the corporation, he also coined the phrase that later became his trademark: "If you can find a better car, buy it."

conjunction of Sun with Orcus and Toro and he has laboured under numerous allegations of employing dubious working practises, including the use of slave labour in mines owned and operated by his company in Kazakhstan.[87] Larry Page, the founder of Google is currently America's 14th richest person and, quite fittingly for somebody who has made a fortune from technology, he has a precise square from Orcus to an unaspected Uranus in Libra. It is no coincidence therefore that he made his money through computer innovation and in partnership with Sergey Brin, co-founder of Google and America's 13th richest person.

It seems that there is a case to be made here, although the majority of notable examples of this type fall within the remit of Orcus in Taurus, the sign most naturally compatible with the principle of material abundance. If we understand Orcus to denote near inhuman levels of determination and endurance, and these take on the sign's innate quality, then we see a generation unusually motivated to acquire, if not fame, then certainly fortune.

But once again we see that it is Orcus' single-mindedness of focus that is the key to the acquisition of wealth and, too, his near-contempt for 'mere human concerns' which bestows a rare power of ruthlessness upon his mortal vessel. We can understand that this intensity of focus is engendered by a great and perhaps compulsive desire – which is another quality shared with his counterpart Pluto – or that in some cases it is applied through the medium of fate, as yet another part of the design for life which astrology marks out. Whether or not that fate is wanted is not remotely relevant. The desire for wealth viewed from a certain perspective is not in itself desirable, and it is certainly a burden

---

[87] "*Workers employed by Lakshmi Mittal, Britain's richest man, are accusing the billionaire of cashing in on 'slave labour' conditions after scores have died in accidents in his mines. Coalminers working in Mittal's Kazakh mines claim his firm is endangering their lives by using dangerous, outdated equipment and by cutting corners. More than 90 have died in the mines since 2004.*" From *UK's richest man in slave labour row*, The Sunday Times, June 10 2007 written by Mark Franchetti in Shakhtinsk, Kazakhstan, and Robert Winnett.

when life is marked by poverty; in that instance a desire for simple living would better align with reality and cause less internal dissonance and therefore, less distress.

And it is within the contemplation of this philosophical Gordian knot that we might grasp some sense of the underpinning sentiment of the meaning and purpose of torture. Not torture as applied with racks, thumbscrews and hot coals perhaps, but rather in the subjective sense of torture as suffering and the internal alchemy which it invokes. Through enduring, whether pain, anguish, loneliness, isolation or torture, the inner spirit grows broader, deeper and stronger.

The astrology of torture-victims is difficult to track down; rarely do these individuals become celebrities. Archetypally, when we look at the process of torture, what we see is a dialogue between the torturer attempting to 'break' his opponent (the negative energy of Orcus) and his victim attempting to resist and to endure the suffering (the positive energy of Orcus). I intend to describe this dialogue from the perspectives of two men, both far removed in terms of culture and expectations, but both of whom endured remarkably similar Orcan dialogues.

Jean Moulin and the Butcher of Lyon

In the first case, that of the French resistance leader, Jean Moulin, we are fortunate to also have the astrology of his torturer at hand, and this sets up a fascinating astrological case study. Moulin was born at 4:00 a.m. on 20th June 1899 in Beziers, France, and after serving in the First World War, he forged a successful legal career for himself, eventually securing a prestigious role as Préfet of the Eure-et-Loir department to the West of Paris. After the Nazi occupation of France, Moulin was pressured to sign a false declaration blaming French Senegalese soldiers for a massacre of civilians perpetrated by German troops. He refused and, as a result, was arrested and badly beaten in prison by his German captors. Such was his determination to resist signing the false document that he attempted suicide in prison after breaking a window and using a glass shard to cut his own throat. He was released shortly afterward whereupon the Vichy government made their displeasure with him known by giving his job to somebody else. Moulin went to live in the far South of France and joined the resistance. His political and organisational skills soon brought him to the attention of Charles de Gaulle, whom he met in London, and Moulin was tasked with uniting the various factions of French Resistance groups under a united command. He parachuted back into France and set about this new task with great success. In 1943 he was betrayed and arrested by the Gestapo while meeting at a Resistance safe-house in Lyon. He was interrogated by Klaus Barbie and later died, it is alleged, as a result of the beatings he received at the hands of Barbie himself.

Klaus Barbie, known as the 'Butcher of Lyon' was a devout Roman Catholic who had wanted to train as a priest but instead pursued a career in Hitler's secret police. Barbie's nature was unremittingly sadistic. A Jewish girl, denounced to the Gestapo by her neighbours, recalled her first meeting with Barbie, "*dressed in grey and caressing a kitten.*"

"*He was caressing the cat. And me, a kid 13 years old, I could not imagine that he could be evil because he loved animals. I was tortured by him for eight days.*"[88]

Barbie personally collected her from her prison cell each morning, dragging the slight 13 year old girl by her hair and punching at her open wounds in order to cause her the maximum pain.

Another survivor of the Lyon dungeons, Lise Lesevre, recalled how Klaus Barbie tortured her for nine days in 1944, beating her repeatedly and using simulated drowning techniques (waterboarding) in a prison bathtub. She recalled how she was ordered to strip naked and get into a tub filled with freezing water. Her legs were tied to a bar across the tub

---

[88] From the records of the American-Israeli cooperative enterprise, 2010. See http://www.jewishvirtuallibrary.org

and then Barbie would pull on a chain attached to the bar to pull her underwater. During her last interrogation, Barbie ordered her to lie flat on a chair and struck her on the back with a spiked ball attached to a chain. It smashed a vertebra, and she endured considerable pain for the remainder of her days as a consequence.

Another survivor, Ennat Leger, said Klaus Barbie *"had the eyes of a monster. He was savage. My God, he was savage! It was unimaginable. He broke my teeth, he pulled my hair back. He put a bottle in my mouth and pushed it until the lips split from the pressure."*

Although he was the acting commander of the Lyon division and could have delegated interrogation duties to his subordinates, Barbie took charge of numerous 'interviews' personally. He is credited with causing the deaths of over 14,000 people, 4,000 of whom are purported to have died at his hands in a little less than 4 years. You will note that this suggests that he personally murdered an average of 3 people per day during his time in Lyon. Ironically however, Barbie's notoriety, especially within France, is derived in great measure from his responsibility for a single murder: that of Jean Moulin who was mercilessly tortured by Klaus Barbie at the Gestapo headquarters in Lyon. Moulin was interrogated after his capture and pressed to give up the names of his fellow resistance leaders. He endured having his fingernails pulled and the bones in his hands being repeatedly broken by having a door slammed on them. Barbie placed ratchet handcuffs of Moulin's wrists and tightened them until his wrists broke. And through all of this, his face a bloody, swollen pulp, his arms hanging, broken and useless at his sides, he still refused to give up the names of his fellow resistance fighters. Another inmate, Christian Pineau, later described Moulin's condition as *"unconscious, his eyes dug in as though they had been punched through his head. An ugly blue wound scarred his temple. A mute rattle came out of his swollen lips."*

Moulin was beaten and tortured until he fell into a coma. Even then Barbie placed him on display, his mangled, unconscious body draped over a chaise longue, in an office at the Gestapo headquarters so that other prisoners could see his pitiful state as they were marched past the window; as an example to those determined to resist. Although no official record of the cause of Moulin's death of July 8th 1943 exists, his biographer maintains his belief that he was 'personally beaten to death,' by Klaus Barbie.[89]

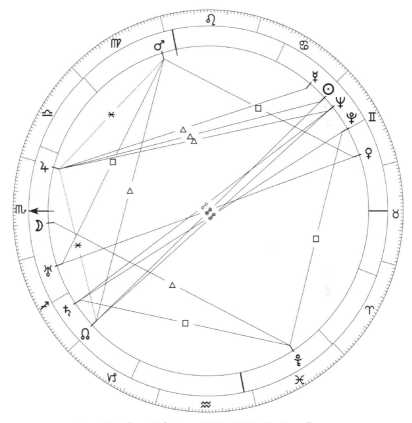

Jean Moulin: 20th June 1899, 1600, Beziers, France

The astrology between these two men, particularly when the matrix of transiting aspects at the time of Moulin's death is given full consideration, is nothing short of remarkable.

---

[89] *The Death of Jean Moulin: Biography of a Ghost* (2001), Patrick Marnham, Pimlico

We see immediately, the chart of Moulin contains a difficult placement for Orcus in Pisces, not only is he the focus of a tee-square from Saturn opposition Pluto, but he is at the precise midpoint of the two, by a distance as close as 14 minutes of arc. This suggests that Orcan energies are realised through the blend of Saturn with Pluto. There are numerous connotations here: forces of authority that are overwhelming in power and scope (like the invading Nazis), the principle of fanaticism, hard-labour or protracted suffering at the hands of faceless and impersonal bureaucracies, hard-heartedness (a common Saturn-Pluto manifestation) and an enormous drive to be in authority, but one that is psychologically born out of a fear of being at the mercy of authority figures oneself ("if I'm the biggest fish in the pond, then who is going to eat me?") Now if isolation, suffering, coming up against the implacability of the eternal are all experienced as manifestations of Orcus and these themes are realised through the medium (midpoint) of Saturn with Pluto, then we have a pattern that suggests that Moulin was destined to experience isolation, suffering and punishment through a faceless and incompassionate authority system, a harsh bureaucracy and that suffering would be hard and uncompromising in the extreme. With Saturn in the 2nd (a great struggle with personal and actually physical security or safety) and Pluto in the 8th (extreme power struggles and survival issues, brutal endings) we immediately see how desperately high are the stakes that are being uncomfortably expressed through the medium of Orcus as the focal point of this uneasy tee-square. Moulin experienced Orcan suffering and loneliness (and what loneliness is greater than facing eternity without comfort, with only the ugliness of brutality and corruption for company?) the terrifying threat of violence, of feeling abandoned and forsaken and ultimately of knowing that he was lost.

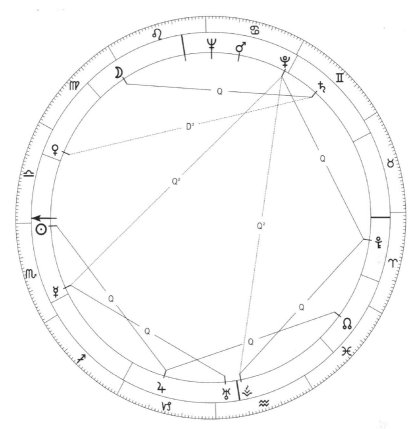

Klaus Barbie: 25th October 1913, 07:00, Bad Godesberg, Germany

Barbie's nativity, by contrast, exhibits Orcus = [Pluto/Vesta] = [Mercury/Saturn] and that is too perfect, but grim and (potentially at least) punishing in the extreme. While Pluto/Vesta speaks of Hadean work, of control, power and fear through work, service and duty Mercury/Saturn with the intermediary of Pluto and Vesta relates harsh and brutal communication as a duty. It is a chilling vocation. Forcing communication because it is one's duty – and the shadow side of Vesta says "I was just obeying orders!" – Barbie was cut out to be a torturer: the duty (Vesta) of oppressing (Saturn) in order to coerce (Pluto) communication (Mercury) could be realised through the medium of torture, incarceration and punishment (Orcus).

Echoing this midpoint picture in Barbie's nativity is a "Golden Triangle" or "Golden Bowl"[90] aspect pattern formed between Orcus, Pluto and Vesta. In this case we can see the pattern of energy exchange very clearly: Orcus mediates between Vesta and Pluto and because the halfsum of formation of these three energies is precisely expressed within a closed circuit of aspectual energies, they are exponentially ramped up into a new dimension of power expression. There are an astonishing number of 5th harmonic aspects in Barbie's nativity and this is typical of people who inexplicably appear to fall into positions of control and power without necessarily having any obviously apparent 'power potentials'. I have explored this conundrum at length:

"...but really, the most remarkable feature of this configuration is its power. It is like a Yod, but supercharged, and without the element of hunting dissatisfaction found in that pattern; it becomes, once activated, innate and in some manner overwhelming and undeniable... Many iconic film stars' charts evidenced Golden Yods, or what I call 'Golden t-squares[91] ' (two quintiles joined by a biquintile), such as Joan Crawford, Charlie Chaplin and James Dean. James Dean has an incredible configuration of quintiles if you take a look at his chart."[92]

The quintile then, in practice, requires some measure of activation, and this is difficult to pin-down or explain comfortably. The 'power' of the quintile is innate, but unrealised until it is recognised and taken in hand and it has this potential, to be activated in a positive, exalting mode, or a base, but crucially, no less powerful mode. David Hamblin explains it thus:

---

[90] By the way, what you refer to as a "Golden T-Square", I call a 'Golden Triangle.' And when there's 4 adjacent points on the Grand Quintile (Joan d'Arc), I refer to this as a 'Golden Bowl' Comment by astrologer Rick Levine on the article Hitler and the Golden Yod on my online astrology journal: http://chirotic.wordpress.com/2008/07/10/hitler-and-the-golden-yod/

[91] See Rick Levine's remarks (71).

[92] From Hitler and the Golden Yod (see 71), by Jeremy Neal, October 2008.

"*When we move on to the fifth-harmonic (H5) chart, we move for the first time into unknown territory... the H5 chart is concerned with the unfamiliar principle of Fiveness.*"[93]

Hamblin goes on to say: "*My own research has convinced me that Fiveness is essentially connected with the idea of making, arranging, building, constructing, structuring, forming. It is to do with the creation of order out of chaos: the bringing together of things that are naturally separate into a formal relationship with one another. It is therefore the first number in which man asserts his power over the world. Within the principle of Twoness he accepts the world as it is and struggles to find his place in it; within the principle of Threeness, he accepts the world as it is and revels in it; but within the principle of Fiveness, he strives to change the world and to make it other than how he found it.*"[94]

The activated quintile, then, has this new potential to impose one's vision upon the fabric of existence and create a new reality, and that is comfortably a definition of power in its truest sense. If this is the case we can see through a matrix of 5th harmonic contacts between Orcus, Vesta, Pluto and Mercury, the same elements that are described in the midpoint pictures being reiterated. Barbie had genuine power to use power, or rather to abuse it, to his own advantage and to the detriment specifically, of the many thousands of individuals whose lives were blighted – and often ended – by him.

So, if Barbie had a 'power of punishment and torture' and, too, a power to extract information by it, then it is small surprise that we see one very significant contact within the synastry of these two charts: Barbie's Ptolemaically[95] unaspected Saturn at 17° 38' Gemini and the 8th house is precisely square Moulin's Orcus at 17° 51' Pisces, by only 13 minutes

---

[93] *Harmonic Charts* (1983), David Hamblin, The Aquarian Press, Chapter 5.
[94] *Harmonic Charts* p 48.
[95] No aspect recognised by Ptolemy: conjunction, square, opposition, trine or sextile. For more on the theory of aspectual peregrination see *Synthesis and Counselling in Astrology* (2005), Noel Tyl, Llewellyn Publications, pages 155-190.

and crucially, therefore, Barbie's Saturn also squares Moulin's Saturn/Pluto midpoint by a single minute of arc. That is a very powerful contact and puts all of those forces in motion when the two men become aware of each other. Barbie becomes the embodied authority against whom Moulin is unwittingly pitted, doomed to fail, and ultimately to perish.

We can draw fate from the condition of Moulin's chart with ease; Pluto perches broodingly on the cusp of the 8th manifesting threat into endings of all kinds, and here he is precisely conjunct Kassandra, who, as we know from the Trojan stories, prophesied truthfully but was not believed. Her pronouncements could not change her fate, and wherever Kassandra is placed there is this communication issue; sometimes she manifests into unsolicited advice, people who will not listen, people who cannot make themselves heard, or, configured with Pluto, people who hold on to their knowledge until their last breath. Pluto opposes Saturn and squares Orcus (as does Kassandra of course). So here we see the last desperate hours of Jean Moulin encoded into these fleeting glyphs. The potential was always there and – with the inclusion of Orcus – the triggers and dependencies are crystal clear.

The transits of Orcus alone make a fascinating study. In Moulin's final days Orcus was experiencing a period of unprecedented activity through his natal configurations. Moulin was arrested on the evening of June 21st 1943 and Saturn squared his natal Orcus for the first and last time in his life at 2:11 am on the 22nd, a few hours later. On June 5th, only a fortnight earlier, he had experienced the final pass of Orcus conjunct Pluto, and this only 6 days after Orcus transited across his 8th house cusp for the final time.

If any further proof of the power and relevance of Orcus as a major astrological player were needed, we see that for Klaus Barbie, Saturn fell sesquisquare Orcus in his nativity on the night of June 21st, at 9:40 pm, the exact time that Moulin was arrested by him! These two men, who became inseparably entwined in heroism and infamy, through the medium of incarceration, torture and death, experienced major Saturn-Orcus transits within 5 hours of each other and Moulin died as Saturn squared Orcus, Orcus fell conjunct Pluto, and crossed the 8th house cusp in the company of Saturn.

How could these final, fearful moments be understood without Orcus? His dread signature is the defining feature of both these disparate astrologies and of both these lives.

The Stockdale Paradox
Admiral James Stockdale, one of the most highly decorated officers in the history of the US Navy, was an aviator who witnessed the infamous Gulf of Tonkin incident in 1964. The Gulf of Tonkin incident refers in fact to two separate incidents, the first being a naval engagement between the USS Maddox, an American destroyer patrolling the seas off Vietnam, and three North Vietnamese gunboats. There was an exchange of fire between the protagonists which resulted in no US casualties, although it heightened tensions at the time. The second incident was a further engagement at the same location which became a pretext for the US declaration of war on the North Vietnamese nation.

After the initial contact, the North Vietnamese claimed that they thought the USS Maddox was a South Korean warship, and it transpired that the destroyer had been following, with suspicious accuracy, the patrol routes of the South Korean Navy. Conspiracy theorists claim that this was a deliberate ploy by the United States to provoke an international incident. The second Gulf of Tonkin incident, remarkably, never even happened; James Stockdale, then a Navy pilot, flew into combat on that fateful day in August 1964:

"[I] *had the best seat in the house to watch that event, and our destroyers were just shooting at phantom targets—there were no PT boats there.... There was nothing there but black water and American fire power.*"[96]

---

[96] Fairness and Accuracy in Reporting (FAIR) article, Media Beat 27th July 1994: *30-year*

The grim possibility exists therefore that the pretext for the Vietnam War was deliberately disingenuous[97]. James Stockdale knew this first-hand, and it caused him untold anguish when he was shot down over North Vietnam and captured by the enemy.

"As the senior naval officer among the prisoners of war in Hanoi for seven and a half years, he was tortured fifteen times, put in leg irons for two years, and confined in solitary for four years. This experience was the crucible for his philosophical thought on issues of character, leadership, integrity, personal and public virtue, and ethics."[98]

Locked in leg irons in a bath stall, he was routinely tortured and beaten. When told by his captors that he was to be paraded in public, Stockdale slit his scalp with a razor to purposely disfigure himself so that his captors could not use him as propaganda. When they covered his head with a hat, Stockdale beat himself with a stool until his face was swollen beyond recognition. He told them in no uncertain terms that they would never use him. When Stockdale was discovered with information that could implicate his friends' 'black activities', he slit his wrists so they could not torture him into confession.

Little did Stockdale know that the actions of his wife, Mrs. Sybil Stockdale, had a tremendous impact on the North Vietnamese. Early in her husband's captivity she organized The League of American Families of POWs and MIAs, with other wives of servicemen who were in similar circumstance. By 1968 she and her organization, which called for the President and the U.S. Congress to publicly acknowledge the mistreatment of the POWs was finally getting the attention of the American press and consequently the attention of the North Vietnamese. Mrs. Stockdale personally made these demands known at

---

Anniversary: Tonkin Gulf Lie Launched Vietnam War, Jeff Cohen, Norman Solomon.
[97] Nearly three decades later, during the Gulf War, columnist Sydney Schanberg warned journalists not to forget *"our unquestioning chorus of agreeability when Lyndon Johnson bamboozled us with his fabrication of the Gulf of Tonkin incident."*
[98] *Thoughts of a philosophical fighter pilot* (1995) Jim Stockdale, Hoover Institution Press

the Paris Peace Talks and private comments made to her by the head of the Vietnamese delegation there indicated concern that her organization might catch the attention of the American public, something the North Vietnamese knew could turn the tide of world opinion against them. The result could not have been more fortunate for James Stockdale at the very time he slit his wrists.[99]

Here we have a man who is dreadfully concerned with perjuring the American government throughout the period of his captivity, which bears a host of Orcan trademarks: punishment, torture, isolation and questions of truth and integrity. James Stockdale became, much like Moulin, the man who would not break; who would rather die than break the faith of his comrades and countrymen. His wife too played an important role in this tale of Orcus and upon his eventual release he wrote a book with her about their shared experiences during the period of his incarceration. [100]

When we look at Stockdale's nativity we immediately see the pivotal role that Orcus plays. Indeed, the inclusion turns what would otherwise be a rather passive grand water trine into an altogether more dynamic Kite configuration. A Grand Trine alone contains no developmental tension because there are no 8th harmonic aspects within the energy exchanges, it is all easy come, easy go. A Grand Trine is innately self-sufficient and requires no external validation, in this case for its feelings, as astrologer Noel Tyl explains it:

---

[99] Wikipedia

[100] *In Love and War: The Story of a Family's Ordeal and Sacrifice During the Vietnam Years* (1984), Jim Stockdale, Sybil Stockdale Harper Collins

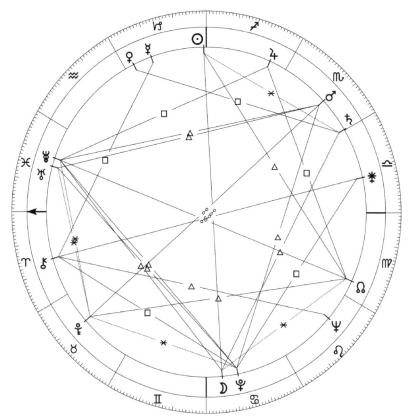

James Stockdale: 23rd December 1923, Abingdon, IL, USA

"*When we see a Grand Trine among planets in the horoscope, we are seeing a classic defense mechanism: a closed circuit of practical (in Earth), motivational (in Fire), social (in Air), or emotional (in Water) self-sufficiency. The Grand Trine isolates and protects by assembling the symbols of behavioural faculties to form a three-sided moat surrounding our ego castle. Very little traffic comes in or goes out. We are safe.*"[101]

The classic exposition of the Grand Trine, therefore, is formatively passive; it creates an unquestioned comfort zone which, due to the very

---

[101] *Noel Tyl's Guide to Astrological Consultation* (2007), Noel Tyl, Llewellyn Publications p33.

nature of its subjective comfort, does not register in consciousness. People can go on for an entire lifetime never truly becoming aware of this structure although they will often wonder at why they feel so uninvolved and disconnected from life. It will simply not occur to them that this 'problem' exists as a direct result of their own conceptual apprehension of life.

The Kite, though, differs in that the fourth planet, at the midpoint of one of the trines, creates oppositional tension and the opposition is the aspect of awareness. Through other people, then, the Kite contains the inbuilt lens through which to view the isolating function of the Grand Trine. A Grand Water Trine alone creates a sense of emotional self-sufficiency which gradually isolates one from nurturing emotional connection, but the opposition (in this case from Orcus to Mars) provides a 'breakout clause' which, when activated by transit, progression or direction, gives one objectivity and allows the native to evolve the pattern, thereby becoming (if you like) its master, rather than its slave.

It is important to appreciate that the sextiling planet is not the focal point of the Kite, rather it is the planet opposite. In Stockdale's case therefore, Mars would become the focus of the Kite configuration, but it is through the opposition to Orcus that Mars receives the focus.

Bill Tierney describes it in this way: "*I interpret it as a more dynamic indicator of success in life. The planet that is sextile to the two points of the Grand Trine represents a stimulating (often mental) outlet for the creative outpour of this configuration. Any special benefits indicated by the Grand Trine usually channel themselves into the natural activities indicated by the drives of this focal planet, often filtering through its natal house position. The Kite may actually be more versatile in its creative application, since the sextile influence encourages eagerness of self-expression. The natal area where the planet of the Grand Trine opposing this pivotal fourth planet is found can indicate where special talents and skills are prone to direct themselves; the planet will suggest the nature of the drive to be expressed, but the fourth planet will act as the catalyst. The stimulation derived from the presence of these other supplementary aspects serve to heighten the individual's awareness of the Grand Trine's vast creative or spiritual potential, encouraging a fuller activation of its promise within a wider range of circumstantial experience. With the inclusion of the opposition aspect there is heightened awareness of how this Grand Trine can be applied to the social environment. This type of configuration becomes thus less self-contained."*[102]

If we apply this insight to James Stockdale we can see that Mars is the area through which he can realise the special talents and abilities of emotional self-sufficiency that are promised by the Grand Trine, but it is through Orcus that these talents are activated. Orcus is the catalyst for the gifts of Mars in the context of the Water element: feelings, security, inner resources. Stockdale could feel safe and content in himself (requiring no external validation) which enabled him to be a more complete man of action (Mars is the focus) but it is through Orcus that this latent skill-set became manifest. The 40 year old Stockdale was a Squadron Commander in the United States Navy at the time of the Gulf of Tonkin incidents in 1964 – well within the remit of his unconscious Grand Trine of Mars – Moon/Pluto - Uranus, but by 1992 he had been awarded the Medal of Honour, had achieved the rank of Vice-Admiral and was running for Vice-President in Ross Perot's bid for the White House (won by Bill Clinton, who was ultimately impeached for lying, which is yet another Orcan story!) Stockdale's Kite had been triggered allowing its enormous creative and spiritual potential to manifest, and great success was the result.

Transiting Orcus made a final conjunction with Stockdale's radix Pluto in May 1964, two months before the Gulf of Tonkin incidents; this was the trigger for the Kite to raise its frequency in his life. Orcus had been trining Mars since mid-1963, with the crucial middle transit (3 of 5) occurring on June 26th, six days before the Gulf of Tonkin began, while

---

[102] *Dynamics of Aspect Analysis* (1980), Bill Tierney, CRCS Publications, p.78

on August 24th (a fortnight after the Gulf of Tonkin) Orcus made the first of five trines to natal Uranus. Since any aspect pattern is a matrix of interconnected energies, they are all affected by contacts to any component. If you pluck one note, other notes begin to resonate into a harmony (or sometimes a discord!). The Grand Trine was being activated by transits from the catalyst planet, Orcus, throughout 1964. The Kite was in full swing by September 9th 1965, when he was captured by the North Vietnamese (a month after the crucial middle transit of Orcus trine Uranus). It is possible, too, to glean greater accuracy from these proceedings by looking at the critical degrees within the Grand Trine structure. On the day of his capture, Orcus was transiting at 35° 23′ of the modulus 45° chart, while the natal midpoints for Juno/NN and Mars/Pluto fall at 35° 26′ and 35° 29′ respectively, effectively rendering the midpoint structure Orcus = Mars/Pluto = Juno/Node with astounding precision (only 3 minutes of arc) on the day of his capture. Since Mars/Pluto defines the Grand Trine structure while the catalyst or trigger planet transits the Moon-Pluto apex of the pattern, it is easy to appreciate how powerful and precise this is. Since we do not have a birth time for James Stockdale, even the three minutes of arc may be rendered superfluous in the reckoning of reality.

There is so much information here that it becomes a trial to keep it in good order. Juno may appear innocuous in this context, but it is utterly crucial to the nativity. Natally, Stockdale's Orcus – Uranus sextile forms the base for a Yod to Juno, which in truth is a marginally focussed Yod when the Chiron – Juno opposition is accounted for. Clearly the marriage partner has a role to play in the story of her husband's Grand Trine. If you follow the language of the earlier discussion of Stockdale's wife, Sybil, it ties in perfectly with his Grand Trine and the resulting Yod to Juno. The organisation she founded: The League of American Families of POWs and MIAs, is inherent in the structure. Prisoner (Orcus) of War (Mars) James Stockdale's wife (Juno) formed an organisation to put pressure (Pluto) on the nation's government (Pluto is in Cancer) to acknowledge the maltreatment (Chiron) of American prisoners (as Orcus transited through the Cancer midpoint). Without Orcus, we simply would not understand or be able to mark these triggers: because they would not be available for measurement by the astrologer.

The rest of James Stockdale's story is a remarkable testament to the singular energies of Orcus. It is in every fibre of his being and his subsequent impact on the world. He wrote a book after these events called *Thoughts of a Philosophical Fighter Pilot*, in which he expounds his various theories on integrity, truth, and the range of Stoic philosophy. It is an entirely Orcan dialogue. Of his time in the Vietnamese internment camps he wrote:

"The fact was, nobody could beat the ropes. The three-cornered squeeze play – the anxiety of having the blood circulation stopped in your arms and upper torso by bindings, the pain of sometimes having your shoulders dislocated, and the claustrophobia and vomiting resulting from being bent double by a man standing on your back, your head stuffed down between your feet – could reduce every member of Stanford's defensive line to a sobbing, compliant, self-loathing wreck in fifteen minutes.

We first had to establish the tradition... of freely reporting to your prison mates the key material you had given up in the ropes... We had to openly admit how we all fared in this circumstance to defuse the guilt feelings, else some would freeze up, eat their hearts out, grow distrustful of others, and become vulnerable loners. We were in a place where within mere months, or even weeks, men made or destroyed their lifetime reputations. We seemed to be scanning reams of data on the problems of good and evil in fast time. The extortion system could quickly drive to the surface weaknesses of moral integrity, which at the pace of normal life could take years to fester and erupt into public view. Epictetus[103] said that the

---

[103] Epictetus 55-135AD was a Greek Stoic philosopher who taught that philosophy should be a way of life and not just a theoretical discipline. He believed that while people could not control external forces they could control whether to react to people and events with compassion, which is the only reasonable response to adversity. He argued that suffering arises from trying to control the uncontrollable or from neglecting

invincible man was the one whom nothing that happens outside the sphere of his moral purpose can dismay. Here we had to check dismay within his sphere of moral purpose too."[104]

And herein is yet another clue to the relationship between Orcus and integrity, both the negative, unevolved exposition which might be best characterised as expedience, and the empowering, exalting, but hard-won quality of Orcus, which seems most accurately described as consistency. This consistency is not easily understood by those who do not possess it: like other profound human qualities it cannot be imagined. After all, what is unconditional love to somebody that has never attained it? A foolishness, an aberration, or a myth? A consistency of integrity is based upon applying a rigorous standard of behaviour, even to one's own detriment. Those who do not understand Orcus assume that it is enough to have an *appearance* of integrity, while behaving badly in ways that are undetectable to others – and possibly even to themselves. Of course, in keeping with Nietzsche's[105] maxim these individuals are hardly likely to understand their inner dichotomy, because self-awareness is required, and very few possess that level of insight, being compulsive and reactionary for the most part.

---

what is within one's power to affect. The 'it isn't what happens to you but how you respond to it that counts' school of life philosophy if you like, which is the clearest underlying truth of astrology too in my own opinion.

[104] *Thoughts of a Philosophical Fighter Pilot* (1995) Jim Stockdale, Hoover Institution Press p 216

[105] Nietzsche argued that there are no moral phenomena in nature, only moral judgements and that the natural world operates just as it is without apology. Predators predate, warriors make war, and that therefore there cannot be conscious evil in the Universe. It is a style of nihilistic Buddhism perhaps, but one which presents a strong argument even so and in relation to astrology, we can say that as a learning paradigm, the nativity must contain polarities, of self-awareness, of behaviour, of insight. We cannot become enlightened without first being compulsive and egotistical. Orcus must therefore allow the soul experience of expedience before moral integrity can have meaning, without the contrast of shadow, all things would be invisible. For more on Nietzsche's view of morality see *Beyond Good and Evil: Prelude to a Philosophy of the Future* (2002) translated by Judith Norman and edited by Rolf-Peter Horstmann: Cambridge University Press

The Orcan philosophy of integrity is, like Orcus' entire realm, uncompromising in the extreme. Jim Collins, a writer and teacher on the theme of self-improvement and the qualities of success, conducted a memorable interview with James Stockdale:

"Stockdale came out of the prison camp even stronger than he went in, by his own account. In preparation for a day I was about to spend with Jim Stockdale, I read his book 'In Love and War', and as I read this book, I found myself getting depressed, because it seemed like his systemic constraints were so severe and there was never going to be any end to it. His captors could come in any day and torture him. He had no sense of whether or if he would ever get out of the prison camp, [it was an] absolutely depressing situation, it's like we can all survive anything so long as we know it will come to an end, we know when, and we have a sense of control. He had none of that. Then all of a sudden it dawned on me: wait a minute, I'm getting depressed reading this book and I know the end of the story. I know he gets out, I know he reunites with his family, I know he becomes a national hero and I know even that we're going to have lunch on the beautiful Stanford campus on Monday. How did he not let those oppressive circumstances beat him down? How did he not get depressed? So I asked him. And he said 'well you have to understand it was never depressing because despite all those circumstances I never, ever wavered in my absolute faith that not only would I prevail, get out of this, but I would prevail by turning it into the defining event of my life that would make me a stronger and better person. And not only that, but I'm the lucky one... because I know the answer to how I would do [in those circumstances] and you never will. Later... I asked him who didn't make it out of those systemic circumstances as well as him. He said 'that's easy... the optimists... They were the ones who said we're going to be out by Christmas. And Christmas would come and it would go. And there would be another Christmas, and they died of a broken heart... You must never, ever, ever confuse the need on one hand for absolute unwavering faith that you can prevail despite those constraints, with the need on the other

hand for the discipline to begin by confronting the brutal facts whatever they are: we're not getting out of here by Christmas."[106]

Collins coined a term for this dissonance of philosophy wherein one can maintain hope only through the absolute denial of optimism: he called it the Stockdale Paradox. It is a Stoic philosophy of sorts.

When we consider Stockdale's nativity, there is no question that this philosophy is eloquently expressed by an unaspected Jupiter in his domicile; that's a very powerful dose of faith that, because it is disconnected from the wider nativity, stands alone. But this cannot explain the duality of faith and optimism. The power of endurance, of near superhuman pragmatism, can only be explained by Orcus. Jupiter contains one side of the paradox, the faith that he would endure, but Orcus describes the other side, the sense that he must not delude himself with false hope.

Orcus is the trigger of the Kite pattern, of course: it renders the gift of Mars, and Mars gives energy, courage and is the natural resistance fighter, it does not countenance depression as a solution. The gift of Martian resistance is therefore rendered through the grim determination of Orcus.

So where Orcus represents the torturer, it represents simultaneously the resistance to torture; it represents the incarcerator and incarcerated, and it represents both the expedient and the resolute. Orcus' implacable determination can be used to punish and terrify but, too, it can be used to stand firm and undaunted. Which is the greater power?

---

[106] Jim Collins, *The Stockdale Paradox*, see http://www.jimcollins.com/media_topics/brutal-facts.html#audio=59 Collins argues that success can only be assured for those who are prepared to face reality as it is, without making excuses for situations and without maintaining false hope that things are different from the way they really are.

It is not any sort of astrological coincidence that at the time of his capture, James Stockdale was engaged in the process of his completing Uranus half-return, which finished some three weeks previously. Barbara Hand-Clow espouses the view that major astrological life-transitions are reflected in the procedural clearing of the subtle body's chakra system:

"Mid-life is the time to take on power without abusing it. At this time, by means of a series of relational dramas, the solar plexus can be cleared and purified by assuming our personal integrity and ending all manipulation of others. The key to successful opening of the solar plexus is to find a way to take our power without harming other people, thus creating negative karma. Like love, power is unlimited, and only by holding it or trying to control another with it does it become destructive. The trick, scary though it may seem at times, is to freely offer power, not hold it or give it in a way that lacks integrity. The solar plexus is the personal power centre, the seat of the emotional body. From this chakra, we size up other people, and as it opens we become honest and discriminating. The more we are clear in the gut, the more easily we can see the truth or the degree of manipulation in the motives and actions of others. As the solar plexus opens, it raises questions of what do we want to get, to grasp and how do we feel in the gut? It is time to build our personal power without abusing others. Outrageous dramas are created to better understand 'power over' versus 'taking on our own power'... In learning about taking on power, all power-abuse tendencies must be looked at, and they can be very subtle and graphic. When the solar plexus is blocked, people are either too defensive or deferential, or they are busy trying to control and abuse others... During mid-life crisis there also are many frustrating encounters with others that involve 'grasping and getting'. As these are played out, we begin to develop discrimination about the intentions of others. Disturbances are felt in the gut that are caused by projections – energy invasions from others. Inevitably somebody appears who causes a lot of stress and pain, because he or she got right into our gut, totally penetrating our energy field. Maybe they want money, maybe they want sex, maybe they want

to swindle us, maybe they want love. Whatever it is, instead of approaching us in a way that's safe and honest for us, they invade our boundaries. They seem to take whatever they want, even if it is under the control or ownership of another."[107]

James Stockdale recognised the connection between Orcus, integrity and the solar plexus chakra intuitively:

"In Hanoi I realised that my captors had all the power. I couldn't see how I was going to keep my honour and self-respect intact. The one thing that I held onto was my knowing that if you don't give up, compromise and literally spill your guts, you can't be had."[108]

The connection here between Orcus, the condition of one's guts and the solar plexus chakra is quite unmistakable, and it is only one example among a multitude which affirms the relationship between the subtle body system and its astrological correspondence. Orcus is innately connected with the solar plexus chakra and this is why people who abuse their power and, too, those who are the targets of the abuses of others – in the form of the energetic invasions which are the result of control agendas – subsequently struggle with imbalances in the digestive system, of the liver, the pancreas, the gallbladder and the upper intestinal tract, as a consequence. If somebody cannot commit a ruthless act – by which we usually understand it to mean an incompassionate act – they are said to not have 'the stomach for it." Astrologically, it is possible to identify the common avenues through which these control-plays are routed by looking at aspects to Orcus. From the Sun, fathers, husbands; from the Moon, mothers and wives. Mercury suggests siblings and to some extent children and so forth. For James Stockdale, Orcus was conjunct Siva 1170 and precisely square Siva 140, both asteroids emphasising contacts with *"Far-Eastern locales, people and culture (including China, Vietnam, Korea, Japan, India and*

---

[107] *The Liquid Light of Sex: Kundalini, Astrology and the Key Life Transitions* (2001), Barbara Hand Clow, Bear and Company, p108-109.
[108] *Thoughts of a philosophical fighter pilot* p 25.

Malaysia)"[109] providing the perfect medium for power-abuse dramas to be played out, to activate (and massively) Stockdale's solar plexus chakra, creating a man of profound power and integrity in the process.

---

[109] *The Orders of Light* (2000), Martha Lang-Wescott, Treehouse Mountain, p255.

Alienation

Loud rang the battle-cry they uttered in their rage, just as eagles
scream which, in lonely grief for their brood, rowing with the oars
of their wings, wheel high over their bed, because they have lost
the toil of guarding their nurslings' nest.

Aeschylus: Agamemnon

Orcus vs. Pluto

A few days past, one of my friends, wishing to understand the quality of
Orcus a little better, asked me to explain to him the difference between
Orcus and Pluto. It was not a question that I could answer easily – not
because the sense of dissonance between the two energies was not
keenly felt when I contemplated his question – but rather because the
quality of these two behemoths of the outer reaches of space are so
very weighty and fundamental. They are difficult to see clearly, not
because they are insubstantial, but for exactly the opposite reason:
they are *profound*. Man has struggled throughout millennia to
adequately describe in language the fundamentals of existence. Alan
Watts intimated this precise conundrum when he said that "*no one's*
mouth is big enough to utter the whole thing."[110] Language runs out
when attempting to frame spiritual experience because it is, by
definition, *immaterial*, and language is primarily materially descriptive.

Astrologers talk about outer-planet experience being *impersonal*. By
this they mean that the themes of the outer planet are unlikely to be

---

[110] *This is it: and other essays on Zen and spiritual experience* (1967), Alan W. Watts,
Collier Books, p 104

experienced directly by an individual. Instead – the logic goes – outer planet energy is considered to be generational; that is to say, the hallmark of the outer planet energy is more likely to manifest across an entire chronological subset of humanity. In my own view, this is entirely fallacious, at least potentially. I do agree that the generational effect of outer planet placements in astrological signs is easy to divine across the generations; there is no question that the Pluto in Cancer generation was – for example – concerned, perhaps arguably *obsessed* with nationalistic themes, as evidenced by the fact that Pluto made final ingress into Cancer only 32 days before the Archduke Franz Ferdinand was assassinated in Sarajevo, the act which precipitated the First World War, and made final ingress into Leo only 79 days before the start of the Second World War. I do not, however, concur that outer planet energies are not felt individually: on the contrary, they are so intrinsic to human experience that they become invisible due to their very profundity. The majority of behaviour in the majority of people is, to one extent or another, *compulsive*, which simply means that most people are not fully conscious of their motives for action and reaction. This is because outer planet energies are responsible for the deep and unconscious drives of human experience, and the only humans who have freed themselves from this trap of unconscious motivation are the spiritually enlightened[111].

So rather than being generational, outer planet energies are as deeply personal as it is possible to be. It is better to say therefore that, rather than being impersonal, outer planet influence is compulsive, but that it is one of the greatest motivators for human behaviour at the individual level.

---

[111] It should be noted that spiritual alignment is not binary, even if the term 'enlightenment' suggests that it is. Spiritual alignment is a spectrum, from self-unconsciousness to self-consciousness, and every shade of grey exists between them. We understand enlightenment to refer to the state of complete self-awareness.

Having said this, when contemplating the difference between Orcus and Pluto, it struck me that both these planets – when operating compulsively – are capable of causing enormous damage. However, they operate in markedly different paradigms. Pluto is very attached, while Orcus is very detached. In order to appreciate this, you only need to observe the classic traits of the Plutonian. Pluto likes to control, indeed, *control* is the true heart of Pluto, exposing a philosophic irony of epic proportions: the enlightened are in control of their Plutonic energies, are self-aware of their control needs, and manage, through that facility of awareness, to rein them in. The self-*unaware* have no such insight and are led by the nose into their own power and control dramas, seeking to control people and situations in their lives. Ironically, therefore they are compulsively controlling of *others* as a symptom of their lack of *self*-control. Even this tells only half of the Pluto story though, because Pluto, with his mask of invisibility, is completely transparent to the habitually compulsive who comprise a majority of all humans alive today. The unenlightened Plutonian needs *attachment* in order to operate because his (or her) greatest weapon and greatest desire is humiliation. Compulsive Pluto loves nothing more than to see his opponent humiliated, shamed, judged, found wanting and cast down into misery, an object of revulsion for all to see. That is the worst of Pluto in the power struggle, but of course, in order for that power struggle to occur, for the battle to commence, there must be *connection*. The combatants must lock horns. Pluto needs attachment.

Orcus, like Pluto, shares an overweening need to be right, but his approach is diametrically opposed. Rather than getting in close enough to rub the opponent's face into the dirt, Orcus simply executes them. Orcus' contempt is as detached as Pluto's is attached. They share an agenda – the subjugation of the enemy – but their methods are as different as can be imagined. The real danger occurs when both planets are operating compulsively in tandem, because then the need to humiliate is coupled with inhuman detachment, and truly monstrous behaviour might be born.

Orcus without Pluto, though, has this astonishing element of distance. It is not the hyper-intellectualised distance of Uranus, it is the distance of a God stepping on a bug. Orcus appears as cold as Pluto is hot, but this impression is not entirely faithful; Orcus wears a mask of implacability, but the inner core is nonetheless in turmoil, as we shall see.

Parental Alienation
And it is that same apparent coldness which creates another manifestation of Orcan energy in the form of alienation. The Journal of Family Law has recognised the rise of the alienating mother in contentious divorce litigation, citing the fact that "[t]*he courts are increasingly aware of the control over contact proceedings that may be attempted by an implacably hostile parent, usually the mother,"* who comprises a unique problem for the courts since "*a judge these days is much less likely to be persuaded that contact is not in the interests of the child, and an order for contact is usually made. However, what can the court do when a parent has alienated a child to the point where he is expressing what appears to be a genuine desire not to have any contact with the non-residential parent? To set the scene, the case will be one where the parent appears to espouse contact wholeheartedly in principle - yet the child is expressing anxiety or even fear at the idea of contact. Although the court welfare officer talking to this child may suspect that the mother is the real obstacle to contact and that she has coached the child, nevertheless it appears that the child is expressing genuine views; it may be difficult for the welfare officer to support his suspicions with concrete facts. The court has to rely on the recorded views of the child and, depending on the age of the child, more or less weight will be attached to his view."*[112]

---

[112] *The Emerging Problem of Parental Alienation* (1997) Caroline Willbourne and Lesley-Anne Cull, Barristers, from Family Law, Jordan Publishing, p 807-8

According to psychiatrist Richard Gardner, Parental Alienation occurs when one parent – usually after a divorce or family breakdown – successfully manipulates children to turn against the other parent. In the most severe examples of parental alienation, a child becomes convinced that the rejected parent is without redeeming qualities. They profess hate and disgust for that parent, often claiming to fear them. In these cases it is seen that before the divorce the relationship with the targeted parent did not warrant such an extreme reaction and the child previously had no reason to fear them. One of the key tools of the alienating parent is to create a sense of anxiety and insecurity about the targeted parent, eventually brainwashing the child fully into the view that the rejected parent is worthless, irresponsible, out of control, dangerous or violent.

The legacy of successful alienation is devastating for all parties involved in the strategy. The rejected parent is left out in the cold, isolated completely from their once loved child. The child is frequently subject to myriad psychological and emotional consequences, which begin to manifest as they grow to adulthood themselves. Eventually, the child comes to understand that they were manipulated into despising a previously loved parent, at which realisation they invariably reject the alienating parent because they cannot reconcile the scope and the depth of the breach of trust that occurred.

One of the most high-profile cases of parental alienation occurred between the Hollywood actors Alec Baldwin and Kim Basinger. They were married in 1993, their daughter Ireland was born in 1995, they separated in 2000 and were divorced in 2002. It was after their separation, in December 2000, that Baldwin began to experience alienation from his daughter.

"Early on, I sensed that Kim wanted me to see my daughter at my ex-wife's whim. There was never any discussion with her, not once, about my rights, responsibilities, or the importance of my contribution as a parent. Very quickly my daughter had one parent, as far as I understood a

parent's role in the life of a child. I was relegated to a role that was more akin to an uncle or even less than that."[113]

This sense began to assume more concrete proportions very quickly however. *"One day, early in the process, I was sitting in a car with my daughter who was then five. We were on our way to the movies. This was one of the first times that my daughter seemed overtly thoughtful and uncomfortable about the situation. I asked her if she was alright. She nodded stiffly. Then she said 'Mommy says we can all be together again if you go and get help. Mommy says you're sick.'"*[114]

Thus, the alienation began and Baldwin became enmeshed in a seven year battle to be allowed to enjoy a normal relationship with his daughter. He battled throughout this period against character assassination, innuendo and relentless badmouthing by his ex-wife, all of which was designed to create distance between him and his daughter. In most cases of alienation, the targeted parent is reinvented as dangerous and potentially abusive. There are a number of means of achieving this goal (and a full examination of the methods of parental alienation is clearly beyond the scope of this book[115]), but for our purposes, it is important to appreciate that alienation is only another form of enforced isolation that is meted out as a punishment for perceived transgression. The principle of alienation is therefore absolutely concomitant with the principle of imprisonment. As discussed in the previous section (Imprisonment), Nelson Mandela was aware of the pressure of time and isolation, *"In jail,"* he said, *"You come face to face with time: there is nothing more terrifying."* The same can be said of the alienated, who universally share a sense of deep personal powerlessness and disconnection due to the isolation from a previously

---

[113] *A Promise to Ourselves, A Journey Through Fatherhood and Divorce* (2008), Alec Baldwin, Mark Tabb, St Martin's Press, p 65.
[114] Baldwin, Tabb p 65-6
[115] For full discussion of the themes and tenets of parental alienation, refer to *Divorce Poison: How to Protect Your Family from Badmouthing and Brainwashing* (2010), Dr Andy Warshak, Harper.

loved child. It is intriguing to note that, exactly as in the case of physical imprisonment, this type of psychic imprisonment must be presaged by a judgement, a 'guilty' verdict, before the criminal is 'sent down'.

When we look at the astrology of Kim Basinger we cannot easily conclude that she is an alienator, however, there is a close (0°14") parallel[116] between Orcus and Pluto. We have explored the fundamental qualities of these two planets already, so we might wonder what happens when these two distant and dark energies are joined in a nativity. I would suggest that this bond creates a person who utilises alienation (Orcus) as part of a power struggle (Pluto), and in this sense we can see that the use of alienation was, for Basinger, completely compulsive[117]. It was not a conscious strategy to separate Baldwin from her daughter, but it was an unconscious effect that was a chain reaction once Pluto was triggered by her ex-husband's opposition to her wishes. The Plutonic power struggle is a concept that is easily understood by the majority of astrologers, and I find it fascinating to delineate the tools and weapons which a person uses in the power struggle based upon the various contacts of Pluto. A Moon-Pluto person might use their moods to gain the upper hand, or they take control of the family, the home, Saturn-Pluto uses authority and social standing, perhaps even their achievements and qualifications, Jupiter-Pluto has a tendency to take control of all the resources (a kind of slash and burn tactic that can be remarkably effective), while Mercury-Pluto has a knack for communicating the devastating observation that leaves their opponent at a loss for words. The list goes on, but the point here is that when combined with Orcus, the combatant opts for alienation.

Of course, alienation in the Orcan mould cannot be effective unless there is a crime, and the easiest methodology for formulating a crime in parent – child relationships is to make an allegation of abuse. Baldwin

---

[116] Much underrated, the parallel is a type of minor conjunction that nonetheless can be very noticeable. A close parallel is easily as powerful as a wide conjunction.
[117] Conversely, it also describes somebody who uses alienation as a means of humiliating their opponent.

experienced this when, by 2004, their ongoing custody saga was becoming increasingly bitter and damaging to both their reputations. Basinger made *"claims that her former husband was 'emotionally and physically abusive'. Both stars seem ready to trash each other's reputations over their daughter, currently living with her mother in Los Angeles... The first shots were fired in a National Enquirer article that claimed Pearl Harbor star Baldwin had beaten his estranged wife in a drunken rage... In a deal reached after their divorce, Baldwin agreed to see an anger management therapist and call his daughter only at agreed hours. Living in New York, he was allowed to see Ireland at set times on one weekend each month in California. Baldwin is said to have become increasingly unhappy at the restrictions. A friend said: 'Kim has gone out of her way to be cruel and to use her daughter as a pawn.'"*[118]

It is interesting to note that in 2000, when the couple first split, their separation appeared to be amicable but by 2002, according to Baldwin, the alienation strategies were already in evidence and it was between January and November 2002 that Basinger experienced transiting Pluto conjunct her natal Sun (January 8th 2002 – November 8th 2002). Pluto was triggered via the power struggle with her husband (Sun) and alienation was her compulsive response (Pluto parallel Orcus).

Intriguingly, during the exact same time period, Alec Baldwin experienced an opposition between transiting Chiron and his natal Orcus (January 18th 2002 – October 10th 2002), thereby suffering the isolating energy of Orcus as a painful reality of life as a direct result of another's actions (opposition). You will note that these transits (her Pluto-Sun, his Chiron-Orcus) began and ended within days of each other).

When we look at their daughter, Ireland's astrology, we see that on January 5th 2002, she experienced Chiron sesquisquare Orcus. The sesquisquare is an aspect where regrets are made, so we can assume

---

[118] *Film Stars in Custody Battle*, The Daily Mail, January 15th 2004

that Ireland embarked upon a life experience of painful alienation at this time which would later be a cause of regret for her. Ultimately, Basinger's attempted alienation of her ex-husband was broadly unsuccessful, but Baldwin is lucky and perhaps his profile and resources gave him the means to keep the fight alive far beyond the point where many alienated parents would have been forced to give up. Indeed, many do give up, and on average, where alienation is used as a strategy in divorce scenarios, of those children who are able to eventually reconcile with an alienated parent (others cannot because the parent has died or no longer desires a reconciliation, and many do not because they feel too ashamed of their rejection of a loving parent), the *average* period of separation is 20 years. The irresponsible use of Orcus by vengeful parents is as remarkably effective a tool for punishment, as the responsible use of Orcus by the criminal justice system. The principles and methodologies of correction are identical, only the judgement becomes debased.

Parental alienation is only one specific *style* of alienation strategy, however. Alienation manifests into myriad human interactions, and like Pluto, its expression is primarily compulsive. Pluto compulsively *gets in close*; consider the child with Pluto rising who has little respect for other people's personal space. Orcus, conversely, pushes away, and just as compulsively. It is not the same distancing energy as Uranus, which is rather indifferent and detached, because Uranus is truly impersonal, whereas Orcus' distancing is entirely *personal* in motivation. Alienating strategies in relationship are invariably motivated by very intense feelings, whereas Uranus' detachment is qualitatively different. It may be that Uranus has a problem with feeling and therefore it amputates the emotions in order to not have to feel them at all, but the Orcan style certainly feels the emotions, this is what fuels the desire for vengeance which compulsively manifests as alienation. The rage and hatred of Orcus is felt in every fibre of the being, which is why Orcus is so devastatingly implacable, but the heated feelings are hidden behind a mask of cold detachment. The Orcan punisher wants to see their opponent isolated and all alone in the world, and will appear dispassionate to third parties, but the feelings will still be apparent in interactions even so.

In Aspect

So Iris came
on dewy, saffron pinions down from heaven,
a thousand colours on her radiant way,
from the opposing sun. She stayed her flight
above that pallid brow: "I come with power
to make this gift to Death. I set thee free
from thy frail body's bound." With her right hand
she cut the tress: then through its every limb
the sinking form grew cold; the vital breath
fled forth, departing on the viewless air.

Virgil: Aeneid, book IV

Mercury and Orcus

In my view, this is an uncomfortable pairing in the extreme. Mercury's rather whimsical predisposition to flightiness suffers inordinately under the implacable dictate of Orcus, and considerable work is required to mitigate the brutal tendency toward 'plain-speaking' that this pairing engenders. Even plain-speaking may be entirely too understated. Orcus' implacability applies to the Mercurial, so very often there is genuine ruthlessness in speech coupled with a lack of compassion for the listener's sensitivities, but also desire for knowledge and communication.

The British comedian Tony Hancock provides an excellent case study for the contact between Mercury and Orcus. Hancock had a close conjunction of Orcus with Mercury in Taurus and the 10th house, squaring Neptune rising in Leo. His mistress, and later wife was quite familiar with his Mercury-Orcus square to Neptune:

"Freddie Hancock tried everything - suicide included - to stop her husband drinking, only to be rewarded with a barrage of verbal or physical abuse... Snappy one-liners are Freddie's forte. Had the right opportunities come along she would have flourished as a comic, the same profession as the man she married: Tony Hancock, the genius of Hancock's Half Hour. Not that Hancock would have allowed it: obsessed with success, ruthless in his ambition, he brooked no competition. Not even from her. "There will be only one comic in this family," he told her many times. "Only one star: and it will be me."[119]

With Orcus in the 10th, he was obsessed with success, and with Orcus quincunx Jupiter and square Neptune there are various pressures relating to status here, we can envisage Orcus – Jupiter in quincunx as a never-sated drive for creative/artistic status, (Orcus/10th, Jupiter/5th) and the square to Neptune is where the tension is expressed, through drinking. Hancock was hailed as a comic genius, but his wife understood the double edged sword this represented to him:

"Tony was the kindest, most gentle, most thoughtful man I have ever known . . . when he wasn't drinking. When he was . . . that was a very different Tony. He was a tortured man, a man who would dwell upon the slightest error he had made. He would lie awake at night worrying that the audience's laughter would stop. When he was like that, no one could help him. No one could convince him of his ability."[120]

It seems that Hancock's introspection and self-doubt was ultimately his nemesis. In early 1960, Hancock appeared on the BBC's Face to Face, a half-hour in-depth interview programme conducted by former Labour MP John Freeman. Freeman asked Hancock many searching questions about his life and work. Hancock, who deeply admired his interviewer, often appeared uncomfortable with the questions, but answered them frankly and honestly. Hancock had always been highly self-critical, and it is often argued that this interview heightened this tendency,

---

[119] *Laugh at Tony? I very nearly died*, Olga Craig, the Daily Telegraph, 10 Nov 2004
[120] Olga Craig

contributing to his later difficulties. According to Roger, his brother, *"It was the biggest mistake he ever made. I think it all started from that really. ...Self-analysis - that was his killer."*[121]

In another intriguing homage to this placement, Hancock read extensively, in an attempt to ascribe meaning to his existence. He read philosophy, religion, politics and sociology almost ceaselessly.

We see here the structural themes of Mercury – Orcus with startling clarity:

- A voracious appetite for reading, learning and communication.
- A tendency to harsh, even brutal, speech.
- A propensity to ceaseless worry.
- A sense of intellectual isolation.
- Deep and uncomfortable introspection.
- An obsession with the themes of Orcus' house, coloured by close aspecting energies, thus status (10th) as a creative, comic (Jupiter/5th) communicator (Mercury). The result was a kind of divine discontent, as is often the case with Jupiter quincunxes.

These are easily gleaned observations too, underlining once again the accessibility of Orcus in the chart. At the time of his death (from a drink and drug overdose – square Neptune), Hancock's Orcus had transited precisely from a waxing to a waning quincunx to Jupiter.

Another good example of Mercury-Orcus energy is provided by Clint Eastwood, who also has a close conjunction of Orcus with Mercury in Taurus. It provides that rather implacable voice tone made famous in many of his roles, from the taciturn hero of many westerns, to Dirty Harry whose immortal line *"do ya feel lucky punk?"* is delivered with typically Orcan deadpan style.

---

[121] Wikipedia entry: *Tony Hancock*

In the sign Aries we find Stewart Granger, an overtly leading man, with myriad Arian qualities. His roles were typically Martian, romantic and swashbuckling both, neither of which are qualities easily reconciled with a classically peregrine 2nd house Taurus Sun. Mercury conjunct Orcus (by a mere 8 minutes) ruled by a 1st house Mars, trine its ruler Neptune (providing the charisma) and square Pluto, adding in a little danger and menace, seems to tell the story more succinctly. Once again we feel the quality of Orcus under the rulership of Mars when we examine the underlying themes of a life. His determination to be *authentically* swashbuckling was so great that when he was preparing for his roles in *The Prisoner of Zenda* and *Scaramouche!* he took lessons with a retired Olympic fencing champion and wore out "*a dozen or so pairs of fencing shoes.*"[122] In Granger's case the Mercury – Orcus conjunction applies to the 2nd house cusp, so we see Venusian themes, too, brought into play, and Granger's love affairs were notorious. He said himself that this was an area of weakness: "*I don't know which was the greatest disaster: my career or my wives,*" and "*I made King Solomon's Mines and I became popular because Quatermain was a mysterious man with a leopard skin around his hat. It was Africa romantic. Deborah Kerr and I made love up a tree. I said to Deborah -- I had a six month affair with her -- that we should never have come down from that tree.*" So here we see the Venus-influenced, Mars-ruled Mercury paired with Orcus. It's bold, rather 'plain' and direct speaking, forthright, ardent and concerned with affairs of the heart.

Moving into Gemini, we have the case of Brian Wilson, founding member of the Beach Boys, who lost many years battling drug addiction and mental illness. He famously spent three years locked in his bedroom sleeping, taking drugs and overeating. Wilson has a Gemini Sun tee-squared from a Neptune-Ceres opposition, ruled by an otherwise unaspected Mercury conjunct both Orcus and Terpsichore[123].

---

[122] http://www.imdb.com/name/nm0001289/bio
[123] For more on Terpsichore refer to the discussion of Carl Lewis page on page 54, Terpsichore was the muse of dance and body movement.

Mercury, unaspected, retrograde, a final dispositor and rising is a very big deal however you want to cut it, and here he is conjunct Orcus. Years of drug abuse (Mercury opposes Panacea!) left Wilson with serious difficulties:

"[W]hen circumstances required Brian to have face-to-face contact with old friends or family members, they often came away dismayed to discover that he could no longer remember some longtime friends and would often lapse into incoherence or even fall asleep in mid-conversation. Brian had also taken on some disturbing facial tics which were often accompanied by shaking hands and a visible trembling in his legs. Some observers concluded that he had suffered a stroke or was showing the latter-day side-effects of the mountains of cocaine and rivers of alcohol he had ingested in the 1970s and early 1980s. But when Brian made a surprise appearance at a Beach Boys' fan convention in the summer of 1990, it didn't take long for Peter Reum, a longtime fan who happened to work as a therapist in Colorado, to realise something else. Reum had met and spoken to Brian on several occasions during the previous fifteen years, and so he knew that the man standing before him in San Diego had changed in distressing ways. Given his professional training, Reum suspected that Brian's twitching, waxen face and palsied hands, pointed to tardive dyskinesia, a neurological condition that develops in patients whose systems had become saturated with psychotropic medications..."[124]

Every astrologer knows that Mercury and Gemini are restless, nervous, fidgety and rule such issues as tics, nervous conditions and disorders and the arms, hands and gesticulatory movements. Here, Orcus combines with Terpsichore (physical movement and coordination) and Panacea (prescription drugs) to create – through isolation and withdrawal – a difficult and transformative process of inner change. The tee-square to the Sun receives pressure from a Neptune – Ceres

---

[124] *Catch a Wave: the rise, fall & redemption of the Beach Boys' Brian Wilson* (2006), Peter Ames Carlin, Rodale books, p.271

opposition, so themes of drugs and food are part of the dual-identity problem (Wilson was incorrectly diagnosed with schizophrenia), and he *"began most of his days with a dozen eggs and an entire loaf of bread,"* [125] and though he hardly produced any new musical material during this solitary period, he could be lured *"to the music room with a sack of McDonald's hamburgers and a few grams of cocaine."* [126] The tension received by the Sun therefore manifested into his identity as a clichéd rock star, and via Mercury's rulership, that same tension eventually manifested into tardive dyskinesia, which is very much the opposite condition to that of Parkinson's disease which results in chronic *immobility*, since sufferer's cannot help but be constantly on the move. It is the most Mercurial of conditions, and it caused Wilson to become singularly isolated and withdrawn.

Moving into the sign of Cancer we have another fascinating example, this time manifesting through the medium of the aforementioned converse condition to that of Brian Wilson. With Michael J. Fox, we see a close conjunction of Mercury with Orcus in Cancer, and his battle with exceptionally early-onset Parkinson's disease is well-documented. Fox's Mercury is conjunct Orcus, Bacchus and Cupido. Bacchus has association with wine (alcohol, drugs and addiction issues in general), while Cupido concerns itself very much with looks, physical appearances and attractiveness:

"After he was diagnosed with Parkinson's disease, but before he started writing books about optimism, Michael J Fox went through a period of seeing himself as he thought others saw him. 'Peculiar,' he says, was the overall impression. 'Funny looking. [Parkinson's] makes me squirm and it makes my pants ride up so my socks are showing and my shoes fall off and I can't get the food up to my mouth when I want to.' Fox had been a movie star for five years when he was diagnosed, and was used to being

---

[125] *Catch a Wave* p.196
[126] *Catch a Wave* p.239

stared at. But of course this was different. 'I hate the way it makes me
look,' he thought. 'That means that I hate me.'" [127]

The Bacchus connection manifested through a hard-drinking lifestyle in
his twenties, a mode of living to which he ascribes his later difficulties:

*"'I have a lot of compassion for my younger self. It's funny. I wouldn't have
an appreciation for the things I do now if I didn't have those experiences. I
was so... it really is a course correction - at that point in my life, when I got
Parkinson's, I had to look at the way I was living: the drinking. It wasn't
like a little warning sign at the side of the road. It was a big caution in
flashing lights. I don't know that I would have the family that I have now,
the life I have, the sense of purpose, if none of this had happened.'*

*After he was diagnosed in 1991, Fox's drinking got much worse. The alarm
call came a year later, when he woke up on the sofa one morning, stinking
of booze, with his baby son crawling on him and half a can of beer on the
floor next to him. When he opened one eye to see his wife looking down at
him, she didn't seem angry or disgusted, but, worse, indifferent. Fox made
arrangements that day to get help with his drinking and hasn't touched
alcohol since."* [128]

Hearing Fox describe his subjective experience of Parkinson's disease is
singularly compelling and heartbreaking, and much of his narrative is
focused on the frustration and dislocation of the symptomatic
communication blocks and challenges that are associated with
Parkinson's disease:

"*When I'm 'off,' (medication) the disease has complete authority over my
physical being. I'm utterly in its possession. Sometimes there are flashes
of function, and I can be effective at performing basic physical tasks,
certainly feeding and dressing myself, as well as any chore calling for
more brute force than manual dexterity. In my very worst 'off' times I*

---

[127] *It's the gift that keeps on taking* by Emma Brockes, The Guardian 11th April 2009
[128] *It's the gift that keeps on taking.*

experience the full panoply of classic Parkinsonian symptoms: rigidity, shuffling, tremors, lack of balance, diminished small motor control, and the insidious cluster of symptoms that makes communication, written as well as spoken, difficult and sometimes impossible.

My ability to form thoughts and ideas into words and sentences is not impaired; the problem is translating those words and sentences into articulate speech. My lips, tongue, and jaw muscles simply won't cooperate. What words I do smuggle through the blockade can be heard, though not always comprehended. Try as I might, I can't inflect my speech to reflect my state of mind...

These impediments to self-expression are not the most painful or debilitating features of Parkinson's disease, yet they madden me more than even the most teeth-rattling full body tremor. When the meds are "off" and P.D. has already rendered me a prisoner in my own body..."[129]

This is a fascinating account that describes with absolute clarity the juxtaposition of Mercury with Orcus, the nervous system has made a *prison* of the body. His first symptoms appeared in 1990, just as a series of Orcus-Neptune squares came to a conclusion and Jupiter opposed natal Orcus by Solar arc.

Intriguingly, the same conjunction is found in the chart of the A list actor, Tom Hanks. I am reminded of his various film roles like Cast Away, which fairly abounds in Mercury/Orcus themes, he plays a postal service worker, who when travelling by plane is stranded alone on a remote desert island, which effectively becomes a prison. He won an Academy Award for his portrayal of a gay lawyer dying of AIDs in *Philadelphia*, another profoundly Orcan role.

This discussion posits the question as to whether or not the contacts of Mercury with Orcus are a primary indicator of nervous system diseases. Muhammad Ali has a close trine between Mercury and Orcus and my

---

[129] *Lucky Man: A Memoir* (2003), Michael J. Fox, Ebury Press p.255

own stepfather has Parkinson's and a close conjunction between Mercury and Orcus. The key indicator though has to be Mercury, ruler of the nervous system. The televangelist Billy Graham, another Parkinson's sufferer, has no contact between Orcus and Mercury, but Mercury is the focus of a tee-square from a Saturn-Uranus opposition, which denotes enormous internal tension of course. Orcus alone lends so much implacable and pitiless energy to whichever point he contacts that he does the job of a Saturn-Uranus opposition single-handedly!

One other intriguing observation about this combination: Orcus appears to affect the voice markedly. Many singer-songwriters of note have this contact, very often their voices have a cracked or broken quality, or some other notable vocal 'style' which is not considered ideal, but which somehow adds a plaintive or compelling quality to the voice-tone, and other notables with a distinctive voice quality frequently evince the contact. Consider the following examples:

- Karen Carpenter (trine).
- Ray LaMontagne (partile conjunction).
- Billy Bragg (opposition).
- David Byrne (sextile).
- Belinda Carlisle (sextile).
- Patsy Cline (square).
- Sean Connery (trine).
- Aretha Franklin (square).
- Cary Grant (sextile).
- Goldie Hawn (opposition).
- Dustin Hoffman (square).
- Whitney Houston (sextile to Mercury conjunct Pluto: supercharged).
- Janis Joplin (trine).
- Annie Lennox (opposition, Mercury cazimi!)
- Madonna (sextile).
- Willie Nelson (semisquare).

- Olivia Newton-John (trine).
- Edith Piaf (square).
- Diana Ross (sextile).
- Tina Turner (opposition).
- Tom Waits (opposition).

Especially intriguing is that one can discern the quality of the voice according to aspect, from smooth trines and sextiles (Sean Connery, Karen Carpenter, Diana Ross) to the more edgy, cracked squares and oppositions (Aretha Franklin, Tina Turner, Tom Waits). Fascinating!

Venus and Orcus
When we come to Venusian contacts with Orcus, we have to modify our insights to account for the differing applications of Venus in male and female nativities. For the most part, traditional male perspectives tend to project the Venusian energy onto prominent women in the life, especially those with whom there is romantic interest. For this reason, we can expect that Orcan dialogues in the realm of love will be more apparent in the female horoscope, and in the male, through their choice of partner. The 2nd house quality of Venus will manifest into a male chart just as keenly in financial and material terms however.

A truly fascinating example of the contact is to be found in the case of Brenda Frazier, who began a career as a *celeb-utante* long before such undertakings were considered to be especially normal, as they might be in today's celebrity-obsessed culture. Frazier was one of the first people to be famous simply for being famous, evincing no especial talent, ability or claim to fame. Frazier's renown derived solely from being invited to every glamorous social occasion of her day, and this was in the 1930s and 40s. She made the cover of time magazine for no reason other than that her debutante party attracted an unprecedented number of guests of good standing within the New York society of the day. What the smiles and glitz concealed, however, was a small girl, starved of love and affection by a domineering line of matriarchs who were determined that she would marry into a good station and reflect well upon her family line.

"*It happened in a Boston hotel suite on March 16th 1961. I sat awake all through the night, alone in my bedroom thinking my thoughts, finally writing a letter. At 5.30 a.m. I swallowed all the sleeping tablets I had and lay back to die.*"[130]

Brenda Frazier was born with a close conjunction of Venus with Orcus in Taurus, Venus' natural domicile, in the 4th house. We are immediately alerted to a strong *family perspective* or perhaps a tribal tradition. Without Orcus, we might see this as a blessed placement, a strong Venus in the 4th house ought to speak of a loving family base, a childhood of fond memories, a warm and loving tactility, traditional and happy family meals, Venus trines Jupiter and sextiles Pluto too, so while there may be some transformative relationships in the future, the early years at least ought to have been jovial, filled with love and light and recalled with affection.

"*I had been the most publicised debutante in history; the newspapers never called me just Brenda Frazier, they called me 'glamour girl Brenda Frazier.' I was supposed to be the envy of all American women. But here I was just two decades later, at the end of my line.*"

Brenda's childhood had appeared to be idyllic. Born into a wealthy Boston family, she seemed to have every advantage, but the dazzling picture of social perfection was a mirage, bought at the cost of near-fanatical strivings for prestige and position:

"*My Grandmother Williams-Taylor aspired to be a social power, not only in Canada but in Europe: in time she managed to become acquainted with Queen Mary and with the King and Queen of Spain. She even had lunch once with Adolf Hitler, who gave her his portrait done in oil. I'm afraid it*

---

[130] *The most famous deb of all denounces the life she lived: My Debut – A Horror*, by Brenda Frazier, LIFE Magazine, December 6th 1961

made very little difference to my grandmother whether a man was a beast or a hero, as long as he was a head of state... To my grandmother, my mother was never a living, breathing child, never a real individual with a life of her own to lead, but merely an embellishment to the family's glory."

Her childhood was lonely and devoid of warmth and even when she managed to forge a connection with one of her nannies, it always came to an abrupt end:

"I myself was brought up by a succession of outsiders. Until I was 5 I had a nanny of whom I was terribly fond; then – I suppose at the time that my parents finally separated – I have vague but terrible memories of being in Montreal, and Nanny was suddenly gone, and afterwards going to a house in New York where I suddenly was in the care of a woman from Russia... I was so miserable that I cried myself to sleep for several months. When I was about 7 I acquired yet another governess, a Frenchwoman whom I called Mademoiselle. She was terribly strict, a tyrant in fact. We rose at 6 o'clock in the morning so that I could practise piano for an hour and a half before going off to school. Evenings I had to practise for another two and a half hours. Unless I placed first, or at the worst, second, Mademoiselle hardly spoke to me for days at a time. Yet with my music and my riding lessons and all the rest of the regimen that was imposed upon me, I had no time to study before lights-out, which came as promptly and as rigidly as in a prison... Christmases, I suppose, were the worst. My mother always seemed to be visiting friends at Christmastime, often in places as far away as Europe, and I was left to open my presents alone, except for the company of a maid or the butler."

So we see all of these themes in the context of Venus – being charming, sociable, musical, poised and feminine. In Taurus the Venusian energy is focussed through a lens of wealth, tradition and material values, and in the 4th house the emphasis is placed on family traditions and the matriarchal line, the tribal heritage. All ought to be well, but in contact with Orcus the entire experience becomes chilled with an isolating, punishing and lonely shadow, and through its implacability, her childhood and family heritage begins to resemble not so much a desirable position of luxury and privilege, as a prison: *a gilded cage.*

The "delights" of Venus became, for Brenda Frazier, a kind of Orcan wasteland, devoid of human warmth and contact.

In a male chart, the quality of Venus is more likely to be experienced through resources or the object of affections. John Paul Getty III was the grandson of oil magnate John Paul Getty, founder of Getty Oil. Getty senior was a notorious miser, to the extent that, despite having a fortune of around $2 billion, he had payphones installed in his home to prevent his domestic staff from making free calls.

In 1973, aged 16, John Paul III *"was kidnapped by a gang of Italian petty criminals who blindfolded him and chained him to a stake for five months. Eventually they cut off his right ear as evidence of their willingness to kill him unless a ransom was paid. Eight years later, and by then addicted to a cocktail of alcohol and hard drugs including heroin and cocaine, Getty was the victim of a near-fatal stroke that left him a quadriplegic, almost blind, and confined to a wheelchair. For the rest of his life, unable even to enunciate his own name, he had to be spoon-fed, dressed, bathed and cared for around the clock by his mother, Gail, and a team of carers. With only peripheral vision, Getty had problems communicating, and could emit only a high-pitched scream. Worse, his relationship with his father, Sir John Paul Getty II, had broken down when his parent – who in 1976 had inherited a quarter of the Getty Trust, worth at least $1.3 billion – refused to pay his son's medical bills, running at £16,000 a month."* [131]

John Paul's astrology contains a near partile square between Venus and Orcus.[132] To add to the dynamic, Venus is precisely conjunct the Transneptunian Cupido which constellates family attitudes toward

---

[131] The Telegraph, Obituaries, 7th Feb 2011.
[132] John Paul Getty III born 4th November 1956, time unknown, Minneapolis, Minnesota. Venus square Orcus occurred at midday, resulting in a potential maximum orb of half a degree if Getty were born within 12 hours of that time.

money and financial considerations of the home and of property in general. The correlations with Getty Junior's Orcus are remarkable. Pluto is parallel Orcus in his case also, so it is small surprise that *other people's wealth* becomes the focus of a power struggle in his life, which in turn led to his kidnapping, torture and eventual substance abuse issues.

John Paul was kidnapped on 10th July 1973 and released on December 15th. Remarkably, on the median day – September 27th – transiting Sun was partile conjunct Getty's natal Cupido and Venus, while transiting Pluto was at 4° 16" Libra: conjunct Getty's Venus (4°43 Libra), his Cupido (4°08 Libra), and square his Orcus (4°43 Cancer).

In April 1981, suffering a severe depression as a result of his kidnapping experience and feeling rejected and isolated by his father, Getty junior took a cocktail of alcohol and drugs, causing a catastrophic liver failure. At this time, both Jupiter and Saturn were transiting at 4° Libra precisely conjunct Venus and Cupido, square Orcus. Getty's excesses had taken their toll on his health, he went too far under the auspices of Jupiter, and was imprisoned by Saturn. He spent 30 years locked inside his body until he died in February 2011.

Mars and Orcus

In my research I have noted the very high incidence of difficult aspects between Mars and Orcus in the nativities of the most brutal murderers. The energy combination constitutes a tendency toward brutal and inhumane violence where other factors exacerbate violent tendencies. Orcus has this potential for cruelty and a complete lack of empathy or care for the other person's sensitivities. These contacts, therefore, have the power to turn a violent type into something quite heinous and brutal. Klaus Barbie (discussed at length in Chapter 6) had the square which he shares with Ian Brady, Jeffrey Dahmer, Erik Menendez and Allan Menzies, brutal murderers all. Ted Bundy had the opposition, Edward Gein the sesquisquare and John Hinckley the conjunction. In general terms the conjunction is not nearly so violent as the hard aspects, but the sign plays an important role in determining the quality of Orcus with Mars. Even so, it can be brutal in other ways, as we shall discover.

Louis Braille, the inventor of the alphabet for the blind was born with perfect sight in both eyes. He was the youngest of 4 children and his indulgent father enjoyed his company in his workshop, where he worked as a saddle-maker. On a summer day in 1812, tragedy struck the Braille household:

"One day at the age of three, sitting beside his father, who was working and lovingly thinking about his little Benjamin[133], the boy wanted to work too, and imitate the movements he saw his father make. In one of his little hands he seized a leather strap, and in the other a serpette (a slender, curved knife, rather like a small pruning hook) and there he was at work. Weakness often invites trouble: and it did. The sharp tool veered out of control at an angle and stabbed the poor worker in the eye. Medical knowledge at that time could not save the eyesight of their Benjamin. Lily water, thought to possess healing powers, was applied by an old woman from the village, probably doing more harm than good to the injured right eye. Louis' other (left) eye became inflamed, and the sight in that eye was eventually lost too. The right cornea became totally opaque, and the left eye partially so, with blue striations. His eyes would have been very painful during this period: he would have cried a lot and needed much mothering. It is not known how long the process continued, but by age five, two years after the accident, Louis was completely blind."[134]

---

[133] Louis' parents, Simon-Renee and Monique were enamoured of their last-born who arrived unexpectedly when they were 44 and 39 respectively; Simon-Renee proudly announced that Louis would be his companion in old-age. They gave Louis the pet-name 'Benjamin', a reference to the beloved son of the Biblical Jacob. From *Louis Braille: A Touch of Genius* (2006), C. Michael Mellor, National Braille Press, 2006 p14.
[134] From the account of Hippolyte Coltat, former schoolmate and friend of Braille. From *Louis Braille: A Touch of Genius* p 16.

By the age of 15 he was formulating his first alphabet for the blind using the very same tool from his father's workshop that had originally blinded him.

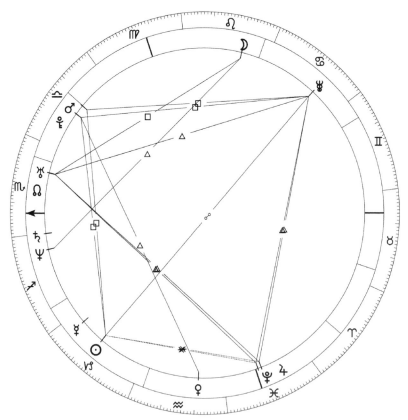

Louis Braille: 4th January 1809, 04:00, Coupray, France

L ouis Braille's nativity is such a wonderful expression of his life story (and vice-versa of course) that it is an excellent study: and nowhere is this more in evidence than through the opposition of Sun with Hygeia. Louis' Capricorn Sun in the 2nd house opposed Hygeia in Cancer and the 8th and this spine of energy carries developmental tension throughout the chart, in the form of a tee-square to Mars conjunct Orcus and a Kite pattern. The Kite, as discussed previously, is a remarkable pattern built around a Grand Trine – in Louis' case in both the water element and through the water houses – which is best understood as an emotional defence mechanism created out of the necessity indicated by the opposition of its spine: in this case, therefore, due to Sun opposition Hygeia. In a Kite pattern the planet at the oppositional apex conjoining the two sextiles is considered the trigger point for the opposing planet's realisation. That is to say, in Louis' case, the Sun would have been the motive energy for the exposition of Hygeian qualities.

The tension of the Sun – Hygeia opposition therefore would have created the necessity for emotional self-sufficiency, which is the hallmark of the Grand Trine aspect pattern. Sun – Hygeia speaks of a constitution somewhat weakened and very often there is an *identification* with health; clearly a strong factor for Louis, as evidenced by the many letters that he wrote to his lifelong friend and colleague Dr Pignier[135]:

"Farewell Sir, Stay healthy for your children's sake, live before you work: health is a treasure whose value is recognised only when it is lost. These are old wives' tales that are still true... The countryside is my only remedy."[136]

Many of his letters contain references on the theme of health, of this nature. If we are *identified* by the Sun, then an opposition challenges our identity: in some way or other, therefore, Louis related to health as an adversary: not just for himself, but to various important male role models in his life. His father, throughout Louis' life a kind of anchor and support, died when Louis was 22, leaving him emotionally devastated for the remainder of his life, and it was at this time that his friends became especially concerned with Louis' health, and particularly the possibility that he had contracted tuberculosis: the disease which would eventually kill him at the age of 43. It is plain to see from his letters,

---

[135] Dr Alexndre-Renee Pignier was a teacher and director of the Paris Institute for the Blind between 1821 and 1840, which Louis attended from childhood; eventually becoming a teacher there himself.
[136] Letter to Dr. Pignier October 2nd 1831.

however, that the loss of his father was the fateful event which first nicked the tenuous thread of the young Louis' life, and he never fully recovered. Sun, representing both father and constitution were to be irrevocably entwined with Hygeia, *health*.

One other point of especial note with the Kite pattern: we see that Uranus conjoins North Node in Scorpio and the 12th house, thus a sudden and fated event catapulted the young Louis into an institutionalised life path, due to the challenges of his health, of which blindness would have been party of course; Louis was blinded only in one eye but *infection*, a truly Hygeian challenge, assured his total blindness and indeed created his lasting legacy and identity.

What is even more remarkable is that Hygeia is exactly conjunct Hopi 2938, which governs knives, sharp metal objects and sudden cuts and stabbings, but also prejudice, and Braille was often concerned with the ways in which being a blind person was not considered to be a physical disability alone, and this awareness of being different was a major incentive for Braille to develop a new system of reading and writing: "[a]*ccess to communication in the widest sense is access to knowledge, and that is vitally important for us if we [the blind] are not to go on being despised or patronized by condescending sighted people. We do not need pity, nor do we need to be reminded we are vulnerable. We must be treated as equals – and communication is the way this can be brought about.*"[137]

The Sun-Hygeia opposition, however, is not limited to its role in the Kite, but also forms a tee-square to Mars in Libra conjunct Orcus. The tee-square is not nearly so complex as a Kite pattern and it follows the simple rule that the oppositional tension becomes *unbalanced* and therefore problematic, through the trigger of the apex planet. So we could say here that Louis experienced health challenges because of the

---

[137] *Undaunted By Blindness* (2011), Clifford E. Olstrom, Perkins School for the Blind

triggering power of Mars-Orcus. This is in so many ways true and in very straightforward delineation also.

The most obvious insight lies in the fact that his isolation (Orcus) was caused by a sharp metal object (Mars) and this of course had enormous consequences for his health. The conjunction falls in the 11th house, thus we can say that being around the crowds of Paris – and yet being cut-off and alone within that crowd – also gave him health challenges; after all in the cities of his day, Louis would have been exposed to cholera, typhus, trachoma and tuberculosis on a daily basis. Blindness then would have exacerbated a sense of physical, as well as emotional isolation: after all there were no guide dogs for the blind in his day, so his movements would have been severely curtailed, and, indeed, he may only have travelled with a companion (Mars/Orcus are in *Libra*.) So this necessity to rely on others for the merest physical freedom would also have caused great strain on his health and peace of mind.

There are other indicators too: Mercury is peregrine (unaspected) and conjunct the fixed star Facies[138], long associated with *eyesight* and problems with sight. Mercury is ruled by Saturn who rises: Saturn conjunct Ascendant often isolates from the immediate environment also.

As an aside it is intriguing to note that the 8th house is ruled by Mercury, thus (with Facies) this becomes another indicator of isolating factors and Louis' death came through tuberculosis, a disease of the lungs (Mercury), which become gradually constricted (Saturn) by liquid (Saturn is conjunct Neptune). He died just 5 days before the first of five passes of Pluto square natal Hygeia: thus forming a transiting Grand Cross from the Mars=Sun/Hygeia tee-square in his nativity[139].

---

[138] "*It is of the nature of the Sun and Mars, and causes blindness, defective sight, sickness, accidents and a violent death*" From *The Fixed Stars and Constellations in Astrology* (1987) Vivian E. Robson, Taraporevala. Facies is the nebula in the face of the Archer, traditionally linked to the eyes and blindness, primarily because a test of good eyesight in the Roman army was to be able to see that a star was not one but a cluster.

[139] As an interesting footnote, Braille died two days after his 43rd birthday of suspected

Jupiter and Orcus

Combinations of Orcus with Jupiter might be considered more amenable than perhaps other groupings. However, the overall tenor of the nativity and the matrix of qualities associated with Orcus must be considered. It would be a mistake to ever consider Orcus to be 'easy', and we will see that, with the societal influences of both Jupiter and Saturn, Orcus' contacts create their own unique energy signatures.

The first example to consider is that of the legendary boxer Muhammad Ali who, when already a World Heavyweight Champion, refused to fight in the Vietnam War due to his religious beliefs[140]:

"I'm expected to go overseas to help free people in South Vietnam, and at the same time my people here are being brutalised and mistreated, and this is really the same thing that's happening over in Vietnam. So, I'm going to fight it legally, and if I lose, I'm just going to jail. Whatever the punishment, whatever the persecution is for standing up for my beliefs, even if it means facing machine gun fire that day, I'll face it before denouncing Elijah Muhammad and the religion of Islam.[141]"

This is a fascinating statement in the context of Jupiter - Orcus, *"I'm going to fight legally (Jupiter) and if I lose, I'm going to jail (Orcus)."* Here is an implacable statement of intent relating to a range of Jovian themes: race, creed, foreign policy, beliefs and religion with Orcan consequences: ostracism, imprisonment, even death.

In the event Ali was not jailed. However he was stripped of his titles and honours and was forbidden to continue fighting, which caused him considerable financial hardship:

---

tuberculosis; a lung disease. His Solar Return chart for 1852 has a *two minute* opposition from Orcus in the sixth to Moon in Gemini and the 12th on the degree for the lungs.
[140] Ali became a member of the Nation of Islam in 1964, changing his name from Cassius Clay to Muhammad Ali.
[141] *Muhammad Ali: His Life and Times* (2004) Thomas Hauser, Robson Books Ltd p187.

"The power structure seems to want to starve me out. The punishment, five years in jail, ten thousand dollar fine, ain't enough. They want to stop me from working (Jupiter/Orcus in the 10th), not only in this country, but out of it. Not even a license to fight an exhibition for charity, and that's in this Twentieth Century. You read about these things in the dictatorship countries, where a man don't go along with this or that and he is completely not allowed to work or to earn a decent living."

He went on to say: *"What do I need money for? I don't spend no money. Don't drink, don't smoke, don't go nowhere, don't go running with women. I take my wife out and we eat ice cream. My wife is such a good cook I never go to a restaurant. I give her twenty dollars for a whole week and it's enough for her. We can eat on three dollars a day. Look out there at that little robin pecking and eating. The Lord feeds the birds and the animals. If the Lord has this power, will the Lord let his servant starve, let a man who is doing His work go hungry? I'm not worried, the Lord will provide."*

Ali's chart has a close trine from Moon/Mercury to Jupiter/Orcus, and indeed the Moon – Orcus trine is only two minutes from partile. What you see here is a sense of almost implacable faith, which is exactly the key energy signature of Jupiter-Orcus, in its best possible interpretation.

While Ali applied Orcus' implacability to his career in the ring, he utilised Jovian themes relentlessly out of the ring too, never missing an opportunity to lay out his philosophies and perspectives, most especially on the subject of *race* (Jupiter) and *segregation* (Orcus):

"Why ask me if I believe in segregation? I recognise the fact that you believe in it. What do you mean you don't believe in it? Oh man, you're just crazy. Every city I go to I can find a black neighbourhood and a white neighbourhood. How many Negroes live out here in this big old neighbourhood? I'd like to see peace on earth, and if integrating would bring it, I'd say let's integrate. But let's just not stand still where one man

holds another in bondage and deprives him of freedom, justice and equality, neither giving him freedom nor letting him go to his own."

These themes were irrevocably intertwined in Ali's consciousness: race and bondage, ethnicity and freedom, and all underpinned by a profound and unshakeable sense of religious conviction.

For Priscilla Ann Wagner, her Jupiter-Orcus square operated differently, but the same themes of Jupiter and Orcus were writ large upon her life story. At the age of 11, the young Priscilla was uprooted from her familiar life in Austin, Texas:

"My newfound tranquillity ended abruptly when my father announced that he was being transferred to Wiesbaden, West Germany. I was crushed; Germany was the other side of the world. All my fears returned. My first thought was, what am I going to do about my friends? I turned to my mother, who was sympathetic and reminded me that we were in the Air Force and moving was an unavoidable part of our lives. I finished junior high school, my mother gave birth to baby Jeff, and we said our goodbyes to neighbours and good friends. Everyone promised to write or call, but remembering past promises I knew better. My friend Angela jokingly told me that Elvis Presley was stationed in Bad Neuheim, West Germany. 'Do you believe it? You're going to be in the same country as Elvis Presley,' she said.[142]"

Priscilla's early teenage years were made a misery by her time in Germany; she felt lost and alone in a country whose culture and language were so alien to that of her homeland. Immediately we can appreciate the fundamental difference in the Jupiter-Orcus quality, in Ali's case a conjunction, and in Priscilla Presley's, as she was soon to become, a square; from the 5th to the 8th house. Indeed, Jupiter in her nativity opposes Proserpina, the Roman facsimile of Persephone, so there is this theme of being snatched away from home into a culture of scant comforts (Pro/2nd to Ju/8th), and she might well have balanced this

---

[142] *Elvis and Me* (2008), Priscilla Presley, Berkley Publishing Corporation p.24.

more easily were it not for the fact that she struggled with bitter isolation and loneliness (Orcus tee-squared from the 5th). Indeed one of her few avenues of escape from this pervading sense of isolation was to be found at the Eagles Club, a social venue in Wiesbaden for American servicemen and their families, and it was there she found solace in the jukebox, which she visited every day after school. She met Elvis in September 1959 under the auspices of a Uranus-Orcus sextile (unexpected improvement in isolating condition), with Orcus conjunct Saturn, but also at the climax of a series of Pluto-Sun squares. With Moon in Scorpio on the Midheaven, squared by Pluto in the 7th ruling the 7th, her marriage was bound to be triggered by strong Pluto energies, and few characters in the world of show business have more succinctly encapsulated Jovian, Plutonic and Orcan themes than 'the King', before or since. Plutonic wealth, Orcan isolation and Jovian excess.

Saturn and Orcus

Two harder taskmasters would be difficult to nominate within the Olympian pantheon than these, who share a dislike of ease and a love of rigour in all undertakings, great and small. Any Saturn – Orcus contact, no matter how fleeting ought not to be taken lightly. This combination tends to create especial implacability therefore. In the nativity of men it tends to manifest directly, while in a female nativity, it more easily manifests through important male authority figures. During Orcus' sojourn in Aries between 1904 and 1916, there is a singularly combative and persistent quality to the blend, since these are the innate energies of Saturn in Aries. Naturally, the position and quality of Mars is of paramount importance when seeking to understand the agenda of the Saturn – Orcus conjunction. When we consider the two cases of Joseph McCarthy and Simon Wiesenthal, both of whom shared the aspect – they were born scarcely six weeks apart – we can easily begin to understand the nature of this particular combination. Both men engaged in lifelong crusades to root out and destroy what they considered to be evil influences hidden in 'decent' society. Neither man has been entirely free of the intimation of controversy, although few would denounce the motives behind Wiesenthal's incarnation as the world's most high-profile and persistent Nazi hunter.

Wiesenthal survived four years in German concentration camps and devoted the remainder of his life, after the Second World War, to bringing those responsible for the camps to justice. Wiesenthal was frequently criticised for a tendency to exaggerating his achievements, and with his closest natal aspect being Mercury trine Jupiter, we ought not to be surprised. [143] Even this though, as many commentators have said, should not detract from his ceaseless striving to see justice done.[144] Wiesenthal's Saturn-Orcus conjunction fell in Aries, for sure, but crucially it resided within Libra's house, the 7th, and so the obsession with justice was ensured. Bringing criminals to account and making them subject to legal and moral authority is the perfect exposition of

---

[143] "[Wiesenthal's] *reputation is built on sand, however. He was a liar — and a bad one at that. From the end of the Second World War to the end of his life in 2005, he would lie repeatedly about his supposed hunt for Eichmann as well as his other Nazi-hunting exploits. He would also concoct outrageous stories about his war years and make false claims about his academic career. There are so many inconsistencies between his three main memoirs and between those memoirs and contemporaneous documents, that it is impossible to establish a reliable narrative from them. Wiesenthal's scant regard for the truth makes it possible to doubt everything he ever wrote or said.*" Biographer Guy Walters in The Sunday Times: "*The Head Nazi-Hunter's Trail of Lies*" (excerpt from his book 'Hunting Evil') July 19, 2009.

[144] "*Walters's documentary evidence on Wiesenthal's inconsistencies and lies is impeccable. He shows how the Nazi hunter's accounts of his wartime experiences are contradictory and implausible. He demonstrates that he had no role, contrary to his own assertion, in the capture of Adolf Eichmann. He pitilessly dissects Wiesenthal's overblown claims about the numbers he brought to justice, suggesting it was not much more than a handful... When you read Hunting Evil, you know its author is telling the truth. And, above all — above everything — the truth matters. The truth however painful, the truth however embarrassing, the truth wherever it takes you. Jews can never be hurt by the truth about the Holocaust and must never fear it, never run away from it... Ben Barkow, the director of the Wiener Library, the institution that my grandfather established to document the truth, has lent his voice to that of Walters, agreeing that a revaluation of Wiesenthal's contribution was in order. Barkow argues that a nuanced view is possible. That accepting that Wiesenthal was a showman and a braggart and, yes, even a liar, can live alongside acknowledging the contribution he made.*" From It is Right to Expose Wiesenthal by Daniel Finkelstein, The Jewish Chronicle, August 20, 2009.

this placement. Many autobiographical accounts of Wiesenthal's life are muddled and confused by contradictory testimony so it becomes difficult to place major transits into the context of his life story. This creates yet another Orcan thread to Wiesenthal's life situation, because we see that a stellium of Sun, Mercury and Uranus is opposed by Neptune, with Orcus conjunct Saturn forming the focal point of a tee square to this grouping. The stellium is a picture of a rather rash, combative character, quick to argue, and with a motivation toward garnering status without necessarily thinking through the consequences of actions taken. This rashness in the context of a Neptune opposition suggests that the truth may have suffered, since Neptune has a tendency to fill in gaps with more perfect motivations. The oppositional tension, then, was found here: Wiesenthal wanted his life story to be more romantic than it actually was. As an example of this, he claimed that before his arrest by the Nazis, he was working as an architect designing beautiful villas for wealthy Polish Jews in Lviv, when contemporary records show that he was in fact working as a middle manager in a furniture factory. Looked at in this way we can see that the lie is not especially harmful, it certainly has no malice in it, but it is instead geared toward a revision of personal history, to make it more refined, more pleasing , more glamorous and less humdrum. Venus squares Jupiter, an aspect of potential self-aggrandisement and indulgence. Wiesenthal was a man who wanted an aristocratic and luxurious past, but didn't have one to draw from so, without malice, he made one up. For most people, such extravagant untruths as those Wiesenthal liked to tell would be fought down, repressed by the quailing of an uncertain conscience, but here we have a man whose Mercury – Neptune opposition, in particular, is squared by Orcus. Mercury is least comfortable with Orcus because the trickster struggles mightily against the straightjacket of integrity. Mercury cannot easily be mercurial with Orcus in the picture, and with the square there is especial early difficulty with telling it like it is. No doubt Wiesenthal learned the hard way to keep his story straight – *eventually* – but by that time he had created a legacy of half-truths and better-truths which simply could not be avoided as his star rose. With Orcus conjunct an Aries Saturn, there is always this idea of rashness, of going off half-cocked, of not thinking things through before acting (that is Aries' shadow, and Saturn creates an early difficulty with that too), and it was this rashness which upset the Neptune oppositions. A rash tendency to tell a romantic untruth and thereby lose credibility, with the end result of having one's integrity sacrificed. In the end, as is often the case with an Aries Saturn, it all came good, his Nazi-hunter legacy was considered to have outweighed his integrity issues and made him, on balance, a worthy man, but there is enormous ambiguity in it.

Not so ambiguous however, is the case of Joseph McCarthy. McCarthy was an American politician who served as a Republican U.S. Senator from the state of Wisconsin from 1947 until his death in 1957. Beginning in 1950, McCarthy became the most visible public face of a period in which Cold War tensions fuelled fears of widespread Communist subversion. McCarthy claimed that there were large numbers of Communists and Soviet spies and sympathizers inside the United States federal government and elsewhere. Ultimately, McCarthy's dubious tactics and his inability to substantiate these claims led him to be censured by the United States Senate.

The term McCarthyism, coined in 1950 in reference to McCarthy's practices, was soon applied to similar anti-Communist activities. Today the term is used more generally in reference to demagogic, reckless, and unsubstantiated accusations, as well as public attacks on the character or patriotism of political opponents.[145] The fact that our language contains a word that is the legacy of his tendency toward speaking without integrity is enormously relevant. Once again, we see that the precise same themes apply to McCarthyism as to Wiesenthalism: namely an implacable crusader spirit, a hunter that cannot be easily evaded, but whose rashness taints the motivation and ultimately the character. McCarthy did not get away with it however, in

---

[145] Wikipedia entry 'Joseph McCarthy'

the way that Wiesenthal did, because his enemies of the state (communists) were not as easily vilified as Wiesenthal's fascists. For McCarthy, the claim of 'reds under the bed' became a foggy, uncertain and ultimately paranoid campaign which was found to have besmirched the reputations of decent people.

At the time of his election to the US Senate, (January 3rd 1947), Sun was conjunct Mars and square Neptune, Saturn was conjunct Pluto in Leo and Uranus was conjunct Orcus in Gemini. The map of this period[146] came to represent enormous challenges to integrity, and the quality of this time was to be reflected in his subsequent career. Indeed, McCarthy made numerous spurious and misleading claims about the character and motives of his opponents while running for office and even won his Senate seat on the back of a carefully stage-managed lie[147]. As an ex-serviceman, he was forbidden from expressing political views (a convention of that time), and he simply sidestepped it in a way that became something of a hallmark of his personal style. He told a meeting of the Milwaukee League of Women Voters that *"I wish I could discuss the importance of oil and the importance of maintaining a strong army and navy... but I may not do so... If I were able to speak, here's what I'd say..."*[148]

McCarthy's legacy makes uncomfortable contemplative material, as befits a badly-handled Orcus, in the 12th and conjunct Saturn. It is said that Saturn joys in the 12th because it is here that he can invest fully in his shadow-side, and unless absolute spiritual integrity is adhered to,

---

[146] See page 62.

[147] In his campaign, McCarthy attacked his opponent, Robert M. La Follette Jr. for not enlisting during the war, although La Follette had been 46 when Pearl Harbor was bombed. He also claimed La Follette had made huge profits from his investments while he, McCarthy, had been away fighting for his country. In fact, McCarthy had invested in the stock market himself during the war, netting a profit of $42,000 in 1943. La Follette's investments consisted of partial interest in a radio station, which earned him a profit of $47,000 over two years. The suggestion that La Follette had been guilty of war profiteering was deeply damaging, and McCarthy won the primary nomination 207,935 votes to 202,557.

[148] *Senator Joe McCarthy* (1973) Richard Halworth Rovere, Harper and Row, p 97-98

the life becomes unstuck. McCarthy, seemingly drunk on the acquisition of worldly power, came to be regarded with near horror by the American public, and his dubious reputation has only tarnished with the passage of the years:

"As a marine he once fired 4,000 rounds of ammunition in a single day – at coconut trees. He added further luster [sic] to his marine uniform by wearing it (illegally) while making an unsuccessful bid for the Senate. Then, as a judge, he became a legend for his ten-second quickie divorces. Still in his judge's robes (illegally), he campaigned again for the senate, winning this time. As senator, he fought public housing, defended Nazis on trial for the Malmédy massacre of GIs, and, when his career reached its zenith, destroyed the careers (and sometimes the lives) of countless Americans... Senator Joseph McCarthy may never be completely forgotten, but the full, sickening story of his life, and of the era to which he gave his name needs constant restatement as a momento mori of our national morality."[149]

Astrologically it is intriguing to note that McCarthy's Saturn makes no major Ptolemaic aspect, it is therefore feral and lent great power to express itself, in its fall sign of Aries, and in the potentially deceptive and ruinous 12th. Orcus is not especially comfortable under the auspices of Neptune, Pisces and the 12th, which are potentially self-deceptive. Virgo is more comfortable with Orcus because it prefers exactness, an important prerequisite to judgement. For McCarthy, Arian rashness is lent to a clutch for status by any means but with Orcus, there is implacable drive which, unless the commitment to absolute integrity is made, sacrifices everything, including integrity itself. This rather wretched Saturn rules the 10th house of status and reputation. Ironically McCarthy ruined his reputation through a single-minded concern with it. His Moon in Leo and the 5th makes only a single trine to Orcus in the

---

[149] From "The Way We Were: At Our Worst" by Harriet van Horne, New York Magazine, 7 February 1977.

12th house: here is potentially narcissistic energy with an easy facility to go beyond normal limits in self-sabotaging acts of hubris.

So, while Saturn alone, without dignity or reception of any kind, might be a millstone around the neck of ambition, we see here how, when combined with Orcus, the energy is ramped up beyond all mortal measure until McCarthy was left with, as Shakespeare had it ...*no spur, To prick the sides of my intent, but only, Vaulting ambition, which o'erleaps itself, And falls on th'other*...[150]

McCarthy died at the age of 48 within three years of being censured by the US Senate for his overall pattern of behaviour with regard to the Communist witch-hunts which bore his name, 30 days after the last pass of Orcus square Saturn, the astrological trend which had characterised his final year of life. He was, by all accounts a "pale ghost of his former self"[151] for the duration of this year and he eventually succumbed to liver cirrhosis on May 2nd 1957.

---

[150] *Macbeth* Act 1, scene 7. 25–28, William Shakespeare
[151] *The Nightmare Decade: The Life and Times of Senator Joe McCarthy* (1971), Cook, Fred J, Random House. p. 31

The Mundane

Now it is as if a sea of evils pushes its swell onward. As one wave sinks, the sea raises up another, triple-crested, which crashes around the city's stern. In between a narrow defence stretches—no wider than a wall. I fear that the city will be overthrown along with its kings.

Aeschylus: Seven against Thebes 758-765

Orcus, by dint of his slow-moving, ponderous and weighty nature like his counterpart Pluto, leaves an indelible mark upon the fate of nations. In the same way as in a human nativity, the signature of an outer planet is most easily discerned in the mundane chart where he is boldly placed: thus in close aspect to a personal planet, or within proximity of an angle. This is the case, for example, with the 1800 chart of Great Britain, where Orcus is found on the Ascendant. It is arguable, though, that the British 1800 chart has been superseded by a more recent nativity[152].

In the case of the United States, though, Orcus forms the closest aspect in the mundane chart and this, as we shall see, has profound consequences in the ordering of destiny for the American people.

There is some debate about the birth-date which best fits the nativity of the United States, but it seems to me, an Englishman, that this is a

---

[152] In this astrologer's humble view, there are at least *three* pertinent charts for the British nation. The first is the Runnymede chart of 1215 which brought a constitution into effect for the English people with the signing of the Magna Carta and it describes a fundamental of *English* character, rather than British. That said, its influence in mundane matters appears to be minimal, perhaps because it has been marginalised by the 1800 chart, when the Acts of Union were written into law. It is arguable that the Anglo-Irish Treaty of 1921 may have stolen some of the 1800 chart's thunder.

question which most concerns Americans. From my rather unattached perspective, the 4th July 1776 chart describes America most succinctly. Transits of Orcus to this chart are utterly compelling.

Philosophically, I find that the influence of Orcus has been strongest in recent times, which is a reflection of the increasing psychological, emotional and spiritual complexity of the human soul. Indeed, in ancient times, the signature of Mars was so strong upon statesmen and leaders that there was scarce a use for subtler approaches. To read about the lives of Roman leaders and generals is to read the diaries of Mars himself! Of course, this is not to say that there weren't more shadowy figures in ancient Roman life, Crassus might be considered a good example, as might Sulla who was quite overtly Plutonic, however even these were not men who easily made headway in Roman life. Mars was the respected power, whereas today, the sophistication of humanity leaves Mars seeming like a rather crude and blunt instrument; and such overt displays of self-interest, which were to the good Roman simply natural and expedient, are in today's world likely to be denounced as brutish and crass. The self-interest of Mars has to consider outer-planet caveats in the contemporary world. President Obama's Uranian appeal must be tempered by the humanitarian concerns of Neptune and too by the dictates of Pluto: that jostling for power, influence and control is a thing best done in the dark if one's reputation is to remain untainted. In Twentieth Century life, power has evolved into an entirely alchemical business and is habitually handled by mysterious adepts in privileged and secret chambers.

It is clear that when Pluto was discovered in 1930, the Plutonic principle became personal. This is not to say that it is easy energy, but mankind, by bringing Pluto into consciousness, was offered the opportunity to work with Plutonic energy. The spiritual imperative of that 'gift', much like Prometheus' gift of fire is responsibility.

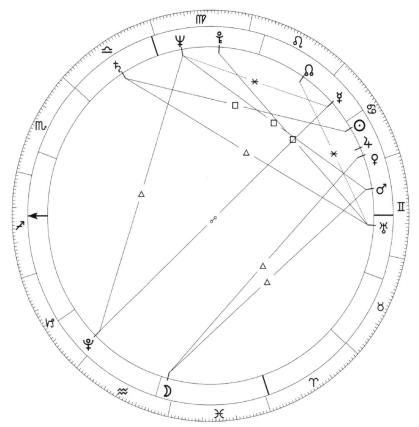

United States: 4th July 1776, 17:10, Philadelphia, PA, USA

The United States failed the first test of Pluto and is to this day the only nation in history to have dropped an atomic bomb in anger, accumulating considerable karmic consequences.

In the US natal chart, Orcus squares Uranus by 9 minutes of arc. Here there is enormous stress around the theme of rationalising foreign policy through less than scrupulous subterfuge (Orcus in the 9th, Uranus on the Dsc: open enemies) . With Uranus conjunct Tisiphone, there is a national dynamic of revenge and retribution. Orcus squares this placement, which suggests that there is a difficulty with being completely honest (Orcus squares always carry the risk of expedience).

While this is easy to understand in an individual, at a national level, it is not so different. Here is a nation that justifies vengeance through not practising scrupulous self-honesty. The United States is not averse to such suspicion either. Indeed, her entry into almost every major war of the last century has been accompanied by the suspicion of a smokescreen, and many commentators have implied that in every case, there is no smoke without fire.

Consider each case:

On May 7, 1915, the RMS Lusitania, jewel of the Cunard Line, was on a New York-to-Liverpool run when it was attacked by a German U-boat 12 miles off the coast of Ireland. At 2:10 p.m., a torpedo ploughed into the ship and exploded. Fifteen seconds later, a massive second explosion rocked the ship again. Within a mere 18 minutes, the Lusitania plunged 300 feet to the bottom of the Celtic Sea. Of the 1,959 passengers and crew, 1,198 were lost, including 128 Americans. The tragedy sparked anti-German fervour that eventually drew the United States into World War I. Controversy has surrounded the event ever since, with no satisfactory conclusion ever having been reached. Survivors recalled how, after the torpedoes hit, a British cruiser steamed into view, only to be inexplicably recalled before picking up any survivors; it wasn't until several hours later that Irish fishing-boats arrived, by which time hundreds had perished in the cold waters of the Irish Sea. German Admiralty records at the time maintain that the German submarine – U20 – fired only a single torpedo, a claim supported by German sailors after the fact; however there were two explosions, with the latter blast being considerably larger than the first. Numerous sources have speculated that explosives were packed into the Lusitania's hold and that this was the source of the second explosion. Myriad other shadows lend a taint of deception to the official accounts of the Lusitania tragedy. In her discussion of the proceedings, historian Diana Preston concluded that "*no government, British, German, or American, was entirely free of blame for the situation leading*

up to the attack. Nor, in its wake, was any government hesitant to twist
the facts, or use the disaster, to its own political ends."[153]

Twenty six years later, history appeared to repeat itself. The main
proponent of the theory that America turned a blind eye to the
possibility of a Japanese attack on Pearl Harbour is Robert Stinnett,
who argued in his meticulously researched book on the subject[154] that
President Roosevelt had advance knowledge of Japan's December 7,
1941, attack on Pearl Harbor. Using documents pried loose through the
Freedom of Information Act, during 17 years of research, Stinnett
provides overwhelming evidence that FDR and his top advisers knew
that Japanese warships were heading toward Hawaii. The heart of his
argument is even more inflammatory: Stinnett argues that FDR, who
desired to sway public opinion in support of U.S. entry into WWII,
instigated a policy intended to provoke a Japanese attack. The plan was
outlined in a U.S. Naval Intelligence secret strategy memo of October
1940; Roosevelt immediately began implementing its eight steps
(which included deploying U.S. warships in Japanese territorial waters
and imposing a total embargo intended to strangle Japan's economy),
all of which, according to Stinnett, climaxed in the Japanese attack.
Stinnett, a decorated naval veteran of WWII who served under then Lt.
George Bush, substantiates his charges with a wealth of persuasive
documents, including many government and military memos and
transcripts. Demolishing the myth that the Japanese fleet maintained
strict radio silence, he shows that several Japanese naval broadcasts,
intercepted by American cryptographers in the 10 days before
December 7, confirmed that Japan intended to start the war at Pearl
Harbor. Stinnett convincingly demonstrates that the U.S. top brass in
Hawaii – Pacific Fleet commander Admiral Husband Kimmel and Lt.
Gen. Walter Short – were kept out of the intelligence loop on orders
from Washington and were then scapegoated for allegedly failing to

---

[153] *Lusitania: An Epic Tragedy* (2003), Diana Preston, Berkley Publishing Group, p 393
[154] *Day of Deceit: The Truth about FDR and Pearl Harbor* (2001), Robert B. Stinnett,
Simon & Schuster

anticipate the Japanese attack (in May 1999, the U.S. Senate cleared their names). Kimmel moved his fleet into the North Pacific, actively searching for the suspected Japanese staging area, but naval headquarters ordered him to turn back. Stinnett concludes – convincingly – that at least 36 people, including the President himself were aware of the impending Japanese attack on Pearl Harbour and that testimony was altered, destroyed, hidden and fabricated after the fact to give the false impression that the attack was a surprise.

I have already discussed in some detail, the infamous Gulf of Tonkin[155] Incident which was the entirely fabricated pretext for America's escalation of war on the North Vietnamese nation.

There are those who assert that the attack on New York's Twin Towers, itself a pretext for the invasions of Afghanistan and Iraq was similarly obfuscated and that the US Administration had advance knowledge of the terrorist's plan. Some have even gone so far as to suggest that, as in the Lusitania incident, explosives were placed within the buildings to ensure that the justification for war would be compelling enough.

All of these stories, regardless of their absolute veracity, are perfectly within the remit of Orcus-Uranus energy, which has this power to hyper-intellectualise a judgemental position. Uranus' style is to consider itself to be above and beyond normal considerations: *a special case*. Where Uranus is involved, there is always the possibility that one becomes so divorced from the human dimensions of any given situation that almost any response is given due consideration, even if, when put into a slightly different perspective, the response would be considered truly heinous. Uranus, God of the Sky, can easily find himself looking at any given situation through the wrong end of the telescope, and zooming so far out that any act of cruelty can be made acceptable. When we add Orcus to the picture, we have another truly

---

[155] See *The Stockdale Paradox* page 88.

inhumane potential, and these two together can become extremely uncomfortable as a result.

When we contemplate the Orcan qualities of the US chart we are drawn to the observation that Mercury opposes Pluto from the 8th to the 2nd, and that this opposition bisects the Uranus – Orcus square: *which is the closest aspect in the US chart,* by a large margin. So we can say that conspiracies relating to business interests and material resources are fashioned from inhumanely rationalised justifications and pretexts. When we look at the US pretext for entering the First World War, the sinking of the RMS Lusitania on May 7th 1915, Orcus was transiting 24° Aries, falling square Mercury and sesquiquadrate natal Orcus (thus triggering the entire matrix of Me = Pl = Ur/Or). When war was finally joined with Germany in April 1917 Orcus was precisely square Pluto, thus Orcus had run the gamut of the intervening degrees of the Mercury-Pluto opposition!

When Britain declared war on Germany in September 1939, Orcus was transiting 9° Gemini, conjunct the US Uranus, incredibly, therefore, square the Lusitania degree of 1915 and semisquare natal Mercury and, by the time of the attack on the US fleet, Orcus was crossing the profoundly sensitive US Descendant.

The Gulf of Tonkin Incident, which became the pretext for an escalation of the conflict with North Vietnam, was in fact *two* incidents on August 2nd and 4th of 1964 where North Vietnamese torpedo-boats allegedly opened fire on an American warship, the destroyer USS Maddox. Many eye-witnesses, including the respected US Pilot and later Vice Admiral, James Stockdale claimed that there was no incident on August 4th and that the August 2nd incident had been manipulated, with the Maddox getting in the middle of the Vietnamese boats while they were deployed on exercise.[156]

---

[156] Stockdale said "[I] *had the best seat in the house to watch that event, and our destroyers were just shooting at phantom targets—there were no PT boats there.... There was nothing there but black water and American fire power."* Stockdale was ordered to

Intriguingly, the Gulf of Tonkin Incident took place against a backdrop of Orcus conjunct the US Sun. More compelling than this was the assassination of President John Kennedy in November 1963, which also occurred under this same transit. The execution (Orcus) of the US Leader (Sun) fits the symbolism perfectly, and transiting Pluto was also sextile the Sun-Orcus transiting conjunction at the same time, which conjures an image of shadowy, but powerful, opportunists pulling the strings.

The Vietnam War officially began on November 1st 1955, when American military advisors were assigned to the South Vietnamese region. At this time Orcus was transiting 3° of Cancer, exactly conjunct the US Venus, while Pluto was semisquare the US Sun. Intriguingly, the US Venus is precisely parallel the asteroid Sisyphus 1866, and so it proved, the Vietnam War became a slow process of attrition and by 1975 the American people had grown weary of the haemorrhaging of American youth in another foreign war, *precisely as Orcus transited the US Mercury* at 24° Cancer!

The case for the USA's entry into conflicts in Afghanistan and Iraq is less clear. Not because there are not conspiracy "theories" in the mix, but because the causal origins of the hostilities are not entirely clear. We could look at the events of 9/11, which was the point at which Orcus transited into the US 9th house, a distinct Crusader motif: a righteous or spiritual campaign. It is intriguing to note that the US entered World War II as Orcus crossed the 7th house cusp. Orcus' transit into the US 8th house began on the same day as China's Cultural Revolution started, whose aim was to remove all traces of capitalism from Chinese society and life. The middle pass of Orcus into the US 8th occurred on the day that China conducted its first successful Hydrogen Bomb test (1967) and by the final pass in 1968, China had ceased assisting the North Vietnamese in their war against the United States. Communism, or at least socialism in general, as the antithesis of capitalism, appears to

---

keep quiet about what he saw that night by his superiors.

feature heavily in the Orcan signature of the US chart. Martin Luther King was assassinated within days of the final Orcus transit into the 8th house – and he as much as Communism threatened vested interests in the US – while Robert Kennedy was assassinated a month later.

McCarthyism and the Hollywood Blacklist

Between 1946 and 1956 Orcus made the long, slow transit between the US Mars, at 21 Gemini, and Venus, at 3 Cancer. Intriguingly, the US Senate elections of 5th November 1946 fell on the day that Orcus was conjunct the US Mars, and this was also the day that Joseph McCarthy was elected to the US Senate. When we put the imagery of Mars together with Orcus, we have a perfect exposition of 'Cold War,' arguably the brainchild of Joseph McCarthy. The Orcus transit of Mars lasted almost two years (11 August 1946 through 24 April 1948), and it is fascinating to note that the term 'Cold War' was first coined by George Orwell in his essay *You and the Atomic Bomb*[157] in October 1945; he brought the term to wider attention when he wrote an Observer article in March 1946, and in 1947, Walter Lippmann published *The Cold War: a study in US foreign policy*[158]. By the time Orcus' Mars transit was complete, the term Cold War was common parlance. It was on the back of these fears of Communist subversion that Joseph McCarthy rose to prominence[159].

And here is a remarkable picture: the Orcus transit of Mars began on the very day McCarthy was elected to the Senate (November 5th 1946) and the Orcus transit of Venus ended on the very last day of his tenure (May 1st 1957), when he died at the age of 48, within a few days of the

---

[157] Published October 19th 1945 in the London Tribune
[158] Harper, 1947
[159] American policy toward the Communist state of Cuba has been a perfect exposition of Orcus-Uranus, with an isolationist strategy and blockade (Orcus) chosen as the means to humble its ideological enemy (Uranus = Dsc). The missile crisis arose from the failed US operation to overthrow Castro's government at the Bay of Pigs in August 1962, as a result of which the Soviets began to build nuclear missile bases in Cuba. On August 10th, CIA director John A. McCone wrote a memo to President Kennedy, in which he warned that Russia was about to introduce ballistic missiles into Cuba. On August 12th transiting Pluto fell conjunct the US Orcus!

final pass of transiting Orcus squaring his natal Saturn. Joe McCarthy was, without doubt, the personification of America's Orcus.

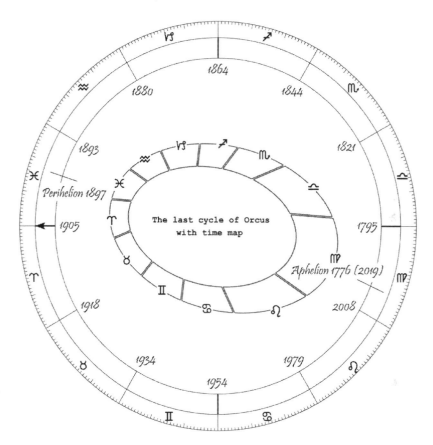

Orcus moved through the intervening years of McCarthy's term of office until he made contact with the US Venus in 1955. By this time the anti-Communist fervour that McCarthy had traded on to get ahead in his career had taken on a life of its own and was insidiously wrecking the lives of Americans in Venus' own domain, the arts, especially in film and television. The first 'Hollywood Blacklist' was publicised on November 25th 1947. At the exact moment that Orcus made square to US Neptune on November 24th, ten writers and directors, later to be known as the Hollywood Ten, were cited for contempt of Congress for refusing to give testimony to the House Committee on Un-American

Activities[160]. Both Ronald Reagan and Walt Disney[161] testified before the committee, lending their support to the program. Richard Nixon sat on the committee also. In all, over 300 artists were blacklisted, Charlie Chaplin was forced to leave the US to find work, many committed suicide and only around 10% of those smeared by Communist innuendo were able to subsequently resurrect their careers after the witch-hunts were done.

Watergate

Watergate was a political scandal during the 1970s in the United States which arose after five men were arrested for breaking in to the Watergate office complex in Washington, D.C, the Democratic National Committee headquarters. It was later discovered that the break-in was politically motivated and the trail led all the way to the highest office in the land. The Nixon administration was subsequently exposed for its attempt to disguise its involvement, eventually leading to the resignation of Richard Nixon, the President of the United States, on August 9, 1974. This is the only time a US President has resigned from office. The scandal also resulted in the indictment, trial, conviction and incarceration of several top Nixon administration officials.

It should not surprise us to learn that two major transits were assailing the US nativity at the time of the Watergate scandal. The first as transiting Pluto crossed the US Midheaven on November 5th 1971, March 8th 1972 and September 2nd 1972. This was followed by Orcus falling conjunct the US Mercury on September 4th 1973, December 15th 1973, July 18th 1974, February 11th 1975 and June 1st 1975. At the same

---

[160] The House Committee on Un-American Activities was formed in 1938, just as the US' Orcus squares began!

[161] Disney took out an advertisement in Variety Magazine on July 26th 1941, declaring his conviction that "Communist agitation" was behind a cartoonists and animators' strike. According to historians Larry Ceplair and Steven Englund, "In actuality, the strike had resulted from Disney's overbearing paternalism, high-handedness, and insensitivity." from The inquisition in Hollywood: politics in the film community, 1930-1960 By Larry Ceplair, Steven Englund University of California Press, 1983 p 157-8

time, transiting Neptune squared the US Orcus, beginning 29th January 1974 until well into 1975.

Since the US Orcus forms the closest natal aspect in the chart – a square to Uranus of just 0°13″, these Neptune squares in particular added enormous drama to an already fraught situation. Neptune quickly formed a transiting tee-square to Orcus through its opposition to Uranus. It should be noted that the US Orcus falls at 9°Virgo also, the point of Orcus' aphelion, the most distant part of a planetary orbit. It is widely perceived that planets moving at their extremes (in terms of time or distance) have greater weight, and therefore a more profound and far-reaching effect. Such planets operate at a more fundamental level than when they are moving relatively quickly, or when they are not at an orbital minimum or maximum.

The timeline of events between 1972 and 1975 makes fascinating reading in the context of the US chart:

As you will see, the sequence is triggered by an overt demonstration of American power, beginning with an atomic bomb test mere hours after the first pass of Pluto conjunct the US Midheaven[162]. As Orcus, Mercury and Neptune enter the fray, the Watergate scandal begins to unfold, with the all-important median pass of Orcus conjunct the US natal Mercury seeing the resignation of a US President.

---

[162] The Cannikin test, performed on Amchitka Island off the coast of Alaska was the largest nuclear device ever detonated by the United States (what a perfect exposition of Pluto/MC!) It caused an outcry from environmental groups who were concerned that the massive blast would cause earthquakes and tsunamis. The 'Don't Make a Wave Committee' was formed to protest the weapons test and, legend has it, that as one committee member was leaving a meeting he gave the traditional farewell of the peace-activist movement, "Peace." "Make it a green peace." replied another member. The Committee would later become Greenpeace. From *The Greater Vancouver Book, an Urban Encyclopaedia* (1997), Chuck Davis, Linkman Press. The next pass of Pluto=MC saw Nixon sign Executive Order 11652, declassifying all military intelligence files from WWII: *another* perfect exposition of Pluto on the Midheaven. One week later The Godfather was released, showcasing organised crime in the US.

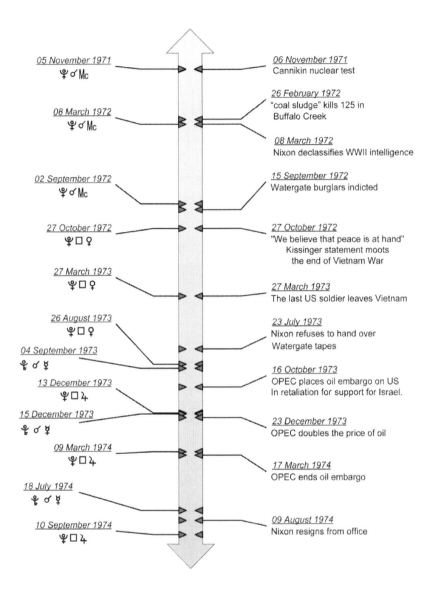

05 November 1971
♀ ♂ Mc

06 November 1971
Cannikin nuclear test

26 February 1972
"coal sludge" kills 125 in
Buffalo Creek

08 March 1972
♀ ♂ Mc

08 March 1972
Nixon declassifies WWII intelligence

02 September 1972
♀ ♂ Mc

15 September 1972
Watergate burglars indicted

27 October 1972
♀ □ ♀

27 October 1972
"We believe that peace is at hand"
Kissinger statement moots
the end of Vietnam War

27 March 1973
♀ □ ♀

27 March 1973
The last US soldier leaves Vietnam

26 August 1973
♀ □ ♀

23 July 1973
Nixon refuses to hand over
Watergate tapes

04 September 1973
♀ ♂ ☿

13 December 1973
♀ □ ♃

16 October 1973
OPEC places oil embargo on US
In retaliation for support for Israel.

15 December 1973
♀ ♂ ☿

23 December 1973
OPEC doubles the price of oil

09 March 1974
♀ □ ♃

17 March 1974
OPEC ends oil embargo

18 July 1974
♀ ♂ ☿

10 September 1974
♀ □ ♃

09 August 1974
Nixon resigns from office

When investigating the mundane application of Orcus, it is quite clear to perceive the manner in which Orcus is directly tied to many of the major events of America's modern history. In some ways this ought not be especially surprising. After all, Orcus makes the closest aspect within the US chart, a square to Uranus and has transited the bulk of US natal planets from before the Second World War until the Watergate scandal rocked the political foundations of the nation in the mid-1970s. It is interesting to note that many of America's current political movers and shakers were placed in positions of great influence as a result of Neptune's squares to America's Orcus in 1976. It remains to be seen if the current transiting oppositions between Neptune and Orcus will elucidate the agendas and motives of this group of individuals.

In the context of the US chart though, Orcus only made subsequent *oppositions*, first to Pluto in the late 1970s, which really ought to be viewed in the context of the Watergate scandal itself, and then to the US Moon between September 2005 and August 2007. Due to traditional lunar associations, it should be no surprise to learn that this period corresponded precisely with the US housing bubble, which was itself the precursor to the so-called 'Credit Crunch' of 2008. The first pass of Orcus opposing Moon occurred on September 19th 2005, exactly as the US housing market bubble was subsequently adjudged to have 'burst'. [163]

By March 2007, the United States' sub-prime mortgage industry had collapsed due to higher-than-expected home foreclosure rates, with more than 25 sub-prime lenders declaring bankruptcy, announcing significant losses, or putting themselves up for sale. The stock of the country's largest sub-prime lender, New Century Financial, plunged 84% amid Justice Department investigations, before ultimately filing for Chapter 11 bankruptcy with liabilities exceeding $100 million on April 2, 2007; just four days before the 4th pass of Orcus opposition the US Moon. It is generally agreed that the so-called Credit Crunch began with the collapse of the US housing market and became irreversible in June 2007, as Orcus made a final pass of the US Moon by opposition.

---

[163] In a report by CNN Money, May 16th 2006, *Real estate cools down*: Prices in the first quarter fell 3% from the fourth quarter, though are still up more than 10% from a year ago. Les Christie wrote that "*Real estate gains came to an abrupt halt in the first quarter of 2006, with the median price of a U.S. home falling 3.3 percent from the fourth quarter of 2005, according to a report released Monday morning. Prices were basically flat or lower during the quarter as inventories of houses for sale rose and their time spent on the market lengthened, according to a survey of 149 markets by the National Association of Realtors.*"

While the main bulk of first harmonic transits are finished the United States has enormous challenges ahead, heralded by the US Orcus returns of 2016 to 2019 and followed almost immediately by the US Pluto return of 2022. One can easily imagine that a country founded on spiritually rigorous constitutional principles will be forced to confront the many ways in which those principles have been subverted, perhaps even perverted, to serve the agendas of those shadowy Plutonic cliques which have grown up around the institutions of American power over the last century.

It remains to be seen if Orcus' punishment for the breaking of those sacred oaths will finish the greatest democratic experiment in history since Athens once and for all.

Part II

In the Old Age of the Soul

I do not choose to dream; there cometh on me
Some strange old lust for deeds.
As to the nerveless hand of some old warrior
The sword-hilt or the war-worn wonted helmet
Brings momentary life and long-fled cunning,
So to my soul grown old -
Grown old with many a jousting, many a foray,
Grown old with many a hither-coming and hence-going -
Till now they send him dreams and no more deed;
So doth he flame again with might for action,
Forgetful of the council of elders,
Forgetful that who rules doth no more battle,
Forgetful that such might no more cleaves to him
So doth he flame again toward valiant doing.

Ezra Pound

The Crucible of Integrity

Integrity is not a 90 percent thing, not a 95 percent thing; either
you have it or you don't.
Peter Scotese

Finally, it remains only to draw together the myriad threads of understanding and weave a tapestry to tell the story of Orcus. This cannot be a small undertaking. It is also, inevitably, a highly personal undertaking, since in my journey through Orcus' desolate reaches I have become changed by the many and often sublime observations and insights which I have encountered on the path.

Even before I set out on this odyssey I was already moving into a certain way of thinking about the disposition of astrology. Some fundamental appeared, to me, to be misaligned. It was as though astrology were missing some crucial part, like a clock without its minute hand. The irony of discovering this missing link is that in finding the missing hand, I came to see that the clock might not be especially important, even when functioning fully, even though it fulfilled its design objectives, because there are deeper eternal truths than astrology, truths which have no need for time. In so many minds, astrology becomes a quest for greater accuracy, to pin down unerringly the most precise of observations. But what is this need to know anyway? It is just anxiety. It is just the fear of uncertainty. If everything is perfect as it is, then there would be no need to know anything, because not knowing ought to be just as good. It is only fear that the next moment might not be as perfect as this one which requires a minute hand.

Astrology has suffered, in my entirely subjective and personal view, from a misapprehension. The discovery of Orcus' message has for me intimated a deep and uncomfortable reality. It is as though, in finding the missing hand, I have repaired the mechanism only to realise that, not only had I overestimated the import of accurately telling the time, but that I had also spent my life operating on an assumption that could I just tell time more accurately, it would greatly improve my chances of realising success. Success is a chimera because the pursuit of it is an unconscious admission that we are dissatisfied with God's plan. Life is much simpler than we can ever believe it to be.

We have all of us lived without clocks, in childhood even if at no other time, and their absence did not make us unhappy. In the same manner, astrology has 'worked' without Orcus, but in some strange way, the repair of finding Orcus and having him in his proper place, while revealing so much more about the inner workings of man, has, instead of promulgating a sense of completion, instead underlined to me the presence of a deeper reality, that casts so vast and profound a shadow that astrology is rendered trivial by it. What is a fine wristwatch in the shadow of eternity? Where is the sense in measuring any part of infinity? This is the conundrum of the astrological Orcus which I must here attempt to relate.

The Misapplication of Astrology

> *Integrity -- When you do the right thing even though no one is watching.*
> *-- Anon*

Astrology alone is only of limited use in making sense of life; at least, as the majority understand life to be. In fact, I would say that I only consider astrology to be useful as a theoretical language; a shorthand for the soul, if you like. In much the same way as a poet attempts to better grasp the mechanics of language in his or her pursuit of the objective of 'describing the indescribable', an astrologer is following this same paradigm in pursuit of the objective of describing the real. What matters is the real; life, existence and experience; the notation is secondary in the same way that the words which create the stanzas of a poem are secondary to the impression or feeling that they create in the reader's mind's eye. But it is within the attempt to describe what is real that the misapprehension at the heart of astrology is to be found. This is because what is 'real' is the soul and the many expositions of that soul's hopes, dreams and aspirations are mere artefacts. They are the wake of the ship only.

For you, as a soul in the world, your intentions, hopes, desires and fears are the compass which sets you into this or that direction. You forge ahead and as you impact the world around you there are consequences. You determine that you want the job and you get it. Somebody else loses out. That's how life goes, these are the consequences, which, like a ship upon the ocean, create a wake as you go along. You observe the consequences and believe therefore that they are the plan. You were destined to get the job, and the other guy was destined to lose. It seems that way because the compass is an esoteric instrument, governed by forces which we cannot see, feel or touch. The wake though, *that* is plain to see. But, of course, the wake is just an artefact of the compass' invisible mechanism.

This is the conundrum of astrology. It is utilised to understand the wake, not the compass.

It is the soul's desire (or compass therefore) which creates the material world, but we assume that the wake of the ship, which is visible to us (the consequences of our choices, needs, beliefs), is the truth of our life. The realisation of Orcus contends that the soul is both less and more than human. It is eternal. The compass is eternal, it will always point to the soul's North, but the wake is gone in moments. All we can meaningfully learn from the wake is to glimpse some element of direction. Aha, we might say, they went this-a-way! Whether or not we 'got the job', like the wake of the ship, tells us nothing of meaning except that, for some reason or other, our soul had a need that the job filled or a fear that it alleviated. The job is a material artefact of a spiritual reality. Nothing more.

The Victorian poet Robert Bridges wrote that 'man is a spiritual animal'[164] and this expresses an Orcan sentiment. The timeless and eternal elements of a human life are entirely spiritual, and the material dimension of life is nothing more than transitory, ephemeral. We employ astrology primarily to measure therefore the meaningless dimensions of human life and thus struggle to make sense of it all. Conversely, the most natural application for astrology has to be found in describing that which is, for most people, incomprehensible. Once the shift of perspective is made which renders astrology truly accurate, it ceases to matter especially. If that is not a conundrum of cosmic proportions then I know not what is! Indeed, once the transition into spiritual orientation is made, very little continues to 'matter' except perhaps the happiness of loved ones.

This is why astrology is, in my view, a roadmap of one's spiritual terrain and nothing more; and the various facets of that terrain – its high ground, its ravines and terraces – are simply descriptive of what 'matters'. Through understanding the terrain, we are gifted the opportunity to understand how and where to let go. Until, eventually, nothing matters at all.

We find ourselves in a splendid and wide solitude where we do not need to be anything. We do not need to be clever, erudite or special. We do not need to look good or travel to exotic destinations. We simply need to focus on the eternal that is within us. In this way, all ephemera is stripped away and we become authentic.

---

[164] From *The Testament of Beauty: A poem in four books* (2007), Robert Bridges, Addison Press, p 171.
In truth " spiritual animal " wer a term for man
nearer than "rational" to define his genus;
Faith being the humanizer of his brutal passions,
the clarifier of folly and medicine of care,
the clue of reality, and the driving motiv
of thatt self-knowledge which teacheth the ethick of life.

Some will disagree, as is only to be expected. There are innumerable philosophies, but every one of them shares a common purpose which is to give the Universe a foundation of meaning, even if, as is the case for example with nihilistic materialism, that meaning is that there is none. Insofar as a meaningful Universe is concerned, all people share a spiritual vantage point that, despite offering a different view from his or her neighbour, is still a position of spiritual observation. This position cannot be fundamental to mankind without being fundamental to astrology. Can the fish be deemed more profound than the sea? If we see that a spiritual perspective is the underpinning perspective of the human condition, then we are led to the inevitable conclusion that astrology is nothing more than a route to meaning. For this reason, because life cannot make sense in isolation from meaning, from the spiritual, then neither can astrology. Astrology is a spiritual map that is primarily employed to focus and define the mundane matters of human life. Put more simply, it is a hologram of the immaterial that is primarily employed to describe the material.

This naturally hints at astrology's true use, since a spiritual map ought to be most useful when applied to a spiritual journey; and of course, when used in exactly this way, it is a tool without compare; it is worth a decade or more of prayer. If, on the other hand, astrology is used as a guide to the material, then it will be, at best, a blunt instrument. Since the material is a shadow of the soul, it cannot be an outright failure when used in this way. The ship follows the compass and the wake follows the ship, so by explaining the wake we inevitably grasp some aspect of the compass. Rather like using a shoe to knock in a nail, it might, in certain circumstances, do the job, but it will never work so well as a hammer.

By the same token, this does not mean for one minute that a spiritual journey without astrology is doomed to failure or frustration. Clearly, the vast majority of humans who have chosen a spiritual mode of life have done so, throughout time, without the benefit of astrology. As with any journey, there are well-trodden paths which can be followed by those who come after and we call these roads 'religion' and they serve well enough. Despite this, they are a route which does not take into account the individual. It is all very well being shown the motorway to salvation, but what is the use of it if you have no car? You have need of a footpath. The overriding truth of a spiritual astrology is that there are as many paths to enlightenment as there are people, and your nativity shows your spiritual challenges with absolute precision. So, while it is possible, with varying degrees of success, to glean clues about one's material life from astrology, it is possible to glean clues about one's spiritual life from astrology, *with absolute precision*. Or at least, it is possible *now*, because Orcus has given into our possession, the previously missing piece of the mechanism.

Plutonic and Orcan Transformation

> *Integrity is not a conditional word. It doesn't blow in the wind or change with the weather. It is your inner image of yourself, and if you look in there and see a man who won't cheat, then you know he never will.*
> *-- John D. MacDonald*

I make a bold claim for Orcus here. However, there is little doubt in my mind that Orcus is a gateway energy, much like that of Pluto. One might argue that this gateway paradigm is applicable to all of the transpersonal planets. The glyph of Pluto defines the circle of spirit within a crescent, a *crucible*, whose function is therefore to transform the spirit. Any crucible is designed to have greater heat resistance than the material it is designed to handle, thus a crucible for melting gold is typically made of graphite. This reflects the process of both Pluto and Orcus which are designed, via their respective media – the power struggle and alienation – to provide sufficient intensity to reach the tipping point over which the soul realigns into a spiritual paradigm. In Pluto's case the necessity is to make the transition from needing to control people and situations in life to finding the point of personal power; wherein one is able to practise *self*-control, rather than power over *others*. Orcus requires a similar transformation of the inner perspective, but rather than a metamorphosis of control needs, Orcus requires a metamorphosis of *integrity*.

Of course the crucible of Orcus is fundamentally different from that of Pluto. Pluto's crucible is, like the fires of hell, a place of infinite pressure, heat, immediacy and closeness. Orcus creates its transformation with extreme cold, distance and eternity. Pluto is Dante's vision of hell, while Orcus is Virgil's. Pluto's transformation is made in a tumult of claustrophobic coercion, you are not left a moment's time or space. Orcus, conversely, has all the time in the world, and leaves you utterly and terrifyingly alone, the better to appreciate the enormity of that dread eternity.

What, though, is the tenuous, invisible connector of solitude with integrity? It is, in my view, simple enough to fathom. When you are left for sufficient time, with only yourself for company, where is the use in deception or glamour? Whom do you deceive? With an audience of one there is simply no sense in trying to create 'impressions'.

 Human experience unadorned is a spiritual minimalism, leaving only the soul and none of the trappings of the material. Impressions become very quickly superfluous and irrelevant. Integrity is the voice of the soul, therefore. Its opposite – which philosophically cannot be easily defined – must be a louder and more strident voice, which drowns out the small, quiet voice of the inner self; its opposite is the voice of the ego. Sufficient solitude relentlessly erodes the human ego, leaving enough space and stillness for the soul to finally be heard. At this point, integrity emerges as a natural consequence of the ego's lack of an audience, and the soul's sufficient maturation.

This does not mean, however, that physical isolation or literal segregation is the only medium which prompts the transformation of Orcus. There are many cold crucibles of the spirit and they only require

Orcan fuel to operate. It is the soul's unconscious dictate which prompts the human spirit to strike out for some destination or other, but it is the soul's maturity which determines the success of the venture. It is only in the doing of it that the wheat will be sorted from the chaff, and where one man will be rendered a madman by solitude, another will be gifted with a deep and abiding integrity. One mother separated from her children might become a hysteric, while another discovers a place of unshakeable conviction and inner calm as a result. One man might head for the nearest bar at the first sign of calamity and strife, while another, another whose soul is ready for the crucible, will head into the wilderness or to the monastery gate.

While these outcomes might appear to be beyond our influence, that is not truly the case. We can maximise our chances of a successful Orcan conversion by practising integrity. Integrity, though, is not at all a simple concept to understand. In some sense, we have to understand, too, that to one extent or another, integrity and spiritual maturity are somewhat akin to the proverbial chicken and egg. But this does not mean that we cannot practise integrity, because our intention – our ship's compass – ultimately determines our wake.

In researching the effects and manifestations of Orcus in my own life, and in those of people that are involved in my life experience, I came to understand a near-esoteric facet of Orcan quality that cannot easily be gleaned from the biographies and news reports of the famous and infamous. I came to the point, in fact, of needing to think very carefully and deeply about the principle of integrity, from personal experience and through the experience and wisdom of others; and, ultimately, to become familiar with a vast range of philosophical concepts and treatises. I realised that as a word 'integrity' is used with enormous license, and in nearly every case is referring to the 'appearance of integrity' rather than to the spiritual quality of integrity itself.

This led me to appreciate that there are different shades of integrity. This in itself sounds like a fallacy, and for the purpose of the human soul, it absolutely is. Spiritual integrity is entirely binary, there are no grey areas. But what most people refer to as integrity is not, in fact, true spiritual integrity. It is something less, and there is no word for it. It is material integrity, which means that it is integrity of the wake and not the compass. That is to say that as long as the intention that can be divined from our wake can be *interpreted* as integrous, then that is enough integrity for most people. True spiritual integrity is integrity at the compass level, and it is exceedingly rare.

We can look at this another way. Etymologically, integrity is derived from the Latin root *integer*, implying oneness, or wholeness. From this we define integrity to mean that one's internal position and one's statements and actions are whole and consistent, consistently – that is, *all of the time*. Put simply it is no good saying one thing and doing another, not even occasionally. This is all very well, but in my observations, I came to the realisation that even people who were clearly behaving in a manner that was inconsistent with their stated motive or perspective were fundamentally unaware of their internal inconsistency or, more accurately, they assumed that because they were consistent the majority of the time (or more pertinently, all of the time in low-risk situations), they had 'earned' the right to behave with less consistency in certain special situations. Invariably, the test of exemption was entirely based upon their own subjective evaluation of the situation which required that they *feel* that fairness and reciprocity had been served. More simply put then, most people appear to feel that they are people of integrity, but when they felt victimised, they were no longer required to adhere to their own code of conduct. They could make an exception to behaving with integrity in certain special situations.

The reason this occurs is because the test of consistency is almost entirely subjective. A person believes, therefore, that if they are acting according to the tenets of their value-system the majority of the time then they are being internally consistent and therefore acting from integrity. On those occasions where they do not follow their code, it is because the normal rules are suspended due to an extraordinary pressure or a unique caveat.

The unique caveat is key because for true spiritual integrity, *there can be no unique caveat.*

The unique caveat takes many forms, but usually it can be 'boiled down' to a single justification. Mostly this occurs because the target individual or situation is made to appear inferior and therefore undeserving of normal consideration. Turned on its head, and put another way, it is because they 'deserved' to be treated without integrity (i.e. they were not deserving of the usual consideration because their rights were less than the rights of others). The moment any person is accorded fewer rights than the basic level of rights accorded to *all other people*, they have become dehumanised; to one extent or another, they are deserving of less than the basic level of human consideration. This is where the negative energy of Orcus comes into play, to dehumanise the target so that there is no impediment to the full exposition of Plutonic power-plays and agendas.

The writer and philosopher Ayn Rand described it this way:

"There can be no compromise on basic principles or on fundamental issues. What would you regard as a compromise between life and death? Between truth and falsehood? Or between reason and irrationality?

Today however, when people speak of 'compromise' what they mean is not a legitimate mutual concession or a trade, but precisely the betrayal of one's principles – the unilateral surrender to any groundless, irrational claim. The root of that doctrine is ethical subjectivism, which holds that a desire or a whim is an irreducible moral primary that any man is entitled to any desire he might feel like asserting, that all desires have equal moral validity, and that the only way that men can get along together is by giving in to anything and by compromising with anyone. It is not hard to see who would profit, and who would lose by such a doctrine.

The immorality of this doctrine – and the reason why the term 'compromise' implies, in today's general usage, an act of moral treason – lies in the fact that it requires men to accept ethical subjectivism as the basic principle superseding all principles in human relationships and to sacrifice anything as a concession to one another's whims.

The question 'doesn't life require compromise?' is usually asked by those who fail to differentiate between a basic principle and some concrete, specific wish. Accepting a lesser job than one had wanted is not a compromise. Taking orders from one's employer on how to do the work for which one is hired, is not a compromise. Failing to have a cake after one has eaten it, is not a compromise.

Integrity does not consist of loyalty to one's subjective whims, but of loyalty to rational principles. A compromise (in the unprincipled sense of that word), is not a breach of one's comfort, but a breach of one's convictions. A compromise does not consist of doing something one dislikes, but of doing something one knows to be evil. Accompanying one's husband or wife to a concert when one does not care for music, is not a compromise; surrendering to his or her irrational demands for social conformity, for pretended religious observance or for generosity toward boorish in-laws, is. Working for an employer who does not share one's ideas is not a compromise; pretending to share his ideas, is. Accepting a publisher's suggestions to make changes in one's manuscript, when one sees the rational validity of his suggestions, is not a compromise; making such changes in order to please him, or please the public against one's judgements and standards, is."[165]

Rand's view resonates strongly with Orcus, her disdain for compromise is clear, and Orcus is innately 'uncompromising', whilst the idea of compromise is fundamentally Venusian. We ought not be surprised to learn, therefore, that Rand's nativity evinces an exact conjunction of Venus with Orcus, both squaring Uranus, which might best be

---

[165] The Virtue of Selfishness (1964), Ayn Rand, Signet, Chapter 7 "Doesn't Life Require Compromise" written July 1962

described in the phrase *"integrity does not consist of loyalty to one's subjective whims, but of loyalty to rational principles!"* Remarkable.

It makes her observation no less valid however. Looked at through this lens, the truth of integrity becomes more lucid; integrity requires consistency with one's principles which are themselves ethical, *no matter the personal cost of maintaining that consistency.* To those without integrity, however, it is easily mimicked, because any stance can be retrospectively rationalised:

"Today's politician... may not lie, but he understands that there is no great reward in store for those who speak the truth, particularly when the truth may be complicated. The truth may cause consternation; the truth will be attacked; the media won't have the patience to sort out all the facts and so the public may not know the difference between truth and falsehood. What comes to matter then is positioning – the statement on an issue that will avoid controversy or generate needed publicity, the stance that will fit both the image his press folks have constructed for him and one of the narrative boxes the media has created for politics in general. The politician may still, as a matter of personal integrity, insist on telling the truth as he sees it. But he does so knowing that whether he believes in his positions matters less than whether he looks like he believes; that straight talk counts less than whether it sounds straight on TV."[166]

This statement gets to the nub of the issue of integrity, because this dilemma applies to all of human life, and is not solely the preserve of politicians. Any human being is faced with this exact choice in pursuing their life objectives. We all are gifted the free will to decide for ourselves how rigorously we harmonise our internal model of integrity with our choices in the world. The remarkable truth, however, is that almost everyone experiences some degree of dissonance between principle and exposition, and it takes a very committed and spiritual

---

[166] *The Audacity of Hope: thoughts on reclaiming the American dream* (2008), Barack Obama, Canongate Books Ltd, p 376-7

being to not experience some small gap between the two, even if only in trivial matters. What Barack Obama calls 'positioning' is, in fact, the curse of Orcus, the simple expedience which ensures that the human soul will occasionally fail the test of integrity and therefore fail to live in the spiritual realm; because to act without integrity occasionally, negates true integrity entirely.

Orcus alone cannot explain this conundrum. In my view, the Orcan transformation (to spiritual integrity) can only occur *after* the Plutonic transformation (to *self*-control). These soul processes are innately and intimately connected. This connection was echoed by one of the initially curious observations that was borne out when looking at the mundane applications of Orcus: the frequency with which Orcan events appeared to be inaugurated by Plutonic agendas. In the history of the United States we can see how the manifestation of Orcus came about as a result of a shadowy power-play. It seemed to be true that in the life of a nation the hint of a cabal of vested interests was present in myriad events heralded by transits of Orcus. The Kennedy assassination may have been the result of Orcus' transit to the US Sun, but before the act of execution became manifest, there was the hint of a power-play in some unknown corridor of power. Conspiracies occur in suburbia after all, where the stakes are far from high: they are as inevitable as those other Plutonic motifs, death and taxes. It seems that in human life as much as in human afterlife, Orcus works in tandem with Pluto.

In this sense we see the curious similarity of the orbits of Orcus and Pluto reflected. Their astronomical resonance is echoed in their astrological collaboration, but they are not so much master and servant, as they are judge and executioner. Hades requires no juries.

In the human quest for equanimity, for peace, the clutch for power is the first spiritual test. It is the human ego which determines that power over others – be that through the medium of wealth, sex, authority or fear – is a desirable aspiration. The spiritually aligned have all been faced with the temptation of power, and given in to it in the past, but at some point they passed the test of Pluto, never to return. Once the lure of power is conquered, it loses its glamour forevermore. The Plutonically transformed are operating at a different frequency and have passed the first test of the spirit and have achieved self-control. This means that they no longer become *compulsively* engaged in power struggles. They no longer believe that power over others is desirable or even *possible*, not, at least, in any meaningful or valuable way. A spiritual being would not even find the possibility of controlling another person attractive; it seems a perversion.

We have all been privy to discussions on this subject, and at no time in human history has anyone ever openly confessed to, or even been self aware of, the fact that their underlying motive for action is to manipulate or control another person, but they *compulsively* seek to control others all the same. Then, in the possession of control, they glamorise their puppet-work. "I'm doing it for your own good", they say, or "it's only fair that I redress this injustice." Those in Pluto's thrall are always, in their own estimation, simply following the natural order of the world, usually as protector of the vulnerable, rescuer of the imperilled or punisher of the unjust. It is just a *side-effect* for them that they happen to be pulling people's strings as a consequence of their unavoidable action.

Midlife: Crisis or Opportunity?

> *Character is doing the right thing when nobody's looking.*
> *There are too many people who think that the only thing*
> *that's right is to get by, and the only thing that's wrong is to*
> *get caught.*
> *--J.C. Watts*

The Plutonic conversion opens the way to Orcus, but we cannot apprehend Orcus succinctly without placing him properly within the context of the spiritualising mechanism of human growth. Once responsibility for one's own actions and, indeed, for the circumstances of one's own life, is accepted and the bolthole of blame is relinquished, then there is sufficient emotional maturity for the shift to integrity, to the healthy expression of Orcus, to begin. For the most part, this process is part and parcel of the general tenor of maturation, facilitated and driven by the major transits of human life. The process undoubtedly begins in a serious way with the Saturn return at 29, and gradually quickens until midlife, and this is when the majority of spiritual work is done. The classic midlife crisis is the long, dark night of the soul from which one hopefully emerges with a new direction, a spiritual direction. Astrologically, this is the crucial paradigm shift from the material to the spiritual, or perhaps we should say, more accurately, from material self-interest, to spiritual self-interest, which both harbour concern for one's own welfare as a prime motivation, but whose expositions and objectives are almost diametrically opposed. The former displays all the pragmatism foreshadowed by the lens of social Darwinism; the latter, an awareness of the spiritual consequence of abandoning philanthropy[167] and compassion as the guiding principle of human life.

Invariably there is, at midlife, some kind of collapse, even if it is a private and subjective collapse, and many people who have acknowledged the need for a deepening at this time will attest to the sense that they were at a low-point for these midlife years. Typically, meaning falls away from those dreams, ambitions, perspectives, possessions and relationships that, at one time, seemed to be of paramount and unquestioned importance. There is a sense of being at rock bottom; at the depth of the abyss, wondering how it might ever be possible to claw one's way back into the light.

---

[167] 'Philanthropy' was first coined by Aeschylus in Prometheus Bound: it was Prometheus' *philanthropos tropos* or humanity-loving character which motivated him to defy Zeus and give humanity the gift of fire, resulting in devastating personal consequences. Zeus chained him to a rock as punishment, and every night his liver was pecked out by a vulture, only for it to regrow ready for the next night's feast.

My view is that life cannot have anything much more than material meaning until you have been through this so-called dark night of the soul. It was the early Christian ascetic, Saint John of the Cross, who first coined this phrase in a poem which described the gradual spiritual tempering of the human soul as it moved closer to God[168]. But even though this particular description has been attributed to a Christian tradition, it describes nonetheless a ubiquitous human journey that is intrinsic to spiritual evolution within all human cultures. Saint John himself was borrowing the idea from earlier writers like Thomas Aquinas and Aristotle and, most intriguingly, he wrote the poem and commentary while imprisoned by his Carmelite brothers[169]. The idea therefore, that life begins at rock bottom is as old as civilisation itself and is ubiquitous, not to a specific culture or tradition, but rather, to a transitioning period of all human life.

It becomes possible to grasp, within this understanding, why it is that astrology ultimately fails, albeit tantalisingly, as a material study. Material reality is the shadow cast by the spiritual body and, like a shadow, it has no features; only a vague outline. We can divine certain dimensions of material life from the shadow, but we cannot determine the face or aspect of it. The texture is lost. The natural course of the soul's spiritual maturation contains a meandering conundrum. The pursuit of the material is designed to be derailed by that objective's intrinsic meaninglessness. It is essential therefore that the fallacy of material objectives is experienced, and the more devastatingly the

---

[168] Saint John, in fact, spoke of *two* dark of nights of the soul, the first being sensual (or material) and the second, spiritual: "*The soul which God is about to lead onward is not led by His Majesty into this night of the spirit as soon as it goes forth from the aridities and trials of the first purgation and night of sense; rather it is wont to pass a long time, even years, after leaving the state of beginners, in exercising itself in that of proficients. In this latter state it is like to one that has come forth from a rigorous imprisonment.*" My view here is that everyone is faced with the *prospect* of the first night, and the spiritually evolved alone will move into the second night. Quoted from Dark Night of the Soul by Saint John of the Cross, Doctor of the Church, 3rd revised edition (1959), translated and edited, with an introduction, by E. Allison Peers. Image Books, p 99

[169] The Carmelites were a Catholic religious order, founded in the 12th Century, at Mount Carmel, Northern Israel.

better, since hard lessons are those most starkly retained, and in the midst of the long, dark night, the soul needs to suspect, and suspect well, that the temptation of 'going back' is a fool's paradise.

Similarly, while the soul is living from the material, which is no more than a cognomen for the ego, there can be no texture to life either. It is the same shadow of meaning, a mere shibboleth, that is cast and while it will have dimension, it will not have depth. The dark night of the soul is the point of ego collapse where one is given the opportunity to consistently see depth and texture for the first time since childhood. Childhood, however, is not simplistically interchangeable with spiritual maturity – a common failing of New-Age thinking in my view. It is the loss of innocence which acts as a catalyst for spiritual awakening, so one cannot simply 'regain' innocence and return to Eden – although this is often the philosophy of New-Age thinkers. Partly this comes about because of the superficial symmetry between the Buddhist objective of living in the now and the child's natural tendency toward being in the moment. The Buddhist, however, is practising self-mastery, while the child is exerting no effort; the former is conscious and the latter entirely unconscious. The irony, however, is that to all intents and purposes, the Zen monk's self-awareness and the child's self-unawareness appear objectively identical, though they are in fact diametrically opposed, albeit upon a shared polarity.

Resistance to the shift is usually vehement, and many manage to avoid committing to meaning altogether, but those who do cannot ever know spiritual truth and therefore are incapable of experiencing a true and consistent background of joy in their lives. It is that simple. They may experience flashes of pleasure – the ego's caricature of joy – as they meet with gain, success, winning and the sating of appetites, but the background to pleasure is dissatisfaction and emptiness, and the search for more pleasure must start over. The situation is precisely reversed in the spiritual realm. The background of life is one of contentment and joy, with only occasional flashes of dissatisfaction, which are the disturbances of the ego attempting to get back in the driving seat. In the spiritual dimension one feels curiously in the flow of life, more of an observer than a participant, but a contented observer, as though one is the audience of a marvellous and inexplicable show. The ego endures dissatisfaction whilst it craves pleasure, and the soul simply allows joy.

And there is no denying the reality that, for the majority, the long, dark night of the soul begins around midlife, which is a period of time between the age of 29, at the first Saturn return, and the second Saturn return at age 58, with the period of criticality falling at around age 42. In our culture we hear Elliott Jacques'[170] mantra for this period and it is given the name 'midlife crisis' which conveys a rather shabby impression of his meaning, for when Jung first talked about this process he was keen to stress the *necessity* of a subjective sense of crisis, because without that experience of pressure, the adoption of a new paradigm could never occur. His view was that the midlife crisis was something to be welcomed because it revolutionised one's perspective to allow for greater richness and joy in life. Indeed, Jung espoused the criticality of midlife almost poetically:

"Wholly unprepared, we embark upon the second half of life... we take the step into the afternoon of life; worse still we take this step with the false assumption that our truths and ideals will serve as before. But we cannot live the afternoon of life according to the program of life's morning - for what was great in the morning will be little at evening, and what in the morning was true will at evening have become a lie."[171]

From the material view, the 'crisis' is become a pejorative, but without the crisis, there could not be improvement. In Jung's view the midlife crisis, which materialists see as an aberration, is a spiritual opportunity. And of course his inclusion of the concept of a revolution of thinking offers another clue to his astrological heritage, since undoubtedly the most compelling astrological event that we can associate with midlife is

---

[170] "Death and the Midlife Crisis", *International Journal of Psychoanalysis*, 1965.
[171] *The Stages of Life* (1930), C.G. Jung, Chap. 8: *The Structure and Dynamics of the Psyche.* p 784

the Uranus half-return between the ages of 38 and 42. In Jung's view as a psychologist – and mine as an astrologer – a human life post-42 which holds the same values and positions as it did pre-38 is a missed opportunity.

So, the process begins astrologically in earnest with the 3rd Jupiter return. I see each return as a winding of the spring, building greater pressure and momentum. The age of 36 is the point where maturity is established; one is at the height of one's powers and normally (historically at least), families are growing, careers settled but there is still plenty of energy left to make new plans, normally with the resources at hand to make things happen. Thus 36 is typically experienced as a good age. But everything changes within a few short years. For current generations, those with Pluto in Leo and Virgo particularly, the Pluto squares come relatively early (even as the Orcus squares come late) and are often the first real challenges of the midlife period. This is quickly followed by the Neptune squares, the Uranus half-return, the second Saturn opposition and the Chiron return at 50. If we follow this trail we can see that the control-needs of Pluto are first challenged perhaps as early as age 36, depending upon when you are born[172]. Then there are the Neptune squares which help in making the shift by ramping up the sense of ambiguity around the material, blurring the boundaries between the mundane and the profound, and deepening the power of desires and dreams, often leading to a deep dissatisfaction with the superficiality of what is. Then comes the Uranus half return, which simply changes the game and puts you at odds with, and at a distance from those things that you once thought mattered – Uranus is gifted the power to bestow sudden, ego-crushing *perspective*. When you get real, 10,000 yard perspective on your own stance, that's when you see how true your position is. It's no real wonder that lives can fall into crisis during midlife because every material tenet upon which you have based your existence is being challenged at this time.

---

[172] My father's Pluto squares occurred at the age of 48, mine at 38 and for my son Teddy, born in 2010, they will occur at the age of 78.

Midlife is a powerful gateway but it is plagued by a lack of emotional and spiritual maturity in our culture's understanding of the rite of passage, an immaturity that is only, in fact, nothing more than a reflection of the immaturity of the wider culture itself. The problematic cultural misconception of midlife lies in the assumption that once a person has attained the gateway age of 21 they are all grown up; an adult, there is little maturing left to do, so one need only carry on being sensible and grown up and wait for the pension to mature. In fact, the human soul has only attained material or ego-maturity at this time; the biggest step of all is yet to come but society labels this most important of all human stages of development a mere crisis; you'll lose your head for a bit, run off with the secretary, buy a sports car and then you'll get over it and go back to being sensible and grown up. Such dismissive debasement of a profound life-passage is the true calamity. The calamity is not in losing your home, your career, your marriage, although those events may well be extremely testing, the calamity is in not letting go of your ego's control needs.

So we can say that essentially the long dark night of the soul begins, faintly and tentatively, around the age of 30, it reaches a crescendo in the early 40s, and it is a done deal, for better or worse, as 60 comes around. Midlife is quite fittingly circumscribed by Saturn returns.

A Spiritual Test has to be Testing

> The measure of a man's real character is what he would do if he knew he never would be found out. --Thomas Babington Macaulay

Some will say that they are more inclined toward the spiritual even though they are not yet at the midlife period of life and this is true enough. People particularly who have strong Pisces or Scorpio placements often evince a facility with spiritual or intangible concepts at an early age, however the midlife experience is still required for these people to make the shift to meaning in their lives. One soul might incarnate with a past-life memory, and thus a facility for spiritual concepts in advance of his or her peers, but it is only when those skills need to be applied under pressure that they are *spiritually* meaningful.

In 1962, psychologist M.M. Berkun and his colleagues at Cambridge University devised an experiment where soldiers were told to make a radio call to seek assistance in the belief that their lives may have depended upon the call being successfully transmitted. When they attempted to make the radio call they discovered that their radio was not functioning correctly. When under no serious pressure, the soldiers would normally have repaired the radio efficiently, but in this high-pressure scenario, the same soldiers took considerably longer to make the repair, they tended to concentrate *"too narrowly on one aspect of the problem while ignoring other peripheral information that would have made their task easier"* and they demonstrated an *"abnormal variability in their approach to the task when compared with controls who were in no danger."*[173]

It is one thing, therefore, to have a natural and innate facility with certain skills or propensities, and quite another to be able to apply them under pressure. This is one of the many conundrums of human character. Some people appear to be fine and upstanding and all might be well but we realise, when disaster strikes, that they were in fact operating within a comfort zone which did not challenge them to dig deep. In the same way that it is easy to be wise after the event, it is easy to be a person of integrity and character from the relaxed vantage point of your armchair. Or *"adversity has ever been considered the state in which a man most easily becomes acquainted with himself"* as Samuel Johnson said it. True depth of character can only be meaningfully measured in times of crisis. Many people behave well in low-pressure situations, but find themselves behaving compulsively and

---

[173] Berkum M.M., Binlek H.M., Kern R.P. & Yagi K. Psychological Monographs 76, No.15 Princeton 1962.

destructively when their security or wellbeing is threatened. This is often the hallmark of the Plutonic character, in fact, because they bury their anxieties and insecurities very deep, only to have them erupt when they feel exposed or vulnerable. Pluto and Scorpio are both prone to experiencing anxiety over loss of control, which is the reason why such types frequently react with surprising and seeming uncharacteristic venom when they feel threatened.

One of the attributes of outer planet energy is that they contain the potential for hubris, a temptation which requires genuine integrity to resist since, after all, most everyone can keep their integrity when the stakes are low and they have little to lose. We all understand hubris as being a type of extreme arrogance, but to the ancient Greeks, hubris had a literal quality. The word was used to refer to the emotions in Greek tragic heroes that led them to ignore warnings from the Gods and thus invite catastrophe. It is considered a form of *hamartia* or tragic flaw that stems from overbearing pride and lack of piety. Fundamentally, hubris for the Greeks embodied in a concept the tragic flaw of considering oneself to be as infallible as the Gods themselves. The myths are littered with tales whose key dramatic premise is the consequence of hubris.

As an example, there is the tale of Oedipus, the story related by Sophocles in his *The Oedipus Trilogy*. In this cycle of plays, Apollo, the God of Truth, warns King Laius of Thebes that he will be killed by his child. When his son, Oedipus, is born, Laius exiles him but the child returns as an adult and kills the king, not recognizing him as his father. King Laius invited catastrophe by attempting to circumvent Apollo's prophecy. The King's actions revealed his hubris because he, a mortal, thought he knew better than Apollo, a God. Taking on the aspect of the Gods, comparing oneself with the Gods, or acting with the impunity of the Gods is what is classically termed hubris, and it is one of the traps of the mortal ego; it is the ego which believes itself godlike and it is the unchecked ego therefore which brings down the wrath of the Gods.

Hubris begins with the trap of rationalising, of comparing one's objective and intellectual faculties with those of the Gods themselves by believing one's perspective to be infallible. We all know that the human mind can rationalise anything in all creation, but very few are able to understand that their own perspectives might be fundamentally flawed. The human mind is capable of rationalising almost any act of cruelty, and it can go even further than making these aberrations seem inevitable: it can refashion them as acts of heroism. Heinrich Himmler said of the extermination of the Jews that *"[t]his is a page of glory never mentioned and never to be mentioned... We have the moral right, we had the duty to our people to do it, to kill this people who wanted to kill us."* The holocaust was repositioned into an act of glory.

It is all too easy to see this kind of expedient rationalisation as a monstrous aberration that any decent person would reject without the slightest hesitation. Unfortunately, this is simply not borne out by the evidence. Myriad studies have proven that the vast majority of people, when presented with the opportunity to wield power, will abuse it, often grossly. In the Stanford Prison experiment, psychologist Philip Zimbardo selected 24 students to play the prisoners and live in a mock prison in the basement of the Stanford psychology building. The participants adapted to their roles well beyond what even Zimbardo himself expected, leading the "officers" to display authoritarian measures and ultimately to subject some of the prisoners to torture. In turn, many of the prisoners developed passive attitudes and accepted physical abuse and, at the request of the guards, readily inflicted punishment on other prisoners who attempted to stop it. The experiment even affected Zimbardo himself who, in his capacity as "Prison Superintendent", lost sight of his role as psychologist and permitted the abuse to continue as though it were a real prison. Five of the prisoners were upset enough by the process to quit the experiment early, and the entire experiment was abruptly stopped after only six days. Zimbardo aborted the experiment early because Christina Maslach, a graduate student he was then dating (and later married), objected to the appalling conditions of the prison after she was introduced to the experiment to conduct interviews. Zimbardo noted that of more than fifty outside persons who had seen the prison, Maslach was the only one who questioned its morality.[174]

It has been demonstrated time and again that the vast majority of people require only official sanction to willingly suspend their own powers of discrimination and behave in ways that – without external authority – they would not have begun to contemplate. All that is required is for a nominal authority figure to give assent, and the majority of people will commit a morally questionable act without demonstrating remorse or self-doubt, or even, in their defence, having any genuine awareness of even the possibility that their chosen action might be immoral, cruel or wrong.

The Harvard historian Daniel Goldhagen promoted a new theory of genocide in his seminal work *Hitler's Willing Executioners*[175] wherein he attempted to explain the enterprise to rid the world of Jewish genes and the seemingly insane willingness of hundreds of thousands of human beings – mostly, but by no means only German – to carry out the evil design. His central, intimated interrogative: is there a beast in each of us waiting to be unleashed by extraordinary fear, greed or fury?

Goldhagen did not originate the theory of collective ethnic guilt. But in his book he provided a scholar's validation for the belief that the crime of the Holocaust was a popular movement, adopted and supported by ordinary, God-fearing German folk. He argued that not only Nazis were the perpetrators of the Holocaust. Rather, those responsible were representative Germans conditioned by an "eliminationist anti-Semitism" so virulent and constant that it needed only the sanction of the Hitler regime to express itself as "right and necessary" mass murder.

---

[174] http://en.wikipedia.org/wiki/Stanford_prison_experiment
[175] *Hitler's Willing Executioners: Ordinary Germans and the Holocaust* (1997), Daniel Goldhagen, Abacus

Whether you agree with Goldhagen's conclusions or not is beside the point. The fact remains that even though many Germans would not have sanctioned the Holocaust, the vast majority were to one extent or another complicit in the marginalisation, alienation and dehumanisation of the Jews in the period leading up to the Holocaust. As Melita Maschmann remarked about that time, anti-Semitism had become nothing more than German 'common-sense.'

All that was required was for those in authority to sanction the prevailing attitudes. All of these experiments and retrospectives demonstrate the worrying principle that a little authority is all that is required for the average person to entirely suspend their moral judgement. When faced with such evidence, the majority of people object, assuming that they would never behave in such a manner. In 1961, psychologist Stanley Milgram devised an experiment to discern whether or not people's assumptions about their probable behaviour in such circumstances were reliable.

Milgram conducted a survey which revealed that only 1.2% of respondents believed that one human being would administer painful punishment to another simply because they were ordered to do so. He then conducted a now famous study to test these figures. He recruited random volunteers and paired them with (unbeknownst to the volunteer) paid actors. The volunteer was assigned the role of 'teacher' and the actor was the 'learner', although the role assignment was rigged to appear random. The learner was placed in an adjacent room while the teacher stayed in the room with Milgram who was the nominal 'authority figure' and the volunteer was then tasked with asking the learner test questions. Whenever the learner gave a wrong answer, the teacher was told to administer an electric shock. In truth, no electric shock was administered and tape recordings of, at first, small cries of discomfort and, later, full-blooded screams were played in the adjacent room to simulate the learner's pain and distress. When teachers became uncomfortable with inflicting pain on their fellow "volunteer" they were ordered, up to 4 times, to continue. If they resisted after the fourth "order" the experiment was halted.

Milgram discovered that rather than a mere 1.2% being prepared to administer pain to another person when ordered to do so, a horrifying 66% were prepared to administer an electric shock, at a *fatal level*, to a completely innocent stranger, simply because a nominal authority figure told them that they should and that they wouldn't be held responsible for any consequences.[176]

"Many subjects will obey the experimenter no matter how vehement the pleading of the person being shocked, no matter how painful the shocks seem to be, and no matter how much the victim pleads to be let out. This was seen time and again in our studies and has been observed in several universities where the experiment was repeated. It is the extreme willingness of adults to go to almost any lengths on the command of an authority that constitutes the chief finding of the study and the fact most urgently demanding explanation. A commonly offered explanation is that those who shocked the victim at the most severe level were monsters, the sadistic fringe of society. But if one considers that almost two-thirds of the participants fall into the category of 'obedient' subjects and that they represented ordinary people drawn from working, managerial and professional classes, the argument becomes very shaky."[177]

In the final analysis, these studies, and many more like them, hint at the depressing truth that most human beings are susceptible to *groupthink*[178] . When a group of people with a common purpose or agenda come together, there is potentially no limit to the cruelty they are able to inflict on others. This phenomenon requires only nominal authority and

---

[176] For a full discussion of the Milgram Experiment, see *The Individual in a Social World: Essays and Experiments* (2010), Stanley Milgram, Thomas Blass, Pinter & Martin Ltd
[177] *Obedience to authority: an experimental view* (2010), Stanley Milgram, Pinter & Martin Ltd, p 5-6
[178] A term coined by Irving Janice in 1972 to describe the phenomenon whereby members of a group arrive at a consensus without realistically appraising alternatives, thus avoiding conflict between group members.

is therefore subject to terrible abuse, especially when character-disordered individuals (e.g. narcissists or sociopaths) assume the authority role. Even where the authority is psychologically healthy and acting in good faith, the consequences might still be heartbreaking:

"*I wish I could say that writing this book was a labour of love; it was not that for a single moment of the two years it took to complete. First of all it was emotionally painful to review all of the videotapes from the Stanford Prison Experiment (SPE) and to read over and over the typescripts prepared from them. Time had dimmed my memory of the extent of creative evil in which many of the guards engaged, the extent of the suffering of many of the prisoners, and the extent of my passivity in allowing the abuses to continue as long as I did – an evil of inaction.*"[179]

The process described intimates therefore, that any individual with a self-interested agenda is able to rationalise cruelty by the simple expedience of finding a nominal authority figure to express approval for their objectives.

That authority need not even be a person; it can be a belief, a deity, a political movement, or a moral imperative. Examine the following statements and the nominal authority or cause in each case. Almost every case of dubious motivation to cruelty is prefaced with a rationalisation according to some precedent or authority, or some shift in perspective which proclaims the superiority or supremacy, the *authority* of the position, often as a parallel to the *inferiority* of the opponent's position. Since the compulsion to take the power-position is Plutonic, and the dehumanisation tactic is Orcan, it is once again possible to follow, most succinctly, the structure of the power struggle in human ego-life. Orcus acts as an agent of Pluto in this sense, dehumanising the opponent to set up the power-play of Pluto.

---

[179] *The Lucifer Effect: How Good People Turn Evil* (2008), Philip Zimbardo, Rider, opening paragraph.

- *"Hence today I believe that I am acting in accordance with the will of the Almighty Creator: by defending myself against the Jew, I am fighting for the work of the Lord."* Adolf Hitler in Mein Kampf.
- *"We, therefore, here in Britain stand shoulder to shoulder with our American friends in this hour of tragedy, and we, like them, will not rest until this evil is driven from our world."* Tony Blair.
- *"But no terrorist state poses a greater or more immediate threat to the security of our people and the stability of the world than the regime of Saddam Hussein in Iraq."* Donald Rumsfeld, Hearing Before the House Armed Services Committee, September 10, 2002.
- *"Those rats ... were attacked by the masses tonight and we eliminated them."* Radio address by Muammar Gaddafi on rebel forces in Tripoli, as quoted in "Libya conflict: Col Gaddafi faces rebel uprising on streets of Tripoli" in The Telegraph (21 August 2011)
- After a loyalist rally in 1968, Ian Paisley commented on the burning of Catholic homes by claiming: *"Catholic homes caught fire because they were loaded with petrol bombs; Catholic churches were attacked and burned because they were arsenals and priests handed out sub-machine guns to parishioners"*; he also said the massive discrimination in employment and allocation of public housing for Catholics existed because *"they breed like rabbits and multiply like vermin"*.
- *"If I can send the flower of the German nation into the hell of war without the smallest pity for the shedding of precious German blood, then surely I have the right to remove millions of an inferior race that breeds like vermin"* Adolf Hitler in a party speech in 1940.

As you can see, all of these individuals are rationalising a position that was subsequently found to be morally ambiguous through an appeal to a superior authority or right. In every case their opponents were described in terms which made them appear to be dangerous, and therefore less than human.

The Perils of Dehumanisation

If moral behavior were simply following rules, we could program a computer to be moral. --Samuel P. Ginder

Indeed it can be seen that *dehumanisation*, disavowing normal human qualities and instead ascribing evil or inferior qualities to a person or a collective, is at the heart of almost every strategy of dominance, and is the key symptom of the Plutonic power struggle. A person of integrity and compassion could not use the negatively Orcan tactic of dehumanisation as a means of winning a power struggle because it negates compassion for other people, and for compassion to be meaningful it has to be consistent. An inconsistency of compassion reflects a lack of spiritual maturity[180].

It is necessary therefore to behave compassionately toward misguided and spiteful people too, although this should always be balanced with compassion for oneself. In this way, one learns to balance that compassion for one's detractors with respect for one's own boundaries. Being compassionate does not mean allowing oneself to be victimised or abused, but the key here is that the spiritual person will withdraw from a toxic relationship rather than engage in conflict.

---

[180] In the brahmavihāras, the four Buddhist virtues, the second is compassion, which is the 'wish for all sentient beings to be free from suffering'. Since the negative state of Orcus is precisely the opposite of this sentiment (that a sentient being should be punished and suffer), it is arguably a position that negates all spiritual value in human life. The Christian gospels similarly exhort the true believer to practise compassion: *"You have heard that it was said, 'Love your neighbour and hate your enemy.' But I tell you, love your enemies and pray for those who persecute you, that you may be children of your Father in heaven. He causes his sun to rise on the evil and the good, and sends rain on the righteous and the unrighteous."* Matthew 5:43-46

It is important, therefore, if you wish to live as a spiritual being, to overcome the temptation to be drawn into the power struggle[181]. In this way one can make the conscious decision to align with a spiritual, rather than a material paradigm. Pluto then shifts focus in the spiritually motivated and the power struggle is internalised instead of being projected. At this stage of human spiritual evolution, there is a struggle against the compulsion to project Pluto, and instead to own it, to become its master rather than its servant, and to finally transform and refine the Plutonic energy in one's spiritual system. All that is required to catalyse the transition into positive Orcan experience is to begin to master Pluto, because this is the birth of integrity. Naturally, integrity has to mature, and this takes time and practice, but the process is begun, which is the most important spiritual milestone in a human life. There is a further significant milestone which is encountered at a later point in development, but without the power struggle with Pluto, it cannot even be envisaged, let alone attained.

As can be seen in the diagram, the evolutionary ideal is to move along the path from the point of blind-compulsion to a more spiritually ideal state of self-mastery. The vast majority of people alive today are locked within the compulsive and material stage of development, and though they might be presented with many opportunities to awaken and move into the higher state of spiritual consciousness, most people are unwilling to let go of their victim-consciousness because that is the perspective which provides most payoff for the ego[182].

---

[181] Of course, it is never quite so simple: the engagement in a power struggle is entirely compulsive, so one cannot simply *choose* to no longer be drawn into such contests. Rather, one retrospectively gains increasing perspective and, with time and practise, the interrupt between compulsion and awareness narrows until they become effectively concurrent. Once awareness of the compulsion is near immediate, the spell is broken.

[182] As an aside, it should be noted that progress on the path toward self-mastery is not smooth even in the best case. In my view, that progression is characterised by a type of oscillation; one hovers within a range that is a subset of the totality of the distance between compulsion and awareness. Envisaged as a numerical scale then, we could say that on a path from 0 to 100, we might be within the subset of 30 to 40 at the current

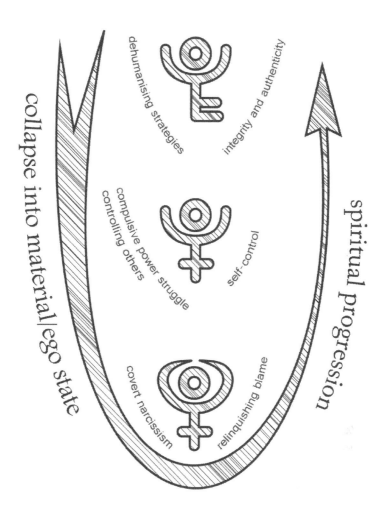

The compulsive (Plutonic) exposition of outer planet energies – via the medium of contacts to personal planets – is the irrigation system of

---

moment. This means that the 'switch' between the material and the spiritual is not a binary movement – one day material, the next spiritual – but is rather a hovering across the threshold: one day raised up into pure consciousness, the next falling back down into ego, and this 'on and off' quality may continue for many years even. Since the movement creates inconsistency, it is not possible to be truly and spiritually authentic until one no longer oscillates into the ego state *at all*. Blame must be relinquished for good.

hubris. The Plutonic transformation allows for the first, unsteady steps on the road toward self-control, which must be a spectrum between blind compulsion and *satori*, as gradually the soul grows in strength and subsumes the ego. All negative Plutonic and Orcan material is experienced in the ego phase of maturation; humiliation, powerlessness, dehumanisation, shame, debt, impotence[183], myriad forms of abuse. All sinister life is there, until the soul through tempering in the crucible of Hades, has gained enough strength, enough tenor, to resist the urge to compulsion.

I believe that this determination to resist compulsion and forgo the power struggle is a system of human soul-processing synonymous with the dark night of the soul as defined by Saint John. When a person is given an opportunity to behave badly and 'get away' with it, some people will take that opportunity, thinking they have found a shortcut to success, to realising their agenda. This can only be an ego-perspective of course, because the soul is not even interested in short-cuts: the soul actively avoids them. Once the shortcut is taken, the gods laugh and offer that person an opportunity to take another shortcut, perhaps this time revealing an even more mendacious path than before. The descent into Hades is a parallel with the descent into hubris; it does not happen all at once, but rather by increments, by a series of small yet fundamental distortions of perspective and motive, until the soul is completely subsumed by the ego[184]. It is the Hadean reflection and reversal of the process of spiritualisation. Nietzsche understood this when he proclaimed that *"there is no such thing as conscious evil."* This seems to echo the findings of researchers in the field of human evil, Zimbardo and Milgram proved as much as did political theorist Hannah Arendt, a Jew who fled Germany after Hitler's

---

[183] The Plutonic markers are these, either manifested in one's own life, or projected onto others. The desire to see others humiliated, powerless, in debt or otherwise helpless and laid low is a typical and unevolved Plutonic response to adversity and conflict.

[184] This is the Ixionic state. Ixion is of course an integral part of this process and will be dealt with in a subsequent publication.

rise to power and later reported on Adolf Eichmann's trial for The New Yorker. In *Eichmann in Jerusalem*, Arendt's famous account of the trial she concluded that, aside from a desire for improving his career, Eichmann showed no trace of an anti-Semitic personality or of any psychological damage to his character. She called him the embodiment of the "Banality of Evil", as he appeared at his trial to have an ordinary and common personality, displaying neither guilt nor hatred. She suggested that this most strikingly discredits the idea that the Nazi criminals were manifestly psychopathic and thereby different from ordinary people. Eichmann himself said he joined the SS not because he agreed with its ethos, but because he needed to build a career.

As an interesting aside, Eichmann joined the SS in 1933 just as Orcus applied to first conjunction with his natal Jupiter. He was invited to join Leopold von Mildenstein's "Jews Section", or Section II/112, of the SD[185] at its Berlin headquarters in mid 1934 as Orcus made the crucial median pass to radix Jupiter; he later came to see this as his "big break". By spring 1946, Orcus had moved to contact Eichmann's natal Pluto by conjunction, and Eichmann was captured by the Americans but passed himself off as a refugee named Otto Eckmann, and he spent the period of Orcus-Pluto transits hiding in an "isolated farmhouse" in Altensalzkoth, an obscure hamlet on the Lüneburg Heath in the North of Germany. Eichmann eventually fled to Argentina, boarding ship only 20 days before the first pass of Orcus quincunx radix Moon. He was captured in Buenos Aires by Israeli agents within a few days of the median pass of Orcus conjunct natal Neptune and was taken to Israel to stand trial. Similarly, he was sentenced to death and executed by hanging within a few days of Orcus' transit to his Midheaven, which is a neat motif for public execution.

Eichmann, who was responsible for organising the deportation of 5 million human souls to death camps in Eastern Europe, was considered

---

[185] The SD, *Sicherheitsdienst* transl. *Security service*. This was the intelligence arm of the Waffen SS.

by many to be "the accountant of the Holocaust," and was said to have the unprepossessing personality of the stereotypical accountant to match. While people would like to believe that mass-murderers and perpetrators of genocide are monsters and raving lunatics, the evidence supports the opposite conclusion: that they are very often boring, unremarkable and generally prosaic types who simply did not have the *character* to resist the gradual decline into a habit of entirely *unconscious* evil. [186]

If spirituality is defined as a set of principles which promulgate compassion, personal integrity and responsibility for one's actions, then it is easy to comprehend how the twofold transformation of Pluto and Orcus describes the shift into spiritual consciousness. One of the energetic components of the Plutonically untransformed is a sense of their being *asleep and unconscious of their egoistic motivations*. They have no awareness whatever of their compulsive behaviour or the hypocrisy of their many self-serving positions. Inevitably, such behaviour garners scrutiny and opposition. Under examination these people claim to be principled, self-aware and in full and conscious control of themselves at all times.

Looked at in this way it's easy to see why the basic currency of a spiritual life is unshakeable – but *conscious* – integrity. Even so, in keeping with many other states of human consciousness, spiritual integrity is only possible to truly comprehend through experience; it is extremely difficult to describe or to intellectualise. This is because language has primarily developed as a materially descriptive toolset and struggles to encompass immaterial concepts, not unlike astrology

---

[186] Stanley Milgram interpreted Arendt's work as proof that even the most ordinary of people can commit horrendous crimes if placed in certain situations and given certain incentives. He wrote: "*I must conclude that Arendt's conception of the banality of evil comes closer to the truth than one might dare imagine.*" However, Arendt did not suggest that Eichmann was normal or that any person placed in his situation would have done as he did. According to her account, Eichmann had abdicated his will to make moral choices, and thus his autonomy. Eichmann claimed he was just following orders, and that he was therefore respecting the duties of a "bureaucrat".

itself. Astrology is *not* a material science; it describes a view of the experiential world which is resultantly ineffable.

You can prove this to your own satisfaction by comparing the number of words we have to describe a fairly limited collection of physical objects: like weapons, with the number of words we have to describe something much more complex and wide in scope but which is immaterial, like love. When we consider even a narrow subset of material objects within this class, such as swords, we can cite many examples such as:

- broadsword
- two-handed sword
- claymore
- foil
- rapier
- scimitar
- bastard sword
- cutlass
- sabre
- katana

When we try to classify immaterial concepts, like love, language runs out. We can say that there is romantic love, filial love and a few others, but even these are describing the object of love, not the love itself. The equivalent would be to describe the sword's target or purpose: thus a 'foreign invader' sword, 'scoundrel who questioned my honour sword' or an 'impressing the tourists' sword. None of these terms describe the actual sword, any more than 'love' helps to elucidate that vast realm of human feeling, with all of its myriad nuances and expressions.

This is only one of the reasons why it is almost impossible to discuss, explain or convey the truth of integrity to another person when they have not made the Plutonic transformation into the spiritual awareness of Orcus.

So, what is spiritual integrity, and if the majority of people are not in possession of it, then why do they believe that they are, in fact, persons of integrity? In my view, humans fall into three distinct groups: those without integrity, those with material integrity, and those with spiritual integrity. It seems clear that there are few people, and those are very low on the scale of human consciousness, who do not care for even material integrity. These are the people who are thieves, cheats and liars, and do not actually care very much if they are known for it. These are the people who would put their hand in the till at the store while the clerk was distracted. The second group comprises the vast majority. These are the people who wish to appear to be persons of integrity, but will make small distortions of perspective to justify their attempts to influence circumstances and other people in service of their own self-interest. A person of material integrity would consider themselves fortunate if they discovered that they were given too much change at the store, they would not return to the store to repay the money, because they would make the small distortion of perspective to gloss over the fact that the money was not theirs to keep by reconceptualising their means of acquiring the sum. A person of spiritual integrity would, upon realising the mistake, immediately return to the store to repay the money, because they understand that *regardless* of how the store's rightful money came to be in their possession, it was still not their money, and therefore they had no right to keep it. This understanding is encapsulated in the Second Precept of Theravada practice: I undertake the training rule to abstain from taking what is not given. Therefore, unless the clerk in the store gave you an extra five dollars and said "here, this extra five dollars is a gift," then you have to return it if you are a person of spiritual integrity. This sounds straightforward enough, and of course it is, but the material ego drives material integrity, so it easy to fall into the trap of rationalising theft. Somebody might say, *"That store is a multinational corporation, so they can afford the five dollars. I am poor and need the money."* They may say, *"It was a mistake, so I have stolen nothing!"*

Dissecting the Power Struggle

Another issue with material integrity is that it polices the integrity of others, ironically, as a tool to dehumanise and thereby disadvantage opponents in a power struggle. Many negatively Plutonic people engaged in power struggles (and all negatively Plutonic people attempt to draw others into their power struggles) will gossip about or slander their opponents to third parties. This assures that those other people (provided they do not adhere to spiritual integrity either) will sympathise with, and in the best case, actively support their agenda. The attempt at dehumanising the target by the Plutonic type will usually consist of a smear-campaign where the following classic Plutonic/Orcan pattern is employed:

1. Discredit and isolate the target
2. Play the victim and/or hero
3. Lie-exaggerate-manipulate
4. Manufacture fear
5. Label the target inferior
6. Hurt the target for spite

These patterns of behaviour vary in visibility, depending on the character of the manipulator, which is nothing more than a reflection of the fact that there is a spectrum of integrity even among the egoistically motivated. Understanding these red flags, it is possible to see that resort to gossip and slander are two very clear indicators of a person who has not yet moved into spiritual integrity. Slander of this type is always designed to fulfil the objectives of the first stage of the compulsive power struggle; to discredit the target and thereby confound the neutrality of third parties as a means of further increasing the target's isolation.

The second stage is to further distort the situation by placing oneself within the victim triangle. This theme was first posited by psychologist Stephen Karpman in 1968[187]. Life counsellor Lynne Forrest describes the process in "an Overview of the Drama Triangle":

"The three roles on the victim triangle are Persecutor, Rescuer and Victim... No matter where we may start out on the triangle, victim is where we end up; therefore no matter what role we're in on the triangle, we're in victimhood... the Persecutor and Rescuer are on the upper end of the triangle. These roles assume a "one-up" position over others, meaning they relate as though they are better, stronger, smarter, or more-together than the victim."[188]

The second stage, then, is characterised by the aggressor assuming one of these roles, and they operate with the unconscious expectation that their target will be drawn into the power struggle as a similarly unconscious function of their compulsive ego[189]. By placing themselves in the role of victim or rescuer particularly, they are creating the overt impression that the target is the persecutor, although they may of course determine to occupy the role of *justified* persecutor.

Eric Berne refers to the construct of power struggles as 'games'. Not all games need be destructive of course, some of these rituals are simply convenient (for example, talking about the weather), but when games are motivated by a hidden power and control agenda, it is usually the case that the protagonist is depending on receiving some form of payoff or satisfaction as a reward for initiating the power struggle:

"...some games are urgently necessary for the maintenance of health in certain individuals. These people's psychic stability is so precarious, and their positions are so tenuously maintained, that to deprive them of their games may plunge them into irreversible despair and even psychosis."[190]

---

[187] *What Do You Say After You Say Hello?* (1975), Eric Berne, London Books, p. 198
[188] http://www.lynneforrest.com/html/the_faces_of_victim.html
[189] *"What we are concerned with here, however, are the unconscious games played by innocent people engaged in duplex transactions of which they are not fully aware, and which form the most important aspect of social life all over the world."* The Games People Play (2010), Eric Berne ,Penguin, p 49
[190] Berne, Games p 62.

This is because the immature soul *needs* to project Pluto. The alternative is to internalise Pluto when there is not sufficient spiritual maturity to handle it. Internalising Pluto is the process of Plutonic transformation and an egoistic focus greatly undermines the probability of a successful conversion. In this case it is as though the crucible cannot withstand the heat of the material and fails, causing irreparable damage. The power struggle is therefore necessary to the spiritually immature as a *defence* against psychological collapse. And this explains comprehensively why it is that Plutonic power struggles of this type are so frequently characterised by remarkable intensity and spite. It also explains why it is that some people become sick or deranged when their targets refuse to take their allotted place within the power struggle. If a spiritually mature individual is targeted and they respond by setting appropriate boundaries rather than by assuming a place on the victim triangle, the protagonist has to begin processing Pluto. When the ego, rather than the mature soul, attempts to process Pluto, the result is normally unhealthy. Of course a 'life and death' illness, heart attack or clinical depression is another form of power struggle altogether, and one that is perfectly apportioned to process Plutonic energy, so this consequence is no great surprise. Projecting Pluto, either in a dehumanising power struggle, through sexual and financial conquest, some form of threat or disease is the only alternative to attaining spiritual maturity and taking responsibility for one's own life and situation.

"We can either choose to let go of the victim archetype... or wait for a significant trauma to force us into the now. In other words, we can either transform our consciousness as a matter of will, or we can wait for a disaster or a life threatening illness to make us do it."[191]

Stage three is designed to destabilise and isolate the target further. We have already discovered some of the Neptunian material that is being employed in the Plutonic process and this is fascinating. I believe that

---

[191] Radical Forgiveness, Colin Tipping, Sounds True 2009 p 173

Neptune is given a fabulously good press by contemporary astrology[192], and one that is scarcely deserved. Certainly, Neptune's reputation is enormously positive compared to his brother Pluto's, and yet I am endlessly sceptical about how deserving of his many generous epithets Neptune truly is. Like the ocean, Neptune seems beautiful, yearning and restive, a vastness of potential and a personification of a gentle eternity, but it seems that way from the perspective of the safe shore. Anyone who has been beyond sight of land in a black and angry sea understands that Neptune's power is just as dread as his brother's; equally as alien and inhumane. Pluto's realm is buried, however; unknown to the living, whereas Neptune's treacherous tides and currents are glamorised by his glittering waves and gentle breezes. Neptune's dreams, poetries and symphonies are spin-doctors *par excellence*. The victim triangle is the hubris of Neptune, as the power struggle is the hubris of Pluto.

The third phase of the power struggle is designed to glamorise the protagonist and besmirch the target. The *reality*, which is undoubtedly painfully prosaic, simply will not do. The reality is undoubtedly as banal as the fact that the "other woman" is just an ordinary woman who formed a relationship with somebody's husband and that she is not a devouring Jezebel, a scarlet woman without a shred of moral fibre whose sole life objective is to seek out contented families and cynically destroy them; but who is going to be taken in by *reality*?

Pluto motivates and, like the third parties who are drawn into the game, Neptune gets into a supporting role. Facts are conjured, repurposed and omitted in order to create the most fruitful impression. All the while, only Orcus' shadow-side is employed; providing implacability and fixity of purpose. Orcus cannot have a positive influence because while Pluto is untransformed, Orcus remains compulsive and base too.

---

[192] The same can be said for Uranus, who is just, if not more likely to be uncooperative rather than unconventional, cranky rather than quirky and brittle rather than brilliant.

In stage four, fear is propagated. The other woman becomes a succubus, threatening *all* selfless and upstanding wives whose only concern is to protect their innocent families from the stain of her lustful corruption. Her low moral character sets her apart as a harlot and temptress luring wayward husbands, siren-like, with her immoral charms, threatening to wreck marriages and destroy happiness, which the argument goes, must be her objective: why else pick on *this* family? How could a person of compassion and humanity wish to destroy happiness? Clearly there is something fundamentally wrong with that woman, something that sets her apart from normal humanity.

Step five is a shoe-in at this point because it is clear that the target is inferior, broken, evil and dangerous. They are undoubtedly beneath human, and therefore undeserving of normal human dignity and consideration. They might be an animal, an insect, a parasite, vermin, or perhaps a person of low moral character, a thief, a prostitute, a criminal, or just simply evil.

Finally, in step six, it becomes acceptable to hurt the target. They are beneath considerations of fair-play and dignity because they are less than human, so it becomes not just acceptable to cause them harm, but in fact necessary to do so. It becomes necessary to destroy their capacity to corrupt others; it becomes necessary to "protect" the innocent from them.

Understanding this process, it is quite straightforward to appreciate how the expositions of Pluto can be identified in the following statements; they consist of a dehumanising Orcan projection, and a target:

- *"We... will not rest until this evil is driven from our world."* Tony Blair (*evil*, Al Qaeda.)
- *"...no terrorist state poses a greater... threat..."* Donald Rumsfeld (*terrorist*, Iraq.)

- *"Those rats ... we eliminated them."* Col Gaddafi (*rats,* revolutionaries.)
- *"They breed like rabbits and multiply like vermin"* Ian Paisley (*vermin,* Catholics.)
- "...an *inferior race that breeds like vermin"* Adolf Hitler (*vermin,* Jews.)

Anxiety is healthy

At its most distilled, Pluto is most easily apprehended as *anxiety.* Untransformed, Pluto is compulsive because unconscious anxiety is so repressed and yet so potent that it promulgates action blindly and without any awareness. Frequently, people who begin to 'wake up' to Pluto do so through an anxiety process of one form or another. For the individual with Venus-Pluto contacts, then, there is anxiety about being lovable. When completely repressed, this anxiety can promulgate very difficult interpersonal behaviours: compulsive flirting, attempting to control others through the affections – men in particular tend to become very emotionally cold when displeased with loved ones, but will warm up and show approval when they want to encourage certain behaviours. Venus – Pluto is decidedly Pavlovian. All of this occurs without conscious awareness. In the next stage of spiritual development, that anxiety begins to creep into consciousness. This phase can last for many years as one shines the light of consciousness further and deeper into the recesses of the buried psyche. Anxiety begins to creep into the persona accompanied by increasingly overt symptoms of experiential distress. It is very easy at this juncture for a person to begin to contend with the symptoms of anxiety, rather than the causes of it, and until this conundrum of misidentification is reconciled, enormous interpersonal difficulties can arise.

Whenever Pluto is subjected to the spotlight in this way, he scuttles away. This is an ironic image, in fact, since the insect-like, chitinous scurry is exactly the imagery that is *projected* by unconscious Pluto.

When considered thus, it is simple to identify Plutonic projection when accusations such as worm, rat and even terrorist or harlot are bandied about. Any entity or activity which dislikes being in full view of 'normal' society inevitably becomes both an invocation of Pluto by the accuser, and reminiscent of Pluto to the listener.

Once the light is directed upon Pluto, however, these compulsive responses to conflict start to become uncomfortable. If the ego is still strong, the subject will balk at the switch into greater humility which is the only antidote to Pluto. Medical doctor and Buddhist philosopher Jon Kabat-Zinn says that these individuals:

"...deal with their insecure feelings by creating conflict wherever they go. They see all their interactions in terms of power and control. Every interaction is made in to an occasion for exerting control in one way or another, for getting their own way without thinking or caring about others. People who have this habit of relating tend to be aggressive and hostile, often without any awareness of how it is perceived from the outside. They can be abrasive, abusive, insensitive out of sheer habit. ... They may act as if all relationships are struggles to assert dominance."[193]

It is of course entirely possible to go too far the other way:

"Some people are so threatened by conflict or angry feelings in others that they will do anything to avoid a blow-up. If you have this habit, you will tend not to show or tell people how you are really feeling but will try to avoid conflicts at all costs by being passive, placating the other person, giving in to them, blaming yourself, dissimulating – whatever it takes."[194]

It is possible to see that both these patterns are, at root, boundary issues, motivated by unchallenged Plutonic anxiety. In the case of compulsively aggressive people, they ameliorate their unconscious insecurity by violating others' boundaries, either overt-aggressively,

[193] Full Catastrophe Living: How to cope with stress, pain and illness using mindfulness meditation (2006), Dr Jon Kabat-Zinn, Piatkus p 368-9
[194] Kabat-Zinn p 368

covert-aggressively or *passive-aggressively*, the latter two of which are typically Plutonic styles of behaviour. In the case of placatory and passive responses to Plutonic anxiety, the control and power issues of Pluto operate through inappropriate timidity. These people have learned to give way, usually at an early age, often in response to an aggressor-parent or sibling. Indeed, like two pieces of a puzzle, passive types and aggressive types are frequently drawn together to play these Plutonic games. The passive parent raises an aggressive child, the aggressive parent raises a passive child, and in adult life those children unconsciously seek their parental fit in the form of a spouse, best friend or boss, and so the game continues.

Or at least the game continues until the ego begins to lose its grip on the persona. This nearly always comes about due to a specific event or series of events that are reflected through major transits to the nativity, which is not an inevitability, but rather a potential predicated upon the truth of human free-will. Misconceptions about the purpose of midlife abound, but this is the time where we are afforded the most accessible opportunity to spiritualise our lives. Inevitably, when viewed from the ego's perspective, midlife can seem to precipitate crisis because of the potential for *loss*, not the potential for gain, a factor that causes me endless amusement when I read studies on the subject:

"Popular culture fuels the notion that the midlife crisis is universal. Television and movies feature pervasive images of fortysomething individuals suddenly shedding spouses and acting like adolescents. Television ads promise that snappy new cars, exotic getaway vacations or expensive jewelry will help soothe the midlife crises that supposedly arise like clockwork... A far different picture emerges from the MacArthur project. Nearly all 750 participants in one in-depth study recognized the term "midlife crisis," but only 23 percent had actually experienced one. When researchers analyzed their responses, they found that only 8 percent tied the emotional turmoil to the realization that they were aging.

The remaining 15 percent said they had experienced a turbulent period in their middle years but the crisis was caused by significant life transitions-- not by aging... Among the events that sent lives into a tailspin were divorce, loss of a job, the death of a child, the serious illness of a close relative or friend or severe financial problems... At the same time, the study found that the number of stressful life events--what the researchers call psychological turning points--peaks during the middle years. But these events don't necessarily trigger a midlife crisis in most people."[195]

Views such as this are founded upon the flawed originating premise that midlife is a time that threatens loss, decline, ruin and chaos. From the ego's perspective, of course, this is simply common sense. The *quantitative* reality of midlife – that three-quarters of people do not experience a 'crisis' – is simply a reflection of the truth that the majority of people are unable to recognise the opportunity to look beyond their ego's perspective. They are able to continue to repress Pluto. The ego continues to run the show, and because the midlife is the life period most stressed by transiting challenges, the likely outcome is that, with the midlife opportunity missed, the ego will remain fully in charge for the rest of that incarnation.

Without the 'crisis' then, there can be no shift to a habit of self-awareness and self-control. Without self-awareness and self-control there can be no shift into spirituality; without facing Pluto, no possibility of facing Orcus; without conscious anxiety, no spiritual integrity.

The Trap of Hubris

So, while integrity is key to spiritual awareness, it must be clear that one's only concern must be integrity for *oneself*, NOT anyone else. It cannot be spiritually meaningful to police other people's integrity. Indeed, once the shift is made into spiritual integrity, one quickly comes

---

[195] *Midlife Without a Crisis*, by Sally Squires. Washington Post, April 19, 1999

to the realisation that a person cannot meaningfully control anyone or anything outside of themselves, and to believe that they can is effectively to claim divine powers. It's hubris. It is the ego's perspective to evaluate the integrity of others. This does not mean that it is egotistical to *believe* that another person does not behave with integrity, any more than it would be egotistical to believe that the sky is blue. It is the ego position however to *police* the integrity of others. In just the same way as it is a starting position for the power struggle to police and evaluate the moral value, intelligence, honesty or ability of others.

True integrity arises as a natural consequence of internalising Pluto. That is to say, once you no longer project Pluto onto other people or situations in your life, then integrity will begin to develop as a natural consequence, and because integrity is the safeguard against hubris, the new spiritual, non-egoistic position becomes self-reinforcing. Integrity is a model of internal consistency that is necessary for spiritual growth. The key component here is consistency, and being consistent means that you follow the rule *even if it is not to your material advantage to do so*[196].

In this, there is the kernel of a spiritual truth that in many ways gets to the very essence of what it is to live spiritually: a material loss is a spiritual gain, and vice-versa. A Course in Miracles states that:

"*To everyone Heaven is completion. There can be no disagreement on this because both the ego and the Holy Spirit accept it. They are however in complete disagreement on what completion is, and how it is accomplished. The Holy Spirit knows that completion lies first in union, and then in the extension of union. To the ego completion lies in triumph, and in the extension of the 'victory' even to the final triumph over God. In this it sees the ultimate freedom of the self, for nothing would remain to*

---

[196] It is to one's spiritual advantage to follow the rule of integrity regardless of any other perceived loss/benefit calculation.

interfere with the ego. This is its idea of Heaven. And therefore union, which is a condition in which the ego cannot interfere, must be hell."[197]

To the ego, then, gain and victory are the hallmarks of success, whereas, for the spirit, curiously, the opposite is true. Success for the spirit can only be attained via the medium of loss and defeat, because these open the heart, foster humility and compassion for oneself and for others and create the most fertile ground for the seeds of integrity to take root and grow. To the spirit, the concept of 'victory' is a chimera, because the spirit knows that victory is a fallacy. What have you 'won' at another person's expense? The spirit has no context for 'winning' because when one views the world in terms of winners, then there must be losers to balance the equation. How would the spirit wish to realise a victory at the cost of forcing another human soul to become a 'loser'. It is a senseless concept *except to the ego*. Only the ego understands, or even believes in, winners and losers. The greatest irony of the ego, however, is that by subscribing to the concept of winning, it creates an unnecessary and meaningless imperative which the ego itself must become enslaved by.

"Most of us believe that there is a finite resource 'pie' from which we all share and that the more we have, the less others have and vice-versa. We believe that all resources are scarce. It's not unusual that so many of us believe this, though. From birth, a mindset of scarcity is ingrained in us. In school we're taught that economics is the science of allocating scarce resources. On television, in magazines, in newspapers, on the Internet, and in virtually every other form of media, we are bombarded with claims that there isn't enough to go around. The theories and strategies of intellectuals like Thomas Malthus articulate such a convincing case for scarcity that it becomes difficult to see the deeper truths beyond what the data seems to suggest on the surface.

---

[197] *A Course in Miracles* (2008), Dr Helen Shucman, Course in Miracles Society, p 206

In the scarcity mindset, we take it for granted that our society does not have enough resources or productive capacity to fulfil everyone's needs and desires. Consequently, we believe that our material gains come only as a loss to others, and that when others possess more, it means less for us. It's easy to see how a culture that accepts the notion of scarcity quickly becomes ultra-competitive and selfish."[198]

This belief becomes self-reinforcing as soon as people act upon it. If people behaved with true spiritual integrity, even if they believed that the world was truly Malthusian[199], then it would make no difference.

Seeing life in this Malthusian way, as a game of winners and losers, opens the door to hubris because, as Aristotle contended, Pluto's hubris arises from a desire to *"cause shame to the victim... for your own gratification ... men think that by ill-treating others they make their own superiority the greater."*[200]

The Authenticity Shift

Integrity is its own reward. This is a truth borne out by experience; however it also yields the benefit of not suffering the fate of the converse egoistic path. The collapse into hubris is the negation of the spiritual life: it is, in a very real sense, the definition of hell.

---

[198] *Killing sacred cows: overcoming the financial myths that are destroying your prosperity* (2008), Garrett B. Gunderson, Stephen Palmer, Greenleaf Book Group LLC p 3
[199] The Reverend Thomas Malthus (1766 – 1834) was an English scholar, influential in political economy and demography who become widely known for his theories about population and its increase or decrease in response to various factors, especially famine and disease: *"The number of mouths to be fed will have no limit; but the food that is to supply them cannot keep pace with the demand for it; we must come to a stop somewhere, even though each square yard, by extreme improvements in cultivation, could maintain its man. In this state of things there will be no remedy; the wholesome checks of vice and misery (which have hitherto kept this principle within bounds) will have been done away; the voice of reason will be unheard; the passions only will bear sway; famine, distress, havoc and dismay will spread around; hatred, violence, war and bloodshed will be the infallible consequence; and from the pinnacle of happiness, peace, refinement and social advantage we shall be hurled once more into a profounder abyss of misery, want, and barbarism that ever by the sole operation of the principle of population!"* From *An Essay on the Principle of Population* by Thomas Malthus, originally written 1803.
[200] Aristotle, *Rhetoric* 1378b

Integrity is an entirely different path, albeit not one that is easily defined. Integrity does not require that you follow rules; indeed, very often you have to break rules in order to maintain integrity. It does require that you maintain a code of behaviour, and that you are able to apply that code to each situation in life that requires an authentic response. The reason that many individuals struggle to apply this internal set of rules appropriately is because they cannot view their own position within the context of the situation with objectivity. This is only another way of saying that they cannot consider the problem independently from the ego. One way of understanding this is through the perspective that the ego is *entirely* self-interested, so any ego-participation whatever, makes *some* self-interest inevitable. The ego is like the mysterious character of Keyser Soze in the movie, The Usual Suspects:

"Who is Keyser Soze? He is supposed to be Turkish. Some say his father was German. Nobody believed he was real. Nobody ever saw him or knew anybody that ever worked directly for him, but to hear Kobayashi tell it, anybody could have worked for Soze. You never knew. That was his power. The greatest trick the Devil ever pulled was convincing the world he didn't exist."[201]

In the same way, nobody who is working for their ego is aware of the fact that they are in the thrall of a shady, underground character. The ego hijacks the internal code of behaviour as a tool to further self-interest, thus ensuring that it deludes the true Self as to its motives, which it can claim is only to 'do the right thing.' This is an easy trap to defeat, providing you adhere to what Immanuel Kant referred to as a categorical imperative. This is an absolute motivator for action rather than a relative one, which he named a hypothetical imperative[202]. The difference between these two modes of motivation is simple enough: a hypothetical imperative is one which causes you to do something, or

[201] *The Usual Suspects*, Polygram Filmed Entertainment 1995.
[202] The philosophy of the Kantian Imperative is discussed at length in Kant's *Groundwork of the Metaphysic of Morals* 1785.

not do something according to the circumstance, so, for example, if you are tired, the hypothetical imperative would cause you to go to bed early and catch up on some sleep. A categorical imperative, by contrast, is one that would cause you to do something, or not do something, *regardless of the circumstance*.

Now the difference between true spiritual integrity and material integrity is that only spiritual integrity actually operates from the categorical imperative. This is because, for the ego, *every* imperative is hypothetical. The ego can justify any behaviour or action dependent upon the circumstance, because there is always a set of conditions which create the exception to the rule. That set of circumstances, the so-called imperative, varies from person to person according to their intrinsic level of ego-investment; so one person might justify keeping another person's possession under fairly relaxed provocation – *"they were rude to me last week"* – while another might have a more stringent imperative – *"well I bought it for her as a gift, and then she ran off with my best friend, so she forfeited the right to keep my gifts"* – but in each case as you can see, stealing another person's property has become a hypothetical imperative. A person of true spiritual integrity simply would not keep another person's belongings, under any circumstance whatever; a categorical imperative, therefore.

According to Kant, the entire system of human ethics is dependent upon categorical imperatives. You do not steal, and you do not make exceptions to the rule of not stealing because human nature being what it is, those without integrity will always find a means of rationalising theft. Not stealing must be a categorical imperative otherwise stealing simply becomes the norm in the world. Kant believed that living according to hypothetical imperatives simply ensures that you live in a world without moral certainties. Put way more simply, Kant's maxim dictates that if you're prepared to cheat, then you simply create a world where cheating is the norm.

As an example of this, consider that if you walk out of the store having been given too much change, you can operate from the hypothetical imperative that you came into possession of that sum "through a mistake", therefore you are not responsible for an act of theft and all might be well. Imagine then that when you get home from the store, you realise that your bank account is empty because the bank has mistakenly credited your month's wages to a different account. By your own rule, the hypothetical imperative of "mistake", the person with the other account should not have to repay your wages, because he or she was not responsible for an act of theft.

This rather mundane example demonstrates the truth that being a person of spiritual integrity requires only a simple and relatively minor shift of perspective. It is not a radical change nor an especially difficult one, it simply requires that you stick to your own rules regardless of whether or not it is to your advantage to do so, in fact, regardless of anything at all.

We create the world we live in through our personal codes of behaviour, and the only person's behaviour we must be responsible for is our own.

This principle, that like attracts like, is spiritual common-sense[203]. If you're a cheat and a liar, you tend to be drawn into situations and

---

[203] Numerous studies affirm that the principle of 'birds of a feather flock together' is true and valid. "*First, emotional similarity coordinates the attention, thoughts and behaviours across multiple individuals. Emotional similarity thus helps individuals respond as a collective to potential opportunities or threats... In humans emotional similarity should guide collective action that would likely be more effective than the efforts of individuals acting alone... Second, when two people feel similar emotions they are better able to understand each other. People who experience similar emotions more easily take each other's perspective, and thus are more likely to accurately perceive each other's perceptions, intentions and motivations. This greater understanding, in turn, should enable individuals to better predict each other's behaviours which would lead to more cooperative and beneficial social interactions. Third, people feel closer to and are more comfortable with others who experience similar emotions. Emotional similarity increases cohesion and solidarity; whereas emotional dissimilarity increases discomfort and the likelihood of interpersonal conflict.*" From The Social Life of Emotions (Studies in Emotion and Social Interaction), Larissa Z. Tiedens (Editor), Colin Wayne Leach (Editor), Cambridge University Press 2004, p 145. It is easily demonstrated that a

circumstances where cheating and lying are the norm. Every human soul eventually finds their field, so if you want to live in a world of integrity and truth then the one thing that will almost guarantee your failure, is to attempt to police the integrity of others. By policing the integrity of others, you will necessarily adopt a habit of being judgemental, evaluative and critical of other people and situations and all you will achieve is to draw judgemental, evaluative and critical people into your life. All you need do is adopt a stance of personal integrity for yourself and be kind to others, and those people who cannot live that way themselves will not be drawn into your field of influence; they will drop away.

Kant's philosophical treatise is no more than an exceptionally thoughtful exposition of the so-called 'Golden Rule', which states very simply that one should treat others as one would like to be treated, or, if phrased conversely, one should not treat others in ways that one would not like to be treated.[204] Almost every human culture throughout time has expressed this principle in its core values. In ancient Egypt for example, in the story of The Eloquent Peasant, which dates to the Middle Kingdom (c. 2040–1650 BCE): *"Now this is the command: Do to the doer to cause that he do thus to you."*[205] In ancient Greece:

- "Do not to your neighbour what you would take ill from him." – Pittacus [206](c. 640–568 BCE)
- "Avoid doing what you would blame others for doing." – Thales[207]
- "What you do not want to happen to you, do not do it yourself either." – Sextus the Pythagorean[208].

---

person who is judgemental will be more likely to associate with other judgemental individuals and that this grouping would mutually reinforce and normalise the habit of judgement. This in turn would decrease the likelihood of association and agreement with people who have a habit of tolerance.

[204] The latter is frequently termed 'the Silver Rule'.

[205] *The Culture of Ancient Egypt* (1956), John Albert Wilson, University of Chicago Press, p 121.

[206] Pittacus, Fragm. 10.3

[207] Diogenes Laërtius, "The Lives and Opinions of Eminent Philosophers", I,36

- "Do not do to others what would anger you if done to you by others." – Isocrates[209]
- "What thou avoidest suffering thyself seek not to impose on others." – Epictetus[210]

From the Quran:

- "Woe to those... who, when they have to receive by measure from men, they demand exact full measure, but when they have to give by measure or weight to men, give less than due"[211]
- "...and you should forgive And overlook: Do you not like God to forgive you? And Allah is The Merciful Forgiving."[212]

The "Golden Rule" has been attributed to Jesus of Nazareth: "*Therefore all things whatsoever ye would that men should do to you, do ye even so to them*" (Matthew 7:12, see also Luke 6:31). The common English phrasing is "*do unto others as you would have them do unto you*". A similar form appeared in a Catholic catechism around 1567 and there are myriad recountings of the Golden Rule in both the Old and New Testaments of the bible.

And in this rendering of a fundamental human principle we have come full circle:

No, Glaucus, no, I think you need not fear,
To bilk your easy creditor, and swear
He lent you no such sum you'll gain thereby
And this consider'd you may death defy
Death of the just alike an enemy.
But know that Orcus has a monster son,
Ghastly of shape who ever hastens on

---

208 The Sentences of Sextus (http://www.gnosis.org/naghamm/sent.html)
209 Isocrates, "Nicocles",6
210 Epictetus, "Encheiridion"
211 (Surah 83, "The Dealers in Fraud," vv. 1–4)
212 (Surah 24, "The Light," v. 22)

To o'ertake perjuries; he'll ne'er forget
Your heinous crime, but with revengeful hate
Send losses, racking pangs, destructive woe,
Till he yourself, with your whole race undo.

For what is a perjury if not the substitution of a hypothetical imperative for one that ought to be categorical? What is perjury if not a changing of the rules according to the supreme dictate of one's own self-interest? What is perjury, if not a violation of the Golden Rule?

And perjury is the hubris which it is Orcus' task to punish. In this sense the ego's self-interest is the soul's ruin, for when viewed from the higher spiritual perspective this self-interest becomes a nonsense, because it rejects the alternative perspective and, with it, any possibility of happiness and contentment:

"*The Self is beyond time and form, and within it, the ordinary consciousness is potentially able to simultaneously function in a worldly manner.*

There was a difficulty in considering the world of ordinary perception to be real and taking it seriously. This led to a sort of permanent capacity to see the world from a humorous viewpoint. Ordinary life seemed to be an endless comedy so that even seriousness itself was humorous. It became necessary to quell expressions of the sense of humour that some people were unable to accept because they were so deeply involved in the perceptual world of negativity.

Most people seem to have a vested interest in the negativity of their perceptual world and resist leaving it for awareness on a higher level. People seem to derive sufficient satisfaction from their endless anger, resentment, remorse and self-pity to actively resist moving on to such levels as understanding, forgiveness or compassion. There seems to be sufficient gain in negativity so as to perpetuate ways of thinking that are obviously illogical and self-serving, much as politicians distort the truth in order to gain votes, or criminal prosecutors suppress evidence of the innocence of the accused in order to gain a conviction.

When these negative 'gains' are relinquished, the world becomes an endless presence of intense beauty and perfection, and love dominates all of life."[213]

This is the conundrum of Orcus. It is an incredible trick, much as though everyone is working furiously to create an environment that most perfectly ensures their own misery: a prison for the soul, a lock-up separating one in a solitary confinement without hope of companionship, peace or ease. By relinquishing the 'payoff' of selfish-interest, and denying oneself true spiritual Self-interest, one realises that their successful life was a gilded cage of one's own making, constructed at the cost of freedom and fulfilment, and that all that was required to escape into happiness was to make the small shift of perspective into personal integrity.

But this perspective shift is normally very hard-won, even if it seems only a minor change of position. It is won through isolation because when you are your only witness, who is there to impress? Perhaps the greatest truth of the astrological Orcus is found in the simplest of questions: how would you change if there was no audience, no one to impress, no one to care?

Alienation, imprisonment, banishment, loneliness, prayer, meditation, solitude; all of these are the agents of Orcus.

At the last we would do well to consider the words of Terry Waite, composed while he was locked, alone, in a cramped, makeshift dungeon under the streets of Beirut:

"My active life is over for a while, perhaps for ever. Maybe I will never leave this place. My life, such as it is, is in the hands of the living God. I

---

[213] *The Eye of the I from which Nothing is Hidden*, (2001), David R. Hawkins, Veritas Publishing

don't feel that God is near. I don't feel comfort from my prayers. All I feel is a searching introspection, as though a light were shining into the deepest parts of my being. Everything will be called to face that light: positive gestures, foolish actions, deceptions great and small, self-importance and insecurity. In these days I must face myself without sham. No false pride, no dodging the questions. Remember Waite, they want to use this experience to break you. They want your mind to be in such turmoil that you will be glad to let them sort it out. I must know if I have compromised my integrity. Have I?"[214]

In this light, all artifice is stripped away and the soul is laid bare. The ego has no narcissistic supply and it gradually starves, until eventually the soul is left stark and small and shivering. If you are not driven mad by the shock of finding yourself so brutally diminished, then the *authentic* life can begin.

Orcus is the transformation, the struggle to liberate meaning from the fake, empty world of form and appearance conjured by the human ego. Orcus is the final gateway into authenticity.

---

[214] *Taken on Trust*, (1993), Terry Waite, Hodder and Stoughton, p27.

Appendix I: The Question of Exaltation

Orcus finds its easiest expression in the sign of Sagittarius whose proclivity toward forthright, uncontaminated, positive self-expression of beliefs is easily the most comfortable medium for authenticity in the entire zodiac. Sagittarius is honest, genuine and endures through enthusiastic conviction. The Sagittarian type will give Capricorn a run for its money in the endurance stakes when it has sincere, reformative motivations and too has a natural affinity with spiritual objectives and perceptions.

At the opposite end of this spectrum lies Gemini, a sign that is too flighty to be comfortable with the Orcan drive and whose mutability simply cannot support the necessary single-mindedness through its multiple perspectives. The shift to dedicated, unshakeable integrity is especially difficult in this most intellectualising and effervescent of signs whose natural tendency is to become distracted by a new perspective that is more appealing. The mercurial trickster, though brilliant and lightning quick, struggles to find the commitment to explore the depths of Orcus.

The Sagittarius – Gemini polarity describes the spectrum of Orcus especially, from depth, belief and commitment to whimsicality and playfulness. The qualities of Orcus, his grim duties, are better suited to serious and deep endeavours and motivations, as pursuer, imprisoner, spiritual adept and executioner; therefore, Geminian lightness, fickleness and changeability can become extremely dangerous when Orcan energy is being expressed. At worst, the native with Orcus in Gemini can change position on a sixpence in order to justify and rationalise Orcus' judgement. Enemies and opponents can be 'sent down' on the slightest whim. Sagittarius, conversely, has a natural reverence for deep and considered perspectives which is better suited to expressing this potentially fatal quality. For Sagittarius, opinion is sacred and profound, whereas for Gemini, it is a plaything, an amusement and easily discarded in favour of the new and delightful.

Both Capricorn and Aries share a 'go it alone' philosophy which seems ideally suited to Orcan single-mindedness. Capricorn however, is undermined by the tendency to status that is implicit in the natural expression of the 10th house. This tends to neutralise the solitary propensity of Orcus with Capricorn. Cancer suffers through a liking for comfort, but at the same time, the private authenticity of lunar quality is a good fit for Orcus. It is very much a case of swings-and-roundabouts with the Cancer-Capricorn polarity.

Aries is another comfortable placing for Orcus, since here the single-minded and independent ardour of the Zodiac's first sign is broadly compatible. Libra conversely has a need to find a consensus with the other person and to some extent is a sign that requires approval. The principle of Venus, with her tendency to compromise is self-evidently a difficult fit for Orcus.

Taurus also struggles because it is the most material of signs and Orcus the least impressed by the fixed earth quality. For the same reason, Scorpio, whose natives demonstrate a singular proclivity for the Spartan, thrives in the realm of Orcus.

The Leo – Aquarius polarity is generally neutral, but the sign Leo desires admiration and is most easily persuaded that it deserves special treatment. The simple, unadorned dictates of Orcus do not sit well with this most easily ruffled of signs, but I personally believe that when Orcus is transformed, this can be a very good fit because Leo also has a very religious and reverent quality when the personal ego is transcended.

Pisces and Virgo have given me the most difficulty in assessment. In some ways these ought both to be happy placements for Orcus. Virgo has a propensity for deep and assimilative consideration, but it is nonetheless a Mercurial sign and is capable of rationalisation. Similarly, the sign of Pisces might be a good fit for Orcus if the soul is purified because there is great self-sacrifice and compassion in it. The lower exposition of Pisces though can create a propensity toward victim-consciousness and again, a habit of obfuscating or romanticising motives and agendas. In these cases the good outweighs the bad and vice-versa, which tends to neutralise the sign influence.

In all cases, it is vital to remember that Orcus is a planet of extremes. In any sign, provided an outright commitment to integrity (to categorical imperatives) is made, Orcus will offer the very best rewards. Certain sign placements make it *easier* to maintain that commitment, but of course, this is only the logic of exaltation extrapolated.

Appendix II: Orcus Sign Ingresses 1821 - 2039

10 Jan 1821	00:24:22	Orcus	Scorpio	D
16 Feb 1821	18:13:50	Orcus	Libra	Rx
7 Nov 1821	12:44:12	Orcus	Scorpio	D
30 Apr 1822	15:15:05	Orcus	Libra	Rx
23 Sep 1822	04:14:10	Orcus	Scorpio	D
15 Dec 1844	21:15:20	Orcus	Sagittarius	D
21 May 1845	20:48:15	Orcus	Scorpio	Rx
28 Oct 1845	19:24:11	Orcus	Sagittarius	D
30 Jan 1864	06:15:41	Orcus	Capricorn	D
5 Jun 1864	20:15:15	Orcus	Sagittarius	Rx
6 Dec 1864	06:50:21	Orcus	Capricorn	D
28 Jan 1880	20:08:17	Orcus	Aquarius	D
24 Aug 1880	08:52:33	Orcus	Capricorn	Rx
25 Nov 1880	13:09:44	Orcus	Aquarius	D
6 May 1892	11:47:58	Orcus	Pisces	D
30 Jun 1892	09:10:59	Orcus	Aquarius	Rx
18 Feb 1893	07:04:19	Orcus	Pisces	D
21 Oct 1893	02:56:33	Orcus	Aquarius	Rx
29 Nov 1893	18:03:10	Orcus	Pisces	D
22 May 1904	01:28:46	Orcus	Aries	D
19 Aug 1904	01:19:03	Orcus	Pisces	Rx
13 Mar 1905	13:41:59	Orcus	Aries	D
24 May 1917	10:39:48	Orcus	Taurus	D
20 Oct 1917	09:25:43	Orcus	Aries	Rx
25 Mar 1918	17:44:15	Orcus	Taurus	D
31 Jul 1932	03:04:13	Orcus	Gemini	D
4 Oct 1932	22:20:08	Orcus	Taurus	Rx
27 May 1933	01:05:59	Orcus	Gemini	D

23 Dec 1933	10:05:29	Orcus	Taurus	Rx
30 Mar 1934	07:07:06	Orcus	Gemini	D
16 Jul 1953	16:54:18	Orcus	Cancer	D
21 Dec 1953	11:48:39	Orcus	Gemini	Rx
30 May 1954	04:30:55	Orcus	Cancer	D
7 Oct 1978	14:30:53	Orcus	Leo	D
23 Nov 1978	01:01:25	Orcus	Cancer	Rx
8 Aug 1979	20:08:51	Orcus	Leo	D
28 Jan 1980	01:02:32	Orcus	Cancer	Rx
25 Jun 1980	00:59:16	Orcus	Leo	D
21 Nov 2007	05:56:58	Orcus	Virgo	D
7 Dec 2007	23:53:44	Orcus	Leo	Rx
12 Sep 2008	07:11:56	Orcus	Virgo	D
19 Feb 2009	15:05:30	Orcus	Leo	Rx
1 Aug 2009	00:18:32	Orcus	Virgo	D
7 May 2010	22:06:29	Orcus	Leo	Rx
21 May 2010	03:30:15	Orcus	Virgo	D
18 Oct 2037	16:05:30	Orcus	Libra	D
15 Mar 2038	08:03:07	Orcus	Virgo	Rx
5 Sep 2038	12:32:20	Orcus	Libra	D
21 May 2039	20:50:19	Orcus	Virgo	Rx
6 Jul 2039	22:30:29	Orcus	Libra	D

Orcus is at the time of publication approaching aphelion at 9 Virgo.

Appendix III: 4th Harmonic transits of Orcus and the US Chart 1900-2025

Ura (12)Sqr	Orcus (9)		7 Jul 1900
Ura (12)Sqr	Orcus (9)		27 Sep 1900
Orcus (3)	Sqr	Mar (7)	10 Apr 1901
Orcus (3)	Opp	Nep (9)	15 May 1901
Orcus (3)	Opp	Nep (9)	11 Aug 1901
Orcus (3)	Sqr	Mar (7)	19 Sep 1901
Orcus (3)	Sqr	Mar (7)	6 Feb 1902
Orcus (3)	Opp	Nep (9)	6 Mar 1902
Orcus (4)	Opp	MC (10)	9 Apr 1905
Orcus (3)	Opp	MC (10)	15 Oct 1905
Orcus (4)	Opp	MC (10)	3 Feb 1906
Sat (3)	Opp	Orcus (9)	28 Mar 1906
Orcus (4)	Sqr	Ven (7)	31 Mar 1906
Sat (3)	Opp	Orcus (9)	12 Oct 1906
Orcus (4)	Sqr	Ven (7)	6 Nov 1906
Sat (3)	Opp	Orcus (9)	13 Dec 1906
Orcus (4)	Sqr	Ven (7)	19 Jan 1907
Orcus (4)	Sqr	Jup (7)	12 Apr 1907
Orcus (4)	Sqr	Jup (7)	24 Oct 1907
Orcus (4)	Sqr	Jup (7)	6 Feb 1908
Orcus (4)	Sqr	Sun (7)	21 Apr 1910
Orcus (4)	Opp	Sat (10)	9 Jun 1910
Orcus (4)	Opp	Sat (10)	31 Aug 1910
Orcus (4)	Sqr	Sun (7)	27 Oct 1910
Orcus (4)	Sqr	Sun (7)	17 Feb 1911
Orcus (4)	Opp	Sat (10)	31 Mar 1911
Sat (6)	Sqr	Orcus (9)	10 Jun 1913
Orcus (4)	Sqr	Mer (8)	21 Jun 1914
Orcus (4)	Sqr	Mer (8)	6 Sep 1914
Orcus (4)	Sqr	Mer (8)	12 Apr 1915
Orcus (4)	Sqr	Mer (8)	19 Dec 1915
Orcus (4)	Sqr	Mer (8)	21 Jan 1916
Orcus (4)	Sqr	Plu (2)	14 May 1916
Orcus (4)	Sqr	Plu (2)	27 Oct 1916
Orcus (4)	Sqr	Plu (2)	15 Mar 1917

Sat (9)	Cnj	Orcus (9)	30 Oct 1919
Sat (9)	Cnj	Orcus (9)	17 Feb 1920
Sat (9)	Cnj	Orcus (9)	20 Jul 1920
Ura (3)	Opp	Orcus (9)	10 May 1921
Ura (3)	Opp	Orcus (9)	20 Jul 1921
Ura (3)	Opp	Orcus (9)	21 Feb 1922
Sat (12)	Sqr	Orcus (9)	24 Nov 1927
Orcus (6)	Sqr	Mon (3)	12 Jun 1931
Orcus (6)	Sqr	Mon (3)	24 Nov 1931
Orcus (6)	Sqr	Mon (3)	18 Apr 1932
Nep (9)	Cnj	Orcus (9)	10 Oct 1932
Nep (9)	Cnj	Orcus (9)	16 Feb 1933
Nep (9)	Cnj	Orcus (9)	12 Aug 1933
Sat (3)	Opp	Orcus (9)	16 May 1935
Sat (3)	Opp	Orcus (9)	28 Jul 1935
Sat (3)	Opp	Orcus (9)	1 Feb 1936
Orcus (6)	Cnj	Ura (6)	1 Jul 1938
Orcus (6)	Sqr	Orcus (9)	10 Jul 1938
Orcus (6)	Sqr	Orcus (9)	16 Nov 1938
Orcus (6)	Cnj	Ura (6)	25 Nov 1938
Orcus (6)	Cnj	Ura (6)	10 May 1939
Orcus (6)	Sqr	Orcus (9)	18 May 1939
Orcus (6)	Sqr	Orcus (9)	17 Feb 1940
Orcus (6)	Sqr	Orcus (9)	24 Feb 1940
Orcus (7)	Opp	Asc (1)	18 Jul 1940
Orcus (6)	Opp	Asc (1)	12 Nov 1940
Orcus (7)	Opp	Asc (1)	26 May 1941
Orcus (6)	Opp	Asc (1)	27 Jan 1942
Orcus (7)	Opp	Asc (1)	22 Mar 1942
Sat (6)	Sqr	Orcus (9)	23 Jul 1942
Sat (6)	Sqr	Orcus (9)	30 Nov 1942
Sat (6)	Sqr	Orcus (9)	11 Apr 1943
Ura (6)	Sqr	Orcus (9)	3 Jun 1944
Ura (6)	Sqr	Orcus (9)	6 Feb 1945
Ura (6)	Sqr	Orcus (9)	25 Feb 1945
Orcus (7)	Cnj	Mar (7)	11 Aug 1946

Orcus (7)	Cnj	Mar (7)	5 Nov 1946
Orcus (7)	Cnj	Mar (7)	16 Jun 1947
Orcus (7)	Sqr	Nep (9)	27 Jul 1947
Orcus (7)	Sqr	Nep (9)	24 Nov 1947
Orcus (7)	Cnj	Mar (7)	12 Jan 1948
Orcus (7)	Cnj	Mar (7)	24 Apr 1948
Orcus (7)	Sqr	Nep (9)	5 Jun 1948
Orcus (7)	Sqr	Nep (9)	1 Feb 1949
Orcus (7)	Sqr	Nep (9)	6 Apr 1949
Sat (9)	Cnj	Orcus (9)	30 Aug 1949
Orcus (7)	Sqr	MC (10)	16 Sep 1953
Orcus (7)	Sqr	MC (10)	17 Oct 1953
Orcus (7)	Sqr	MC (10)	9 Jul 1954
Orcus (7)	Sqr	MC (10)	2 Jan 1955
Orcus (7)	Sqr	MC (10)	22 May 1955
Orcus (7)	Cnj	Ven (7)	12 Aug 1955
Orcus (7)	Cnj	Ven (7)	27 Nov 1955
Orcus (7)	Cnj	Ven (7)	22 Jun 1956
Sat (12)	Sqr	Orcus (9)	30 Dec 1956
Orcus (7)	Cnj	Ven (7)	29 Jan 1957
Orcus (7)	Cnj	Ven (7)	1 May 1957
Sat (12)	Sqr	Orcus (9)	28 Jun 1957
Orcus (7)	Cnj	Jup (7)	4 Sep 1957
Sat (12)	Sqr	Orcus (9)	24 Sep 1957
Orcus (7)	Cnj	Jup (7)	8 Nov 1957
Orcus (7)	Cnj	Jup (7)	8 Jul 1958
Orcus (7)	Cnj	Jup (7)	13 Jan 1959
Orcus (7)	Cnj	Jup (7)	22 May 1959
Plu (9)	Cnj	Orcus (9)	10 Oct 1961
Plu (9)	Cnj	Orcus (9)	16 Feb 1962
Plu (9)	Cnj	Orcus (9)	12 Aug 1962
Orcus (7)	Cnj	Sun (7)	5 Oct 1963
Orcus (7)	Cnj	Sun (7)	23 Oct 1963
Ura (9)	Cnj	Orcus (9)	1 Nov 1963
Ura (9)	Cnj	Orcus (9)	31 Jan 1964
Orcus (7)	Cnj	Sun (7)	24 Jul 1964
Ura (9)	Cnj	Orcus (9)	12 Aug 1964

Orcus (7)	Cnj	Sun (7)	9 Jan 1965
Sat (3)	Opp	Orcus (9)	11 Mar 1965
Orcus (7)	Cnj	Sun (7)	8 Jun 1965
Orcus (7)	Sqr	Sat (10)	8 Aug 1965
Orcus (7)	Sqr	Sat (10)	26 Dec 1965
Orcus (7)	Sqr	Sat (10)	23 Jun 1966
Orcus (7)	Sqr	Sat (10)	3 Mar 1967
Orcus (7)	Sqr	Sat (10)	24 Apr 1967
Sat (6)	Sqr	Orcus (9)	25 May 1972
Orcus (8)	Cnj	Mer (8)	4 Sep 1973
Orcus (8)	Cnj	Mer (8)	15 Dec 1973
Nep (12)	Sqr	Orcus (9)	29 Jan 1974
Nep (12)	Sqr	Orcus (9)	24 Apr 1974
Orcus (8)	Cnj	Mer (8)	18 Jul 1974
Nep (12)	Sqr	Orcus (9)	26 Nov 1974
Orcus (8)	Cnj	Mer (8)	11 Feb 1975
Orcus (8)	Cnj	Mer (8)	1 Jun 1975
Nep (12)	Sqr	Orcus (9)	31 Jul 1975
Nep (12)	Sqr	Orcus (9)	11 Sep 1975
Orcus (8)	Opp	Plu (2)	11 Sep 1976
Orcus (8)	Opp	Plu (2)	13 Dec 1976
Orcus (8)	Opp	Plu (2)	24 Jul 1977
Orcus (8)	Opp	Plu (2)	9 Feb 1978
Orcus (8)	Opp	Plu (2)	8 Jun 1978
Sat (9)	Cnj	Orcus (9)	9 Oct 1978
Sat (9)	Cnj	Orcus (9)	19 Mar 1979
Sat (9)	Cnj	Orcus (9)	28 Jun 1979
Ura (12)Sqr	Orcus (9)	28 Nov 1983	
Sat (12)	Sqr	Orcus (9)	21 Feb 1986
Sat (12)	Sqr	Orcus (9)	14 Apr 1986
Sat (12)	Sqr	Orcus (9)	8 Nov 1986
Sat (3)	Opp	Orcus (9)	19 Apr 1994
Sat (3)	Opp	Orcus (9)	31 Aug 1994
Sat (3)	Opp	Orcus (9)	13 Jan 1995
Plu (12)	Sqr	Orcus (9)	1 Jan 1999
Plu (12)	Sqr	Orcus (9)	30 May 1999

Plu (12)	Sqr	Orcus (9)	31 Oct 1999
Sat (6)	Sqr	Orcus (9)	2 Jul 2001
Sat (6)	Sqr	Orcus (9)	3 Jan 2002
Sat (6)	Sqr	Orcus (9)	14 Mar 2002
Ura (3)	Opp	Orcus (9)	10 Apr 2005
Ura (3)	Opp	Orcus (9)	23 Aug 2005
Orcus (9)	Opp	Mon (3)	19 Sep 2005
Ura (3)	Opp	Orcus (9)	1 Feb 2006
Orcus (9)	Opp	Mon (3)	5 Feb 2006
Orcus (9)	Opp	Mon (3)	7 Aug 2006
Orcus (9)	Opp	Mon (3)	6 Apr 2007
Orcus (9)	Opp	Mon (3)	15 Jun 2007
Sat (9)	Cnj	Orcus (9)	12 Aug 2008
Nep (3)	Opp	Orcus (9)	22 Apr 2015
Nep (3)	Opp	Orcus (9)	3 Aug 2015
Sat (12)	Sqr	Orcus (9)	14 Dec 2015
Nep (3)	Opp	Orcus (9)	19 Feb 2016
Orcus (9)	Sqr	Ura (6)	3 Nov 2016
Orcus (9)	Cnj	Orcus (9)	2 Dec 2016
Orcus (9)	Cnj	Orcus (9)	13 Dec 2016
Orcus (9)	Sqr	Ura (6)	12 Jan 2017
Orcus (9)	Sqr	Ura (6)	12 Sep 2017
Orcus (9)	Cnj	Orcus (9)	21 Sep 2017
Orcus (9)	Cnj	Orcus (9)	28 Feb 2018
Orcus (9)	Sqr	Ura (6)	12 Mar 2018
Orcus (9)	Sqr	Ura (6)	31 Jul 2018
Orcus (9)	Cnj	Orcus (9)	10 Aug 2018
Orcus (9)	Cnj	Orcus (9)	19 May 2019
Orcus (9)	Cnj	Orcus (9)	28 May 2019
Orcus (9)	Sqr	Asc (1)	1 Oct 2020
Orcus (9)	Sqr	Asc (1)	23 Feb 2021
Orcus (9)	Sqr	Asc (1)	20 Aug 2021
Orcus (9)	Sqr	Asc (1)	27 Apr 2022
Orcus (9)	Sqr	Asc (1)	25 Jun 2022
Sat (3)	Opp	Orcus (9)	23 Feb 2024

Bibliography

(1991, November). *Track and Field News* , p. 8.

Baldwin, A., & Tabb, M. (2008). *A Promise to Ourselves, A Journey Through Fatherhood and Divorce.* St Martin's Press.

Bartoletti, S. C. (2005). *Hitler Youth: Growing Up in Hitler's Shadow.* Scholastic Nonfiction.

Berkum, M., Binlek, H., Kern, R., & Yagi, K. (1962). Volume 76, No.15. *Princeton Psychological Monographs* .

Berne, E. (2010). *The Games People Play.* Penguin.

Berne, E. (1975). *What Do You Say After You Say Hello?* London Books.

Bernheimer, R. (1970). *Wild Men of the Middle Ages: a Study in Art, Sentiment and Demonology.* Octagon Books.

Bridges, R. (2007). *The Testament of Beauty: A poem in four books.* Addison Press .

Brockes, E. (2009, April 11). It's the gift that keeps on taking. *The Guardian* .

Bullock, A. (1991). *Hitler and Stalin, Parallel Lives.* Harper Collins.

Carlin, P. A. (2006). *Catch a Wave: the rise, fall & redemption of the Beach Boys' Brian Wilson.* Rodale Books.

Ceplair, L., & Englund, S. (1983). *The inquisition in Hollywood: politics in the film community, 1930-1960.* University of California Press.

Christie, L. (2006, May 16). Real estate cools down. *CNN Money* .

Cohen, J., & Solomon, N. (1994, July 27). 30-year Anniversary: Tonkin Gulf Lie Launched Vietnam War. *Media Beat* .

Cook, F. J. (1971). *The Nightmare Decade: The Life and Times of Senator Joe McCarthy.* Random House.

Craig, O. (2004, November 10). Laugh at Tony? I very nearly died. *the Daily Telegraph* .

De Grummond, N. T., & Simon, E. (2006). *The Religion of the Etruscans.* University of Texas Press.

Dickinson, E., & McNeil (ed.), H. (1997). *Emily Dickinson Everyman Poetry.* Phoenix.

Dowden, K. (2005). *Zeus.* Routledge.

Ebertin, R. (1972). *The Combination of Stellar Influences.* Ebertin-Verlag.

Finkelstein, D. (2009, August 20). It is Right to Expose Wiesenthal. *The Jewish Chronicle* .

Fox, M. J. (2003). *Lucky Man: A Memoir.* Ebury Press.

Franchetti, M., & Winnett, R. (2007, June 10). UK's richest man in slave labour row. *The Sunday Times* .

Frazer, S. J., & Frazer, R. (1936). *The Golden Bough: A Study in Magic and Religion.* Macmillan & Co.

Frazier, B. (1961, December 6). The most famous deb of all denounces the life she lived: My Debut – A Horror. *LIFE Magazine* .

Goldhagen, D. (1997). *Hitler's Willing Executioners: Ordinary Germans and the Holocaust.* Abacus.

Gray, C. *Holocaust Denial on Trial, Trial Judgment: Electronic Edition.* Lewis H. Beck Center for Electronic Collections and Services, Emory University Atlanta.

Gunderson, G. B., & Palmer, S. (2008). *Killing sacred cows: overcoming the financial myths that are destroying your prosperity.* Greenleaf Book Group LLC.

Hamblin, D. (1983). *Harmonic Charts.* The Aquarian Press.

Hauser, T. (2004). *Muhammad Ali: His Life and Times.* Robson Books Ltd.

Hawkins, D. R. (2001). *The Eye of the I from which Nothing is Hidden.* Veritas Publishing.

Herodotus, Rawlinson, G., Rawlinson, S. H., & Wilkinson, S. J. (2010). *The History of Herodotus: a new English version, Volume 3.* Nabu Press.

Hitler, A. (2007). *Mein Kampf.* Jaico Publishing House.

Jacques, E. (1965). Death and the Midlife Crisis. *International Journal of Psychoanalysis* .

Juhasz, S. (1983). *The Undiscovered Continent: Emily Dickinson and the Space of the Mind.* Indiana University Press.

Julian Borger, D. C. (2003, August 8). The Governator. *The Guardian* .

Jung, C. (1957). *The Undiscovered Self.* Routledge.

Jung, C. (1967). *Two Essays on Analytical Psychology.* Princeton University Press.

Kabat-Zinn, D. J. (2006). *Full Catastrophe Living: How to cope with stress, pain and illness using mindfulness meditation.* Piatkus.

Kapleau, P. (1989). *The Three Pillars of Zen, Teaching, Practise and Enlightenment.* Anchor Books.

Keller, H. *Story of my Life.* Dover Publications Inc.

King, C. W. (2009). *The Gnostics and Their Remains, Ancient and Medieval.* Bibliobazaar.

Kornfield, J. (1995). *A Path with Heart.* Rider & Co.

Lang-Wescott, M. (1988). *Mechanics of the Future.* Treehouse Mountain.

Larissa Z., T. (., & Colin Wayne, L. (. (2004). *The Social Life of Emotions (Studies in Emotion and Social Interaction) .* Cambridge University Press.

Leland, C. G. (1901). *Etruscan Roman Remains in Popular Tradition .* T. Fisher Unwin.

Lippmann, W. (1947). *The Cold War: a study in US foreign policy.* Harper.

MacKillop, J. (2006). *Myths and Legends of the Celts.* Penguin.

Marnham, P. (2001). *The Death of Jean Moulin: Biography of a Ghost.* Pimlico.

Maschmann, M. (1964). *Account Rendered.* Abelard-Schuman.

McGuire (ed.), W., Jung, C., & Hull (ed.), R. (1980). *C.G. Jung Speaking: Interviews and Encounters.* Macmillan.

Mellor, C. M. (2006). *Louis Braille: A Touch of Genius.* National Braille Press.

Milgram, S. (2010). *Obedience to authority: an experimental view.* Pinter & Martin Ltd.

Milgram, S., & Blass, T. (2010). *The Individual in a Social World: Essays and Experiments.* Pinter & Martin Ltd.

Moore, K. (1992, August 17th). Ode to Joy. *Sports Illustrated .*

Norman (trans), J., & Horstmann, R.-P. (2002). *Beyond Good and Evil: Prelude to a Philosophy of the Future.* Cambridge University Press.

Obama, B. (2008). *The Audacity of Hope: thoughts on reclaiming the American dream.* Canongate Books Ltd.

Obituaries, John Paul Getty Jr. (2011, February 7). *The Daily Telegraph* .

Olstrom, C. E. (2011). *Undaunted By Blindness.* Perkins School for the Blind.

Orwell, G. (1945, October 19). You and the Atomic Bomb. *The London Tribune* .

Peers, E. A., & Cross, S. J. (1959). *Dark Night of the Soul.* Image Books.

Presley, P. (2008). *Elvis and Me.* Berkley Publishing Corporation.

Preston, D. (2003). *Lusitania: An Epic Tragedy.* Berkley Publishing Group.

Rand, A. (1964). *The Virtue of Selfishness.* Signet.

Robson, V. E. (1987). *The Fixed Stars and Constellations in Astrology.* Taraporevala.

Rovere, R. H. (1973). *Senator Joe McCarthy.* Harper and Row.

Shucman, D. H. (2008). *A Course in Miracles.* Course in Miracles Society.

Slusser, G. E., & Rabkin, E. S. (1986). *Mindscapes: the geographics of imagined worlds.* Southern Illinois University Press.

Squires, S. (1999, April 19). Midlife Without a Crisis. *Washington Post* .

Stinnett, R. B. (2001). *Day of Deceit: The Truth about FDR and Pearl Harbor.* Simon & Schuster.

Stockdale, J. (1995). *Thoughts of a Philosophical Fighter Pilot.* Hoover Institution Press.

Stockdale, J., & Stockdale, S. (1984). *In Love and War: The Story of a Family's Ordeal and Sacrifice During the Vietnam Years.* Harper Collins.

Stutfield, H. E. (2008). *El Maghreg: 1200 Miles' Ride Through Morocco,.* BiblioBazaar.

Tipping, C. (2009). *Radical Forgiveness.* Sounds True.

Tyl, N. (2007). *Noel Tyl's Guide to Astrological Consultation.* Llewellyn Publications.

Tyl, N. (2005). *Synthesis and Counselling in Astrology.* Llewellyn Publications.

van Horne, H. (1977, February 7). The Way We Were: At Our Worst. *New York Magazine* .

Volguine, A. (1973). *The Ruler of the Nativity.* ASI Publishers Inc.

Waite, T. (1994). *Taken on Trust.* Coronet.

Walker, B. G. (1987). *The Woman's Encyclopaedia of Myths and Secrets.* HarperSanFrancisco.

Walters, G. (2009, July 19). The Head Nazi-Hunter's Trail of Lies" (excerpt from his book 'Hunting Evil'). *The Sunday Times* .

Watts, A. W. (1967). *This is it: and other essays on Zen and spiritual experience.* Collier Books.

Wescott, M. L. (1988). *Mechanics of the Future.* Treehouse Mountain.

Willbourne, C., & Cull, L.-A. (1997). The Emerging Problem of Parental Alienation. *Family Law, Jordan Publishing* .

Wilson, J. A. (1956). *The Culture of Ancient Egypt.* University of Chicago Press.

Woodward, R. D. (2007). *The Cambridge Companion to Greek Mythology.* Cambridge University Press.

Zimbardo, P. (2008). *Lucifer Effect: How Good People Turn Evil.* Rider.

Index

About the author:

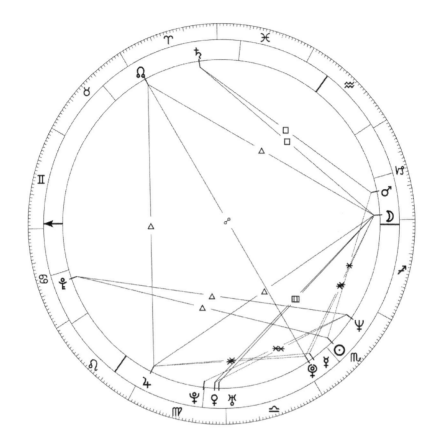

Made in the USA
Lexington, KY
26 July 2013